THE DEFINITIVE GUIDE TO
CANADIAN
ARTISANAL
AND FINE
CHEESE

THE DEFINITIVE GUIDE TO
CANADIAN
ARTISANAL
AND FINE
CHEESE

BY GURTH PRETTY

whitecap

Edited by Elaine Jones
Proofread by Joan E. Templeton
Cover design by Diane Yee
Interior design by Michelle Mayne

Printed and bound in Canada

LIBRARY AND ARCHIVES CANADA CATALOGUING IN PUBLICATION

Pretty, Gurth
The definitive guide to Canadian artisanal and fine cheese / Gurth Pretty.

Includes index.
ISBN 1-55285-760-3
ISBN 978-1-55285-760-1

1. Cheese--Canada--Varieties. 2. Cheesemakers--Canada. I. Title.

SF274.C2P74 2006   637'.35'0971
C2006-900707-1

The publisher acknowledges the financial support of the Government of Canada through the Book Publishing Industry Development Program for our publishing activities. We also acknowledge the financial support of the Province of British Columbia through the Book Publishing Tax Credit.

Thank You Joanne!

If I did not have my guardian angel watching over my shoulder, making sure I selectively sampled small pieces of cheese and exercised regularly with her, this book would not have been completed on time. I would still be sampling cheese, instead of writing. Thank you, Joanne, for your limitless support and love.

Acknowledgements

During my research, travels and writing, I received assistance and support from many wonderful individuals. Without the belief and patience of Robert McCullough, publisher of Whitecap Books, this project would still be in my head. Thank you to fellow members of Cuisine Canada, for informing me of producers unknown to me. To Isabel Gil of Destinations Québec, Diane Rioux of Tourism New Brunswick, Lana Kingston of Tourism Vancouver Island and Susan Jeffries of Nova Scotia Tourism, thank you for your logistical support. Thank you to Heather Mitchell for interpreting legalese in a way I understood. Thank you to Heather MacKenzie and Janice McGregor, fellow Cuisine sub-committee members at the Canadian Tourism Commission, for your words of support.

Sometimes there is help from unexpected sources. For this, I thank my cousin, Marie-Bénédicte Pretty, whom I had not seen for several years. Her knowledge of the Canadian artisan cheesemaking scene opened new doors for me. If not for the co-operation of the cheesemakers, the pages of the book would be blank. Keep experimenting and I will keep writing.

Petra Cooper, Kathy Guide and Vanessa Taylor, fellow members of the Ontario Cheese Society, clarified cheese terminology and provided me with an understanding of the fascinating world of cheese. Elaine Jones, my editor, who taught me as much about English grammar as I taught her about Canadian cheese, thank you. I now know the difference between en dashes and em dashes.

The book would not have been completed as quickly without the support of Darlene Huff, District Manager of Williams-Sonoma Canada. She allowed me the time I needed to complete my research and write the manuscript.

To my parents, Peter and Pauline, and my in-laws, Robert and Kathleen, thank you for your constant positive thoughts, support and proofreading skills.

This book was written by one person, with many hands guiding the pen.

Table of Contents

How *The Definitive Guide to Canadian Artisanal and Fine Cheese* Came About

Three years after the idea of writing this book popped into my head, it is completed. This is how the adventure began.

While enjoying a visit to Montreal's Le Marché des saveurs, a fine food shop specializing in regional Quebec ingredients, I spotted the book *Le Répertoire des fromages du Québec* on the shelf. Wow! A whole book dedicated to the fine cheese produced in Quebec. I immediately bought a copy. I brought it back to Toronto so Joanne and I could learn more about Quebec cheese and taste the ones available in Ontario.

I began wondering what other delicious cheeses are made in Canada. Where are they made? Who are the cheesemakers, and what are their stories? What kind of milk do they use? Where can we buy the cheese? Most international cheese books may have one page about our cheese if we are lucky. I took on the challenge of finding the companies that specialize in making cheese, not realizing the extent of the project I was starting. My search for information took me from coast to coast. I discovered several surprises. Alberta has cheese producers! There are more than just beef cattle in Wild Rose Country.

This book is a journey across Canada, from Nova Scotia to British Columbia. Reading it cover to cover, you will discover the delicious cheese produced in each region, learn about the makers and find out where you can buy the cheese or experience them in restaurants. Many are available only in their home province. Plan to visit some of the cheesemakers on your next vacation in that province. Each listing includes a few suggestions of local activities and attractions. Experience each delicious cheese in its terroir: the region where it was made. Through food, you meet people and truly experience the local flavour.

I haven't provided tasting notes on the cheese as I do not want to bias you, and with so many cheese, I would be sampling for a long time. Go out and experience them yourself, with a clean mind and palate. Enjoy!

The Big Stink!

A comic look at the evolution of the Canadian cheese industry

INNOCENT COWS ARE WAR BOOTY!

(Acadia, 1541)—Mr. Jacques Car tier, French discoverer of Canada, ponders the fate of the cows he brought in 1541 to the Acadian colony.

"The sailors had a terrible mess to clean as our ship trudged up and down the high rolling waves during our Atlantic crossing. Have you ever seen a seasick cow? It is not a pretty sight!" said the navigator.

Mr. Cartier would not state the reason why the cows were brought to the New World on his third and final voyage. This reporter wonders if it was for their meat, their milk, to start up a tannery industry, or for national defense.

With the recent British capture of the French colony of Acadia, the fate of the innocent cows is unknown. Will the cows swear the oath of allegiance to the British king or will they be deported to another French colony? Cartier wants his cows back. He is leading a team to negotiate their release.

"The British will drive our cows MAD! They are French property. We do not want them to be turned into overcooked roast beef!" commented Cartier.

INDUSTRY RETURNS TO ITS COTTAGE ROOTS

(Île d'Orléans, 1610)—Samuel de Champlain, Governor of New France, introduced dairy cows to the Quebec City region in 1610. He discovered he had a problem on his hands. What could be done with the surplus seasonal milk?

Ms. Anne Aubin, a local entrepreneur, helped to solve the problem. She began making cheese and selling it regularly at the Quebec City Farmers' Market. Marie de l'Incarnation, a noted member of New France's religious orders, commented it was one of the best cheeses she ever tasted.

Le fromage "rafiné" de l'île, as it was known, was never made in factories, but in private homes. The production of this 17th-century cheese continued into the 20th century. Between 1940 and 1970, 38 families were producing it for their personal consumption. Little by little, production declined to nil.

Nearly 400 years after its first appearance, the island's cheese is back on the market. Jocelyn Labbé and several business partners established Les Fromages de l'Isle d'Orléans, a modern-day renaissance of the island's cheesemaking industry.

In 1999 Mr. Gérard Aubin, the last master cheesemaker of the island, joined Mr. Labbé's team to commercially produce the artisanal cheese.

Their cheese will be produced in three forms: a fresh, a roasting cheese and a soft. The production quantity is small as only the milk from the island's dairy farms is used. The cheese is available for sampling and purchase, next door to a 17th-century home.

BRITISH TASTES INFLUENCE THE INDUSTRY

(British North America, 1783)—The forced resettlement of over 100,000 United Empire Loyalists from the rebellious American colonies brought a new influx of tastes and cheesemakers to British North America.

As early as 1793, the newly settled British colonists were producing cheese. Six tons (5,455 kg) of mystery cheese was exported from Nova Scotia. Cheesemaker, type of cheese and destination are unknown. Is this the first case of trans-Atlantic cheese smuggling?

Cheesemaking headed west with the gradual settlement of Upper Canada and Rupert's Land. The craft was also well established in the Red River Colony in 1812.

Cheddar was the popular cheese amongst the British subjects of Upper Canada. With no artificial refrigeration, milk spoiled quickly, and cheddaring was a practical method of preserving the extra milk produced in the spring and summer months. Cheddar has a long shelf life. In 1840 Upper Canada's first commercial cheese factory opened near Ingersoll, establishing a cheesemaking industry in both Upper and Lower Canada.

AMERICAN INTRODUCES RADICAL CONCEPT

(Upper Canada, 1864)—Harvey Farrington, a Yankee with big ideas, had the technology to make cheese on a large scale, but lacked the milk. He persuaded dairymen to deliver their milk to his plant, so he could produce large quantities of cheese. The farmers liked his idea and bought into his scheme, whereby they owned shares in the business. Thus the first co-operative cheese factory was established. The Pioneer Cheese Factory began production in 1864 in Norwich, Upper Canada.

The co-operative was farmer-owned, and managed by a board of directors elected by the share-owning farmers. They hired a cheesemaker to produce cheese, hence obtaining a higher return on their milk. As delivery of unpasteurized fresh milk in the mid 1800s was by horse and buggy, co-operative cheese factories popped up every 5 to 6 miles (8 to 10 km) from each other. Three years later at Confederation, 200 such factories existed in the new province of Ontario. Nova Scotia and New Brunswick, also founding provinces, had cheese plants beginning production.

By the early 1900s, over 2,000 co-operative cheese factories were in operation in Quebec and Ontario, producing unique cheese with names like Union Star, Flower Station, Square Deal, Farmer's Own and Highland Chief. Farther west, cheese factories opened north of Edmonton as early as 1906.

The reason for their success was the export market to the United Kingdom. Cheese was the main source of protein for the British labourer, who could not afford meat on a regular basis. Cheese is a highly concentrated source of protein with a long shelf life. British cheesemakers could not keep up with the demand. Canadian cheese companies jumped in to fill the gap. Canada quickly became the largest supplier of cheddar to Great Britain, even surpassing their own production levels.

MAMMOTH CHEESES CRASH FAIRS

(Ingersoll, Upper Canada, 1866)—How big is BIG? Imagine a hunk of cheese 3 feet (1 m) high by 7 feet (2.3 m) in diameter, weighing 7,300 pounds (3,318 kg). This colossal chunk of cheddar was made in 1866 by cheese factories in the vicinity of Ingersoll, Upper Canada. It is understandable why this community became known as the Cheddar Capital of Upper Canada.

The enormous cheese was created to promote the Upper Canadian cheese industry at the New York State Fair in Saratoga and open new markets. The cheese was also exhibited in Liverpool, England, prior to being sold to distributors.

Cheese got even bigger—gargantuan in fact. The Canadian Mammoth Cheddar Cheese grabbed international headlines at the World Columbian Exposition, held in Chicago in 1893. Newspaper reports stated the humongous cheese crashed through the floorboards of its display stage. This is exactly the free publicity the Canadian cheesemakers had hoped for.

It took 207,000 pounds (94,090 kg) of milk to make this gargantuan cheese. Cheesemakers at 12 cheese factories laboured for 2 ½ days to produce the curds. Specially designed cheese presses and

> ## "Newspaper reports stated the humongous cheese crashed through the floorboards of its display stage."

a railway car were built for its production and delivery. The final mass of the cheese was estimated to be 22,000 pounds (10,000 kg).

The cheese received the Exposition's Diploma and a Bronze Medal. It was on display under a glass roof for six months, with temperatures reaching 90°F (32°C) at times.

The cheese was eventually sold to a British importer, who had it cut up and sold throughout the United Kingdom. Three hundred pounds (135 kg) were saved and returned to the original cheesemakers, as a keepsake for their efforts.

Canadian cheddar cheese had caught the world's attention and the world was anxious to gobble it up! Way to go Canada!

QUEBEC'S HOLY CHEESE

(Oka, Quebec, 1893)—With the arrival at Oka of Brother Alphonse Juin, the tradition of Canadian monastery cheese began. The French Trappist monk had made cheese at the Port du Salut Abbey in France for 19 years. Each Trappist abbey was expected to support itself, creating items that could be sold to obtain other items.

In 1974 the monks sold the name of the cheese and the rights to make it to Agropur, the province's largest dairy co-operative. Some say the cheese is not as good as when the monks produced it. It is believed they aged it longer than the modern-day cheesemakers. Oka is one of Canada's best-known cheeses, both domestically and internationally.

In 1912 the Benedictine monastery of Saint-Benoît-du-Lac was established on the shores of Quebec's Lac Memphrémagog. Five monks resided in the small building, devoting themselves to the study of the word of God. Saint-Benedict said that to be a true monk, one must live by the work of one's hands.

Such work is meant to provide for the needs of the monastery and to maintain a happy balance of mind and body. The monks support themselves with a cheese factory, an orchard, a cider factory, a farm and a store where their products are sold.

The cheese factory has been in operation since 1943. Different types of cheese are made: Ermite, a blue cheese; Mont Saint-Benoît, a mild Gruyère; Le Moine, a stronger-tasting Gruyère, and ricotta (made with whey). Some lay people are employed to assist.

The newest religious community to produce cheese commercially is Saint Monastère Vierge-Marie-La-Consolatrice in the hills of the Laurentians. The sisters of the Greek Orthodox order made cheese initially for their own consumption, from the milk of their own goats and sheep. After sampling their cheese at religious events and festivals, the regional Greek community began asking where they could purchase it. As the demand grew for their products, the sisters took on the challenge of producing their cheeses commercially. Today, the sisters have the ability to nourish a new flock of worshippers—cheese lovers, that is.

RETURN OF ONTARIO'S PRODIGAL SON

(Ontario, 1920)—This was a big year in Canada's cheese

industry with the return of James Lewis Kraft, a Stevensville, Ontario, native. Canada's MacLaren's Imperial Cheese Co. Ltd. was bought out by his company, J.L. Kraft & Bros Co., selling processed cheese in tins and loaves across the country.

His education in cheese began when he worked at Ferguson's grocery store in nearby Fort Erie. He invested

dried out quickly, and the taste varied from being strong to bitter. Much cheese was wasted.

After years of experimentation, Kraft created the first commercially produced processed cheese. It was a product that could be packaged without waste, maintain a uniform quality, and be sold in convenient sizes. In 1915, $1,500 of this new cheese was sold. Sales

try, enlarging his commercial empire with the acquisition of Canada's MacLaren's Imperial Cheese Co. Ltd.

CHEESE FACTORIES FACE DOOM BY BIG BROTHER

(Ontario, 1950s)—What happened to the 1,000 cheese factories in Ontario? Where did they all go?

There are many reasons for their demise. Many of them were small, farmer-owned co-operatives that closed down due to low profitability. Others did not upgrade their facilities to meet new government standards. Several mysteriously burnt down and were never rebuilt.

> "In 1916 Kraft received the patent rights for his processed cheese. The next year, the United States government, realizing the long shelf life of the cheese, ordered 6 million pounds to feed its soldiers during World War One."

money in a Buffalo cheese company and was overseeing the Chicago branch, but found himself pushed out of the business by his partners, with only $65 US.

Knowing the importance of delivering high-quality cheese quickly to retailers, Kraft became a distributor. He would arrive early at the Chicago wholesale warehouse district, purchase the cheese and deliver them promptly to the small stores.

He sought ways of making cheese more shelf-stable, with more uniform flavour. The cheese was often mouldy or

increased to $150,000 the following year.

In 1916 Kraft received the patent rights for his processed cheese. The next year, the United States government, realizing the long shelf life of the cheese, ordered 6 million pounds (2.7 million kg) to feed its soldiers during World War One.

To meet the market's demand for his cheese, Kraft established more cheese plants and purchased cheese from co-operative farmers' cheese factories. They had to meet his specific standards to be considered.

In 1920, J.L. Kraft re-entered the Canadian cheese indus-

To continue to exist, many sold their cheese to larger cheese companies and were required to produce to the exact standards of their clients or their cheese would be refused. Thus began the era of mass-produced, bland-tasting cheese. Other factories were bought out by larger companies, such as Kraft and Ault Dairy. Famed Balderson Cheddar Co. was acquired by Parmalat, an Italian multinational corporation.

There are still a handful of small farmer-owned or privately owned cheddar cheese producers in Ontario. St. Albert, Pine River, Bright, Empire and Ivanhoe Cheese continue to thrive in their regions.

NEW WAVE ARRIVES

(Canada, 1950s to present)—With the end of the Second World War, a new wave of skilled European immigrants landed on Canada's shores. Italians, Greeks, Portuguese and Dutch arrived, bringing with them recipes and skills from their homelands.

Within the ethnic neighbourhoods of Canada's large cities, the demand arose for cheese in the style of the Old Country. When there is a demand, an entrepreneur is quick to fill the need. Italian-Canadian cheesemakers began making mozzarella to fill the need for the pizza industry. Ricotta, mascarpone and provolone soon followed, much to the delight of community members.

Whether it's on Toronto's Danforth or in Montreal's Prince Arthur and Duluth neighbourhoods, feta is a popular cheese amongst the Greek-Canadian population. This cheese is now a staple in Canadian grocery stores.

Only recently have Portuguese-styled cheeses become more available outside the local ethnic community. With an enhanced distribution system and marketing program, these lesser known cheeses are being discovered by fellow caseophiles.

Dutch settlers brought their love for their native cheese with them and began making it here. Dutch Canadians make Gouda in Nova Scotia, New Brunswick, Prince Edward Island, Ontario, Alberta and British Columbia. French, Swiss and German cheesemakers have also landed on our shores and are producing new versions of their traditional cheese, with a Canadian twist to them.

Indo-Canadians have introduced paneer to their new communities. Whether it be the Maritimes, Winnipeg or British Columbia, they are filling a need and enriching the Canadian cheese spectrum.

BACK TO THE EARTH & GROWING!

(Canada, 1980 to present)—With corporate downsizing and executive burn out, many Canadians want to re-establish themselves with a simpler lifestyle, going back to nature and producing something tangible.

Many have decided to try their hand at producing cheese. New enterprises sprouted first in Quebec where a greater appreciation for fine cheese and abundant milk allowed entrepreneurs to become cheesemakers.

People within the food service industry, like David Wood of Salt Spring Island Cheese Co., and others who lived in Europe, took the plunge and began making cheese themselves, using cow's, goat's and sheep's milk to create a vast array of cheeses.

Many small enterprises did not survive past a few years. The owners did not realize the effort and capital required; financial return comes only after years of establishing a reputation within a region.

For a Canadian cheese industry to grow and prosper, Canadians must actively support their local and regional cheesemakers. Buy their products and promote them to friends and family.

Public support must diversify so both the industrial producer and the small artisanal cheesemaker has a place and market for their products. Make the time to discover new cheese by visiting the retail outlets of local cheese companies, frequenting farmers' markets and asking your cheesemonger what new Canadian cheese they are offering for sale. The consumer has power. If enough consumers ask for a product, a smart business person will fill that demand.

> "For a Canadian cheese industry to grow and prosper, Canadians must actively support their local and regional cheesemakers."

Milk Terminology

COW

Cows are the main milk producers in Canada. Breeds such as Ayrshire, Brown Swiss, Canadienne and Jersey provide milk high in butterfat and protein. Holstein is the most popular breed amongst farmers, due to the cows' high production volumes. The dairy cow industry is long established in Canada, as compared to the dairy goat and sheep industries.

GOAT

Alpine, LaMancha, Nubian, Saanen and Toggenburg goats are breeds used in Canada for the production of milk. Goat's milk can be easier to digest for people who are lactose intolerant. It's a rich milk, used extensively in producing fresh and soft cheese.

SHEEP

East Friesian is the predominant dairy sheep breed in Canada. Raising dairy sheep is a fairly recent phenomenon here. Sheep's milk is richer than cow's or goat's milk and is very nutritious. Similar to goat's milk, it's more easily digested by those who are lactose intolerant.

RAW MILK

Canadian laws allow raw milk to be used in the production of cheese. The milk has not been heated over 40°C prior to being processed, so all the original bacteria are still present in the milk. Most companies that produce raw-milk cheese obtain their milk from a single supplier or herd. This facilitates monitoring and quality control of the milk. For the cheese to be sold, it must be aged for no less than 60 days. After this date, the potentially harmful bacteria have died off. Amongst cheese connaisseurs, the flavours provided by the good bacteria produce a complex and subtle cheese.

THERMALIZED MILK

Thermalization of milk occurs when the milk has been heated to between 57 and 63.5°C for a minimum of 15 seconds prior to being processed into cheese. It's believed this procedure significantly reduces potentially harmful bacteria. The remaining harmful bacteria die during the ageing period. The potential for subtle flavours still exists depending on the skills of the cheesemaker.

PASTEURIZED MILK

Pasteurization of milk kills all bacteria, good and bad. The milk is either heated to 61.6°C for 30 seconds or to 72 to 85°C for 15 seconds. Beneficial bacteria is re-introduced into the milk to begin the cheesemaking process. Most cheese processed in Canada is produced from pasteurized milk.

Cheese Categories

FRESH

All cheeses begin as fresh, unripened cheese. Those eaten fresh have a high moisture content (up to 80%), as little of the extra whey has been drained. They have a short refrigerated shelf life of two weeks to a month. *Examples are cream cheese, cottage cheese, fromage frais, paneer, quark and ricotta.*

SOFT

Fresh curds are placed into moulds and permitted to drain naturally. Soft cheeses have a 50 to 60% moisture content. They may be: unripened, white and bloomy (due to the addition of *Penicillium* bacterial culture); washed with salt water or other liquid; or a combination of both bloomy and washed (that is, mixed). Their refrigerated shelf life is one to two months. *Examples are brie, Camembert, chèvre and crottin.*

SEMI-SOFT

Firmer than the soft cheeses (40 to 60% moisture content), the semi-soft category is divided into several sub-groups, depending on how it was ripened.

- Unripened: Cheese is cut and stretched after the draining process. *Examples are bocconcini and mozzarella.*
- Interior ripened: Curds have been pressed, cooked and ripened. Ripening occurs throughout the whole body of the cheese. Rinds may be washed or brushed. *Examples are Casata and Monterey Jack.*
- Surface ripened: The cheeses are turned, washed and aged in a cold room. Ripening occurs from the surface toward the centre of the cheese. *Examples are Oka and Limburger.*

The refrigerated shelf life of semi soft cheese is from two to four months.

FIRM

The fresh curds are drained and heavily pressed to remove more whey (35 to 45% moisture content). Some cheeses are cooked, making them even firmer. They are all interior ripened. Their refrigerated shelf life is three months to a year. *They may be rindless such as provolone and cheddar, washed and brushed (Miranda) or covered in wax or plastic (Gouda).*

HARD

Hard cheeses are cooked and pressed and may be aged for a long time. They are used extensively in cooking (gratins) where their sharp flavours are appreciated. They have a very low moisture content (25 to 35%)—and have the longest refrigerated shelf life of over a year. *Examples are chèvretale, Kefalotyri, Leoni-Grana and Parmesan.*

BLUE

Blue is a true category of cheese. A bacterial culture, such as *Penicillium roquefortii*, is introduced onto the rind or inserted into the ageing cheese. These bacteria produce the blue surface mould or veining. Blue cheese is mostly produced in the soft and semisoft categories. *Examples are Baa Baa Bleu, Bleu Ermite, Blue Velvet and Geai bleu.*

To learn more about specific types of cheese, please refer to the glossary.

Production Levels

ARTISANAL FARMSTEAD

- The cheeses are made on the farm, from the milk of the maker's own herd or flock.
- The cheesemaker follows the artisanal production guidelines listed below.
- The flavours of the cheese may vary from season to season, depending on the grazing and feeding of the animals.
- The cheese tends to be distributed regionally or provincially.

ARTISANAL

- The milk from one or several milk producers is delivered to a cheesemaking facility, located off the farm property.
- The processing of the milk into cheese is done in small batches and mostly by hand.
- The cheese tends to be distributed mostly regionally or provincially.

SEMI-INDUSTRIAL

- A cheesemaking establishment processes large quantities of milk from one or several herds or flocks.
- Mechanized equipment is used with a manual component involved.
- The cheese is distributed regionally, provincially or nationally.

INDUSTRIAL

- A cheesemaking company processes large quantities of local milk and milk from outside the region.
- Their highly mechanized and standardized production system creates consistent cheese year-round for a large market.
- The cheese is distributed provincially, nationally or internationally.

Shopping at Whole Foods Market.

Buying and Storing Cheese

Cheese is a living organism of bacteria and protein. It must be properly cared for to permit it to display all its delicious qualities.

BUYING

- Purchase from a reputable cheese-monger, one who is knowledgeable about the products and stores them properly.
- Check the best-before date on the packaging.
- If you're uncertain about the taste of a certain cheese, ask for a sample. Remember the sample is not at its best, for the cheese is in a refrigerated display and will be cold.
- Purchase only what you need for the next week. Buy cheese to be eaten, not to be forgotten or lost in the refrigerator where it can spoil.
- I prefer to have my pieces of cheese cut fresh from the larger wheel or block. Vacuum-wrapped pieces cannot be smelled, nor are you informed as to when the cheese was cut and packaged.
- If the cheese you purchase smells of ammonia, return it to the cheese-monger with the receipt. It may be an off cheese, stored improperly during shipment or improperly stored by the cheesemonger, who may offer a refund or another piece of cheese as a replacement.

STORING

- If you're unable to refrigerate cheese immediately, place it in a cooler with ice packs.
- Refrigerate wrapped cheese 90 minutes before serving them on a platter.
- Cheese should not be rewrapped in its original packaging. It will no longer be airtight and the cheese will deteriorate faster.
- Rewrap cheese in fresh wrapping material each time you open it.
- Blue, bloomy rind, mixed rind and washed rind cheese should be wrapped first in wax paper and then in either plastic wrap or an airtight re-sealable plastic bag. These types of cheese need to breathe and should be protected from extra moisture.
- Firm and hard cheese should be rewrapped in plastic wrap or an airtight re-sealable plastic bag. Unwanted moisture is blocked by the layer of plastic.
- Every second day, turn soft and semi-soft cheese over.
- Cheese such as a feta, purchased in a saltwater brine solution, should be returned to the original container and its brine solution.

Creating and Serving Cheese Platters

There's a renewed interest in serving cheese as a separate course at parties. An old tradition is enjoying a renaissance!

WHEN TO SERVE IT?

Cheese platters can be served at any time of the day or night. They're perfect for a brunch buffet, lunch, picnic snack, tailgate party, dinner or an after-theatre nibble.

At dinner, French Canadians traditionally serve cheese platters before the dessert course. Canadians of British heritage have theirs after the dessert. There are no set rules. Have fun and serve it whenever you want. Joanne and I love having a cheese platter as our dessert course.

I enjoy serving a cheese platter at the end of the meal in the living room. It permits my guests and I to leave the dining room and enter a less formal setting. Guests sit where they wish and begin nibbling at the cheese selection. Port, wine, coffee or tea are offered and the conversations renew. A cheese platter is a great way to end a meal.

- Plan to serve three to four different cheeses on your platter.

- Anticipate each guest will eat 120 g of cheese in total. This amount is generous, and there will possibly be some leftovers for a future snack. The actual amount varies according to the individual person, time of day the platter is served and the social occasion (picnic versus after-dinner cheese platter).

- Decide what types of cheese you are planning to serve. You might have a theme:

    - Cheese made with different kinds of milk (that is cow, goat and sheep)

    - Raw, thermalized, pasteurized cheeses

    - Cheese representative of different categories (that is soft, semi-soft, firm, hard, bloomy rind, washed rind, et cetera)

    - Local, regional, national or international cheese

- Let the cheese warm up at room temperature, unwrapped, for at least 90 minutes.

- Before serving, leave the cheese whole or in large pieces. Do not cut cheese in cubes or wedges, for it will dry out faster. If you cut a double or triple cream too early, the paste will ooze out and spread onto the platter.

- Provide a separate knife for each cheese to reduce the chance of cross-contamination of flavours. You do not want a knife that just cut a blue cheese to slice a piece of brie. You will not taste the true flavours of the brie with the small crumbs of the blue transferred by the knife.

- Place a card on each cheese to identify it. Your guests will thank you for informing them of the offered selection.

- If you're a cheese purist, serve slices of white baguette or water crackers alongside. The neutral base will not compete with the cheese flavours.

- If you're a gourmet, gastronome or foodie, offer a selection of other side garnishes. Roasted garlic, pistachios, caramelized walnuts, fruit chutney, flavoured breads or crackers and fresh or dried fruit are popular choices. Drizzling artisanal honey over the cheese is becoming very trendy.

Nova Scotia

If you know of other Nova Scotia commercial cheesemakers, send details to Gurth@CheeseofCanada.ca for the next edition.

THE DEFINITIVE GUIDE TO CANADIAN ARTISANAL AND FINE CHEESE

1660 Lower Church St.
R.R. # 1,
Port Williams, NS
902-542-3599

OWNERS/CHEESEMAKERS
Richard and Jeanita Rand

MILK TYPE
Pasteurized cow's milk

PRODUCTION LEVEL
Artisanal farmstead

Federally registered

FOX HILL FARM IS A SIXTH-GENERATION family farm located just outside of Port Williams. Richard and Jeanita decided to take the milk of their small herd of 50 Holstein cows one step further and began producing cheese in 2004. They use only the milk from their own animals. This allows the Rands to pay strict attention to the quality of the forage fed to the cows and the production of clean, pure, drug- and hormone-free milk.

The cheese house, located right on the farm, is both their store and the plant. You can sample their wares while watching Richard or Jeanita making cheese in the next room. An outdoor deck invites you to soak in the natural beauty of the Minas Basin or Cape Blomidon. Bus tours are welcome.

This is one of three cheese companies in the Annapolis Valley, including Holmestead Cheese Sales and Ran-Cher Acres, that can be visited in the same day.

LOCAL ATTRACTIONS AND ACTIVITIES
- Acadia University Art Gallery (Wolfville)
- Blomidon Inn Gardens (Wolfville)
- Holmestead Cheese Sales
- Local wineries (Gaspereau Vineyards, Grand Pré Wines & Sainte-Famille Wines)
- Ran-Cher Acres
- Randall House Historical Museum (Wolfville)
- Robie Tufts Nature Centre (Wolfville)

FOR MORE IDEAS, VISIT
www.novascotia.com

CHEESE PRODUCED

CHEDDAR
- Medium
- Blueberry
- Cranberry

CURDS

FETA

GOUDA
- Medium
- Old
- Caraway
- Cumin
- Garlic and Chives
- Herb and Garlic
- Hot Jalapeño
- Peppercorn
- Smoked, rolled in Spanish paprika

HAVARTI
- Plain
- Dill and Chives
- Fenugreek
- Italian

QUARK
- Chocolate
- Country Curry
- Garlic Delight
- Harvest Onion
- Italian Blend
- Lemon Dill

Fox Hill's owners, Richard and Jeanita Rand

1- Lemon Dill Quark; 2- Harvest Onion Quark; 3-Italian Blend Quark; 4- 1-Year-Old Unpasteurized Cheddar (in development); 5- Chocolate Quark; 6- Country Curry Quark; 7- Plain Quark; 8- Cumin Gouda; 9- Herb and Garlic Gouda; 10- Caraway Gouda; 11- Old Gouda; 12- Peppercorn Gouda; 13- Smoked Gouda, rolled in Spanish Paprika; 14- Feta; 15- Blueberry Cheddar; 16- Cranberry Cheddar; 17- Dill and Chives Havarti; 18- Medium Gouda; 19- Cumin Gouda; 20- Hot Jalapeño Gouda; 21- Fenugreek Havarti; 22- Italian Havarti; 23- Garlic and Chives Gouda; 24- Plain Havarti; 25- Medium Cheddar

AVAILABILITY

STORES
- Onsite store
  April to December
  Monday to Saturday
  10 a.m. to 5 p.m.
  Sunday 1 to 5 p.m.
  January to March
  Thursday to Saturday
  1 to 5 p.m.
- Local wineries (Annapolis Valley)
- Halifax Farmers' Market
- Wolfville Farmers' Market

USED AT THE FOLLOWING RESTAURANTS
- ArtCan Gallery (Canning)
- Restaurant Le Caveau (Grand Pré)
- Tempest Restaurant (Wolfville)

For distributor inquiries, please contact Richard and Jeanita.

G. PRETTY

THE DEFINITIVE GUIDE TO CANADIAN ARTISANAL AND FINE CHEESE

HOLMESTEAD
FROMAGE FETA CHEESE

3 Kg

• GREEK • BULGARIAN • ITALIAN •
• GREC • BULGARE • ITALIEN •

SINCE 1985 HOLMESTEAD HAS BEEN PRO-viding high-quality cheese to the Maritimes. Nick has over 60 years of hands-on experience, first acquired in his native Greece. The rest of Canada can also appreciate his cheese, for they are available across the country.

This is one of three cheese companies in the Annapolis Valley, including Ran-Cher Acres and Fox Hill Cheese House, that can be visited in the same day.

2439 Harmony Rd.
Aylesford, NS
902-847-1797

OWNERS
Susan and Nick Tziolas

CHEESEMAKER
Nick Tziolas

MILK TYPE
Pasteurized cow's milk

PRODUCTION LEVEL
Industrial

Federally registered

LOCAL ATTRACTIONS AND ACTIVITIES
• Fox Hill Cheese House
• Oaklawn Farm Zoo
• Annapolis Valley Apple
  Blossom Festival
• Ran-Cher Acres
• Grand Pré National Historic
  Site—commemorative site of
  the deportation of the Acadian
  people (Grand Pré)

FOR MORE IDEAS, VISIT
www.novascotia.com

CHEESE PRODUCED

FETA

KEFALOTYRI

RICOTTA

Grand Pré National Historic Site

1- Feta; 2- Kefalotyri; 3- Ricotta

AVAILABILITY

STORES

- Onsite
  Knock at the door of the house for service
- Cash and Carry Atlantic, Loblaws, Save Easy and Sobey's grocery stores (Atlantic Canada)
- Western Grocer grocery stores

USED AT THE FOLLOWING RESTAURANTS

- Union Street Café (Berwick)

For distributor inquiries, please contact Susan.

THE DEFINITIVE GUIDE TO CANADIAN ARTISANAL AND FINE CHEESE

144 Canaan Rd.
Aylesford, NS
902-847-3895

OWNERS/CHEESEMAKERS
Randy and Cheryl Hiltz

MILK TYPE
Raw and pasteurized goat's milk

PRODUCTION LEVEL
Artisanal farmstead

Provincially licensed

LOCAL ATTRACTIONS AND ACTIVITIES
- Fox Hill Cheese House
- Grand Pré National Historic Site—commemorative site of the deportation of the Acadian people (Grand Pré)
- Annapolis Valley Apple Blossom Festival
- Holmestead Cheese Sales
- Oaklawn Farm Zoo

FOR MORE IDEAS, VISIT
www.novascotia.com

NESTLED IN THE LUSH ANNAPOLIS VALLEY, Randy and Cheryl Hiltz have made goats into a family affair. Since 1985, they have been producing cheese with milk from their herd of Saanen goats. Now their son Aaron has taken over managing the herd, giving Randy and Cheryl time to focus on the cheesemaking. When you visit the farm, look for the white goats in the pastures or watch them being milked.

Ran-Cher Acres is one of three cheese companies in the Annapolis Valley, including Holmestead Cheese Sales and Fox Hill Cheese House, that can be visited in the same day.

❧

While driving with Joanne down the country road to visit the Hiltzes, my mind wandered and I began reading roadside signs aloud. I chanted "Chickens for sale" first before reading the address number on the sign. Too late, we had driven past the Hiltz farm. Ever since then, whenever I make a wrong turn or drive by our destination, Joanne chants, "Chickens for sale."

That day we were on a tight schedule. We crossed the Bay of Fundy aboard the St. John to Digby ferry, planning to visit all three cheese companies of the Annapolis Valley and be in Halifax for dinner. Being the optimist, I hoped to be able to show Joanne the beautiful community of Annapolis Royal and visit Port Royal National Historic Site, the reconstructed buildings of Champlain's first permanent settlement in North America. We also had to time our Sunday visit just right. Randy is the local Baptist minister. He had a few hours available to see us between leading the local church services. We made it in time for our appointment to meet Randy, but had to forego our visit to Annapolis Royal and Port Royal. I promised Joanne we would experience them on our next trip.

CHEESE PRODUCED

USING PASTEURIZED MILK

CHEDDAR
- Plain
- Chive
- Smoked

CHÈVRE
- Plain
- Herbed
- Rolled in ash, known as Canaan Mountain Ash Chèvre

CURDS

FETA
- Plain
- Marinated in oil and herbs
- Rolled in ash, known as Canaan Mountain Ash Feta

GOUDA
- Made with raw milk
- Made with pasteurized milk

HARD CHÈVRE
- Plain
- Rolled in garlic and peppercorns

PANEER

PARMESAN

QUARK

Ran-Cher Acres' goats

1- Paneer; 2- Canaan Mountain Ash Chèvre; 3- Canaan Mountain Ash Feta; 4- Smoked;
5- Feta; 6- Quark; 7- Chive-flavoured Cheddar; 8- Cheddar; 9- Gouda; 10- Feta button;
11- Feta marinated in herbs

AVAILABILITY

STORES
- Onsite
  Knock at the farmhouse
  door for service
- Annapolis Natural Food
  (Annapolis Royal)
- EOS Fine Foods (Wolfville)
- Halifax Farmers' Market
- Valley Natural Foods
  (Greenwood)

For distributor inquiries, please contact Randy or Cheryl.

www.farmersdairy.ca

FARMERS COOPERATIVE DAIRY HAS A LONG history. Originally established as Farmers Dairy in the 1920s, 41 years later it evolved into a co-operative dairy. Today 200 milk producers are owners of the company. Its success permitted the company to acquire Newfoundland and Labrador's Central Dairies in 1981 and distribute product to Prince Edward Island.

Farmers Cooperative operates the largest cheesemaking plant in Nova Scotia. The cheese is made in open vats and prepared by the master cheesemaker. The cheddar is aged naturally through a process the staff have mastered over 44 years of experience.

1024 Salmon River Rd.,
Box 160, Truro, NS
902-895-7906

MILK TYPE
Pasteurized cow's milk

PRODUCTION LEVEL
Industrial

Federally registered

LOCAL ATTRACTIONS AND ACTIVITIES
- Acres of the Golden Pheasant Bird Park (Truro)
- Little White Schoolhouse Museum (Truro)
- The Organery—a collection of 123 melodeons, harmoniums and reed organs (Truro)
- Truro tidal bore—a natural phenomenon of a wave of water moving upstream against the river current

FOR MORE IDEAS, VISIT
www.novascotia.com

CHEESE PRODUCED

CHEDDAR
- Mild
- Medium
- Old
- Old White
- Marble

MARVELLOUS MOZZARELLA

Kayakers at Cape Chignecto Provincial Park

AVAILABILITY

STORES
- Onsite store
  Monday to Friday
  8 a.m. to 4:30 p.m.
- Atlantic Superstores and
  Sobey's grocery stores
  (various locations across
  Atlantic Canada)

USED AT THE FOLLOWING RESTAURANTS
- Casino Nova Scotia (Halifax)
- Lord Nelson Hotel (Halifax)
- Prince George Hotel
  (Halifax)

For distributor inquiries, please contact their sales team.

THE DEFINITIVE GUIDE TO CANADIAN ARTISANAL AND FINE CHEESE

R. R. # 1, Highway 2
Upper Economy, NS
902-647-2751

OWNERS
Maja and Willem van den Hoek

CHEESEMAKER
Willem van den Hoek

MILK TYPE
Thermalized cow's milk

PRODUCTION LEVEL
Artisanal

Provincially licensed

LOCAL ATTRACTIONS AND ACTIVITIES
- Bass River Heritage
  Interpretative Park
- Cobequid Interpretation
  Centre (Central Economy)
- Five Islands Lighthouse (Five
  Islands)
- Fundy Geological Museum
  (Parsboro)
- Ottawa House Museum
  By-the-Sea (Parsboro)

FOR MORE IDEAS, VISIT
www.novascotia.com

MAJA AND WILLEM MOVED FROM THE Dutch town of Soest to Canada in 1970 as newlyweds. After working on farms and in the forests of British Columbia, they eventually settled in Nova Scotia with their family. There they created a little bit of the Netherlands in the Maritimes: Dutch-style farm buildings and a pond with a windmill. Willem and Maja returned to Holland to learn how to make Gouda. They enrolled in courses and worked at a farmstead cheese company where Maja and Willem gained knowledge from the experienced lady cheesemaker.

Since 1980, Willem has been producing his farmstead Gouda. He uses thermalized milk to make his golden wheels with a natural rind. They breathe and interact with the surrounding air, giving them a regional flavour.

A visit to That Dutchman's Farm is about more than just cheese. Willem has created walking trails through his property. You can see the family's rabbits, emus, pot-bellied pigs, Scottish Highland cattle, miniature goats and Bossie, their pet Jersey cow. Sit in the café or on the outdoor deck and enjoy a cup of tea with a light snack.

CHEESE PRODUCED

DRAGON'S BREATH
a soft, blue cheese dipped in black wax

GOUDA
- Mild
- Medium
- Old
- Caraway
- Cumin
- Cumin and Cloves
- Fennel
- Fine Herbs (basil, dill and celery)
- Garlic Mix (garlic, chives and onions)
- Pepper Mix (black peppercorns, chilies, paprika and ginger)
- Smoked

SMEERKAS
a spreadable cheese
- Plain
- Garlic
- Horseradish
- Pepper
- Smoked

SWISS

That Dutchman's store; inset: Willem van den Hoek unmolding gouda

1- Cumin and Cloves Gouda; 2- Garlic Smeerkas; 3- Plain Smeerkas; 4- Fine Herbs Gouda; 5- Plain Smeerkas; 6- Pepper Smeerkas; 7- Caraway Gouda; 8- Smoked Smeerkas; 9- Horseradish Smeerkas; 10- Old Gouda; 11- Extra-old Gouda; 12- Smoked Gouda; 13- Swiss Extra-old; 14- Dragon's Breath; 15- Peppermix Gouda; 16- Garlic Gouda; 17- Nettle Gouda; 18- Cumin Gouda

AVAILABILITY

STORES
- Onsite store
  9 a.m. to 6 p.m.
- Halifax Farmers' Market
- Jost Winery (Tatamagouche)
- Nasstown Market
- Truro Co-op

For distributor inquiries, please contact Maja or Willem.

USED AT THE FOLLOWING RESTAURANTS
- Lord Nelson Hotel (Halifax)

34

SHELLEY EXPERIMENTED MAKING ORGAN-ic goat yogurt for a sick friend in 2000. She discovered that no one in the province was producing any organic goat cheese. It was a natural transition from yogurt to cheese, and she began commercial production herself. Her cheese are certified organic by the Maritime Certified Organic Growers.

R.R. # 5
Tatamagouche, NS
902-857-0264

OWNERS/CHEESEMAKERS
Shelley Roode and Alta MacPherson

MILK TYPE
Pasteurized organic goat's milk

PRODUCTION LEVEL
Artisanal farmstead

Provincially licensed

LOCAL ATTRACTIONS AND ACTIVITIES
• Creamery Square Museum
• Intercolonial Railway Station
• Jost Vineyards (Malagash)
• Sunrise Trail Museum

FOR MORE IDEAS, VISIT
www.novascotia.com

CHEESE PRODUCED

COTTAGE CHEESE

CREAM CHEESE

FETA

PANEER

RICOTTA

Sunrise Trail region

1- Yogurt; 2- Feta; 3- Cream Cheese

AVAILABILITY

STORES

- Amherst Farmers' Market
- Earltown General Store
- Healthy Habits (Truro)
- Stewiacke Farmers' Market
- Tatamagouche Farmers' Market
- Truro Farmers' Market

USED AT THE FOLLOWING RESTAURANTS

- Pictou Lodge (Pictou)
- Piper's Landing (Pictou)
- Train Station (Tatamagouche)

For distributor inquiries, please contact Shelley.

Prince Edward Island

If you know of other Prince Edward Island commercial cheesemakers,
send details to Gurth@CheeseofCanada.ca for the next edition.

79 Water St.
Summerside, PEI
902-888-5088 OR
1-888-235-6455

MILK TYPE
Pasteurized cow's milk

PRODUCTION LEVEL
Industrial

Federally registered

LOCAL ATTRACTIONS AND ACTIVITIES
- PEI National Park
- College of Piping (Charlottetown)
- Founders' Hall—interactive multimedia museum on the confederation of Canada (Charlottetown)

FOR MORE IDEAS, VISIT
www.gov.pe.ca/visitorsguide

IN APRIL 1953, WHEN EIGHT ISLAND CHEESE and butter manufacturers joined together to centralize dairy processing in Summerside, Amalgamated Dairies Limited was born. By joining forces, a stronger company was created that would promote the economic welfare of its members and help to stabilize the dairy industry in Prince Edward Island.

In 1992 the company diversified and began producing European-style cheese as well as its traditional cheddars.

CHEESE PRODUCED

BRICK

CHEDDAR
- Mild
- Mild White
- Mild Light
- Medium
- Medium White
- Old
- Old White
- Extra-Old
- Extra-Old White
- 2-Year-Old White
- Canadian Extra-Sharp
- Cheddar Blend
- Marble

COLBY

CURDS (ORANGE AND WHITE)

FARMERS

HAVARTI (SOLD ONLY IN PEI)

MONTEREY JACK

MONTEREY JACK WHITE

MOZZARELLA

Lupines in Clinton

1- Mozzarella; 2- Colby; 3- Cheddar

AVAILABILITY

STORES
- Onsite factory outlet
  Monday to Friday
  8 a.m. to 5 p.m.
- Local supermarkets and
  convenience stores

*For distributor inquiries, please contact A.D.L. Foods–Bill Corbett,
902-888-5007.*

R.R. # 9
Winsloe North, PEI
902-368-1508

OWNER/CHEESEMAKER
Martina ter Beek

MILK TYPE
Pasteurized cow's milk

PRODUCTION LEVEL
Artisanal farmstead

Provincially licensed

LOCAL ATTRACTIONS AND ACTIVITIES
• Brackley Beach
• Oyster Bed Raceway Track

FOR MORE IDEAS, VISIT
www.gov.pe.ca/visitorsguide

PAUL TOKARCHUK, ONE OF MY PAST CAN-
adian Cuisine students, told me about the
Cheeselady of Prince Edward Island. He discovered her Gouda while on summer vacation on
the island. Knowing I was writing a book on Canadian cheese, Paul sent me a note of his regional food discovery. I am happy he did! Martina
believes in making handmade cheese with only
the finest ingredients. The milk she uses comes
from her husband's herd of cows. Her Gouda is
made according to an old Dutch recipe.

You can buy Martina's cheese only on the island.
Her store and plant are located on the family
farm, a 30-minute drive from Charlottetown.
A six-minute video presentation explaining the
cheesemaking process is offered in both French
and English. You can also watch the cheesemaking through a viewing window in the store and
see a room full of cheese wheels, ripening on the
racks. Such a sight would make a cheese lover
salivate. Both Joanne and I did.

CHEESE PRODUCED

GOUDA
- Mild
- Medium
- Old
- Cumin
- Fenugreek
- 4-Pepper
- Garlic
- Herb and Garlic
- Onion and Red Pepper
- Pepper and Mustard
- Peppercorn
- Red Chili Pepper

1- Cumin; 2- Plain; 3- Pepper; 4- Garlic; 5- Peppercorn; 6- Red Chili Pepper; 7- Pepper and Mustard; 8- Herb and Garlic; 9- Fenugreek

AVAILABILITY

STORES
- Onsite store
  Monday to Saturday
  9 a.m. to 6 p.m.
- Charlottetown Farmers'
  Market
- Mail order

For distributor inquiries, please contact Martina.

USED AT THE FOLLOWING RESTAURANTS
- Delta Prince Edward
  (Charlottetown)
- Culinary Institute of Canada
  (Charlottetown)

New Brunswick

If you know of other New Brunswick commercial cheesemakers,
send details to Gurth@CheeseofCanada.ca for the next edition.

ARMADALE FARM
SUSSEX, NEW BRUNSWICK

MY VISIT TO ARMADALE FARMS, LOCATED just outside of Sussex, the dairy capital of New Brunswick, brought back many childhood memories. My family enjoyed wonderful summer vacations at nearby Fundy National Park. Still in my mind are the images of walking on the tidal mudflats, dancing in the clouds as the Bay of Fundy fog rolled into the park and seeing whitetail deer grazing the fairways of the golf course.

For a special treat, we would drive into Sussex for delicious ice cream. Years later, my father would rush back to Montreal from business trips in Atlantic Canada with an icebox full of ice cream in the car—a special treat for my sister and me.

If Joseph and Regina were open for business back in the early 1970s, I would have been knocking at the door of their cheese shop. Regina began making cheese in 1986, after going back to the Netherlands to learn more about commercial cheesemaking. Now Joseph also makes the cheese. It's a real team effort, using the milk from their own herd of Holsteins.

Joseph and Regina believe in producing homemade products of high quality using no colour, additives or preservatives.

393 Roachville Rd.
Roachville, NB
506-433-6031

OWNERS/CHEESEMAKERS
Joseph and Regina
Duivenvoorden

MILK TYPE
Raw and pasteurized cow's milk

PRODUCTION LEVEL
Artisanal farmstead

Provincially licensed

LOCAL ATTRACTIONS AND ACTIVITIES
- Atlantic Balloon Fiesta (Sussex)
- Fundy National Park (Alma)
- Kings County Covered Bridges Festival. (There is a covered bridge just beside the farm.)

FOR MORE IDEAS, VISIT
www.sussex.ca AND
www.tourismnewbrunswick.ca

THE DEFINITIVE GUIDE TO CANADIAN ARTISANAL AND FINE CHEESE

CHEESE PRODUCED

USING RAW MILK

GOUDA
- Mild
- Medium
- Old
- Caraway
  (in Mild, Medium and Old)
- Cumin
  (in Mild, Medium and Old)
- Cloves and Cumin
- Herbed
- Onion, Paprika and Garlic
- 2-Year-Old
- Smoked

HAVARTI
- Plain
- Basil and Onion
- Caraway

USING PASTEURIZED MILK

CHEDDAR (ALL WHITE)
- Mild
- Medium
- Old
- Extra-Old

EDAM

FARMERS (4% MILK FAT CONTENT)

FETA

QUARK
- 1% milk fat content
- 8% milk fat content

SWISS

Seal Cove on Grand Manan Island

1- Smoked Gouda; 2- Aged Gouda; 3- Swiss; 4- 2-Year-Old Gouda; 5- Quark; 6- Cumin Gouda; 7- Edam; 8- Cloves and Cumin Gouda; 9- Herb Gouda; 10- Onion, Paprika and Garlic Gouda; 11- Caraway Gouda

AVAILABILITY

STORES
- Onsite store
  Monday to Friday
  8 a.m. to 6 p.m.
- Cochrane's Market
  (Saint John)
- Dieppe Farmers' Market
- Fredericton Farmers' Market
- Winterwood Natural Foods
  (Sussex)

USED AT THE FOLLOWING RESTAURANTS
- Broadway Café (Sussex)
- Calactus Vegetarian Café
  (Moncton)
- Paris Crew Café (Saint John)

For distributor inquiries, please contact the Duivenvoordens.

100 Alban Légère Rd.
Sainte-Marie-de-Kent, NB
506-525-9633

OWNERS
Monique Roussel and
André Martineau

CHEESEMAKER
André Martineau

MILK TYPE
Raw cow's and sheep's milk

PRODUCTION LEVEL
Artisanal farmstead

Federally registered

LOCAL ATTRACTIONS AND ACTIVITIES
- Kouchibouguac National Park (Saint-Louis-de-Kent)
- Parlee Beach (Shediac)
- Pays de la Sagouine—thematic park based on the books of Acadian author Antonine Maillet (Bouctouche)
- Irving Eco-Centre: La Dune de Bouctouche—beach and nature interpretive centre (Bouctouche)

FOR MORE IDEAS, VISIT
www.kent.nb.ca AND
www.tourismnewbrunswick.ca

ANDRÉ AND MONIQUE WANTED A BETTER quality of life for their family. Remembering their experiences on their grandparents' farms, they moved to Kent County to establish themselves in the countryside. Originally, the plan was to raise sheep for meat; then they discovered there were very few producers of sheep's milk cheese in Canada. In 2000, their focus changed from meat to cheese production. Making 100% natural cheese, following the French tradition, became André's goal.

The salt air and the organic pastures their sheep graze on give regional uniqueness to their cheese. The sheep are so well taken care of that they spend their summers on Prince Edward Island. Vacationing sheep! Their herd of Jersey cows could become jealous of all the attention the sheep receive.

❧

The first time I tasted André's cheeses in Toronto, several years ago, I was blown away! I did not know such good cheese was made outside of Quebec or Ontario. New Brunswick? La Bergerie aux 4 Vents is the only federally registered cheesemaking operation in the province, hence their cheese can be sold in other parts of Canada.

CHEESE PRODUCED

USING COW'S MILK

Le Gamin
a semi-soft, washed rind cheese

Geai Bleu
a blue cheese

Tomme de Champ Doré
a tomme-style, washed rind cheese

USING SHEEP'S MILK

Sieur de Duplessis
a firm, washed rind cheese

Irving Eco-Centre—Dune de Bouctouche

1- Sieur de Duplessis; 2- Geai Bleu; 3- Tomme de Champ Doré; 4- Le Gamin

AVAILABILITY

STORES
- La Faim de Loup booth at the Saturday Dieppe Farmers' Market
- Croissant Soleil (Dieppe)
- Les Gourmandes (Moncton)
- The Cheese Boutique (Toronto)

USED AT THE FOLLOWING RESTAURANTS
- Delta Beauséjour (Moncton)

For distributor inquiries, please contact Monique.

Les Blancs d'Arcadie

L'ORIGINAL QUI FAIT "SQUICHE SQUICHE"

340 A Saint-Pierre Blvd.
Caraquet, NB
506-727-5952

OWNER/CHEESEMAKER
Alberte Doiron

MILK TYPE
Pasteurized cow's milk

PRODUCTION LEVEL
Artisanal

Provincially licensed

LOCATED IN THE HISTORIC FISHING VILL-age of Caraquet on the Acadian Peninsula, the cheese plant and store cannot be seen from the main road. The company sign at the road directs you down a short drive to the facilities in a country setting with horse corrals and farm cats.

Alberte worked in many different aspects of the food service industry: kitchens, restaurants and bakeries. She loves food! After working for 14 years as the company's cheesemaker, she decided in 2004 to take over the reins and buy the company. Her cheese displays her belief in offering handmade, artisanal products of high quality. You can see Alberte and her staff making the cheese through a viewing window in the store. Guided tours are offered; phone ahead for a reservation.

LOCAL ATTRACTIONS AND ACTIVITIES
- Hôtel Paulin—a grand, historic hotel to be managed soon by the fourth generation of the same family (Caraquet)
- Shippagan Aquarium and Marine Centre (Shippagan)
- Village Historic Acadien— a living history community of restored buildings, showcasing the Acadian lifestyle from the late 1700s to the 1900s (Caraquet)

FOR MORE IDEAS, VISIT
www.tourismnewbrunswick.ca

CHEESE PRODUCED

CHEDDAR
- Plain
- Fine Herbs
- Smoked

CURDS
- Plain
- BBQ

SOFT CHEESES
soft, unripened cheese
- Plain
- Garlic
- Peppercorn

TORTILLONS

Les Blancs d'Arcadie shop

1- Cheddar; 2- Smoked Cheddar; 3- Fine Herbs Cheddar; 4- Peppercorn soft cheese; 5- Garlic soft cheese; 6- Plain soft cheese; 7- Tortillons; 8- BBQ Curds; 9- Plain Curds

AVAILABILITY

STORES
- Onsite store
  Summer and Fall
  Monday to Friday
  8 a.m. to 5 p.m and
  Saturday afternoons
- Atlantic Co-op grocery
  stores (Acadian Peninsula
  region)
- Moncton Farmers' Market
- Tracadie Farmers' Market

USED AT THE FOLLOWING RESTAURANTS
- Café Phare (Caraquet)
- Hôtel Paulin (Caraquet)
- Maribel (Caraquet)

For distributor inquiries, please contact Alberte.

G. PRETTY

Quebec

North shore of the St. Lawrence River

South Shore of the St. Lawrence River

If you know of other Quebec commercial cheesemakers,
send details to Gurth@CheeseofCanada.ca for the next edition.

54

Pied-De-Vent

149, chemin Pointe-Bass
Havre-aux-Maisons,
Magdalen Islands, QC
418-969-9292

FOUNDERS
Jeremy Arseneau, Paul Jomphe
and Vincent Lalonde

CHEESEMAKER
Vincent Lalonde

MILK TYPE
Raw cow's milk

PRODUCTION LEVEL
Artisanal

Provincially licensed

THERE ARE SEVERAL REASONS WHY FRO-
magerie du Pied-de-Vent is unique. It is the only
cheesemaking facility on this archipelago of
islands, located in the Gulf of St. Lawrence.
They produce their cheese using milk from la
Canadienne dairy cows—the first breed to be
developed in North America by the French colonists. The milk has a high fat and protein count.
The cows graze on island vegetation and mature
hay, which have a slight salty taste due to the
sea mist. With such unique milk, Vincent is able
to produce cheese displaying the flavours of the
Magdalen Islands terroir.

LOCAL ATTRACTIONS AND ACTIVITIES
• Aquarium des
  Îles-de-la-Madeleine
  (Île du Havre-Aubert)
• Charcuterie Cochons
  Tout Ronds—delicatessen
  (L'Étang-du-Nord)
• Fumoir d'antan des harengs—
  smoked herring Economuseum
  (Havre-aux-Maisons)
• Espace Bleu—art gallery
  (L'Étang-du-Nord)

FOR MORE IDEAS, VISIT
www.tourismeilesdela-
madelaine.com AND
www.bonjourquebec.com

CHEESE PRODUCED

PIED DE VENT
a semi-soft, mixed rind cheese (both bloomy and washed)

TOMME DES DEMOISELLES
a pressed, dry rind cheese

Cycling on the Magdalen Islands

AVAILABILITY

STORES

- Onsite store
  Daily 8 a.m. to 5 p.m.
- Maison Moisan
  (Quebec City)
- Fromagerie du Marché
  Atwater (Montreal)
- Marché du Vieux-Port
  (Quebec City)
- S. Bourassa Ltée.
  (Mont-Tremblant)

USED AT THE FOLLOWING RESTAURANTS

- La Marée Haute
  (Île du Havre-Aubert)
- La Moulière
  (Havre-aux-Maisons)

For distributor inquiries, please contact Vincent.

56

LES ENTREPRISES DE
LA FERME CHIMO
1 7 6 5
GASPÉ (QUÉBEC) G4X 2W9

1705, boul. de Douglas
Douglastown
Gaspé, QC
418-368-4102

OWNERS
Hélène Morin and Bernard Major

CHEESEMAKER
Bernard Major

MILK TYPE
Raw and pasteurized goat's milk

PRODUCTION LEVEL
Artisanal farmstead

Provincially licensed

BERNARD DISCOVERED THIS PART OF THE Gaspé through an unexpected situation: he was forced to land his Royal Canadian Air Force plane nearby. He liked what he saw and decided to one day return and settle in the area. In 1980 he and Hélène moved from Montreal, bought an abandoned farm, and established a simpler lifestyle amongst people who shared similar values.

Cheese from la Ferme Chimo are made only with the milk from their herd of Swiss Alpine goats. The goats are rotated amongst eight pastures all summer, to permit them to graze on the freshest vegetation available. Under these conditions, the goats produce high-quality milk displaying the flavours of the region's terroir.

During the summer, there are guided tours offered several times a day. At the end of the visit a cheese tasting is offered.

LOCAL ATTRACTIONS AND ACTIVITIES
• Forillon National Park
• Gespeg Micmac First Nations Interpretation Site (Gaspé)
• Haldimand Beach sand castle competition
• Rocher Percé—popular maritime geological feature

FOR MORE IDEAS, VISIT
www.tourismegaspe.com AND
www.bonjourquebec.com

CHEESE PRODUCED

USING PASTEURIZED GOAT'S MILK

CHÈVRE DE GASPÉ
a soft, unripened cheese
- Plain
- Peppercorn

CORSAIRE
a soft, bloomy rind cheese

SALIN DE GASPÉ
a soft, feta-style cheese
- Pasteurized milk version available at local stores
- Raw-milk version available only at the farm

VAL D'ESPOIR
a cheddar-style cheese
- 2-month-old versions available using either pasteurized or raw milk
- 14-month-old versions available using either pasteurized or raw milk
- 40-month-old raw milk cheese available

Gaspé

1- Le Corsaire; 2- Val d"Espoir; 3- Salin de Gaspé

AVAILABILITY

STORES
- Onsite store
  Monday to Saturday
  8:30 a.m. to 7 p.m.
  Sunday
  8:30 a.m. to 6 p.m.
- Fromagerie Hamel (Montreal)
- Fromagerie du Marché Atwater (Montreal)
- Marché du Vieux-Port (Quebec City)
- S. Bourassa Ltée. (Saint-Sauveur)

USED AT THE FOLLOWING RESTAURANTS
- Fairmont Château Frontenac (Quebec City)
- Laurie Raphaël (Quebec City)
- Maison William Wakeham (Gaspé)
- Mon Manège à Toi (Quebec City)

For distributor inquiries, please contact Plaisirs Gourmets, 418-876-3814.

THE DEFINITIVE GUIDE TO CANADIAN ARTISANAL AND FINE CHEESE

THE DEFINITIVE GUIDE TO CANADIAN ARTISANAL AND FINE CHEESE

2292, chemin Plateau
Saguenay, QC
418-543-9860

CO-FOUNDER AND CHEESEMAKER
Martin Gilbert

MILK TYPE
Raw sheep's milk

PRODUCTION LEVEL
Artisanal farmstead

Federally registered

THIS CHEESEMAKING COMPANY EVOLVED from the hobby farm Martin's parents established in 1979 on the Saguenay Fjord. The salty mist deposited on the vegetation his East Friesian sheep graze on gives the milk a slight salty flavour.

Martin's buttery Blanche du Fjord, named after his mother and the fjord of the region, has a nut and mushroom flavour. He is experimenting in the production of a semi-soft, washed rind cheese aged for a minimum of 120 days.

LOCAL ATTRACTIONS AND ACTIVITIES
- D'Arbre en Arbre—tree adventures (Saguenay)
- La Fabuleuse histoire d'un royaume—a multimedia outdoor performance (Saguenay)
- Saguenay Marine Park (Tadoussac)

FOR MORE IDEAS, VISIT
www.saguenaylacsaintjean.net
AND www.bonjourquebec.com

CHEESE PRODUCED

LE BLANCHE DU FJORD
*a soft, bloomy rind cheese, aged for a
minimum of 60 days*

Spectacle La Fabuleuse

AVAILABILITY

STORES

- Onsite store
  Wednesday to Sunday
  10 a.m. to 4 p.m.
- Charcuterie de la Gare
  (Chicoutimi)
- Maison du Pain (La Baie)

USED AT THE FOLLOWING
RESTAURANTS

- Restaurant Le Doyen,
  Auberge des 21 (La Baie)
- Auberge Villa Pachon
  (Jonquière)
- Restaurant Le Privilège
  (Chicoutimi)

For distributor inquiries, please contact Martin.

504, boulevard Tadoussac
Sainte-Rose-du-Nord, QC
418-675-2537

OWNERS
Rhéaume Villeneuve and
Line Turcotte

CHEESEMAKER
Line Turcotte

MILK TYPE
Pasteurized goat's milk

PRODUCTION LEVEL
Artisanal farmstead

Provincially licensed

RHÉAUME AND LINE ARE ENTREPRENEURS.
They realized there were no goats being raised
and milked commercially in the Lac-Saint-Jean
region and believed goats would thrive well in
the local environment.

They named their company Heidi, after their
first goat. Their cheese reflects their belief in
producing a product soft in taste and aroma,
with no goaty flavour association.

LOCAL ATTRACTIONS AND ACTIVITIES

- Croisière La Marjolaine—
  cruise charters
  (Sainte-Rose-du-Nord)
- La Route du fjord—scenic drive
- Musée de la nature—nature
  interpretation centre
  (Sainte-Rose-du-Nord)
- Pourvoirie Québec
  Nature—wildlife excursions
  (Sainte-Rose-du-Nord)

FOR MORE IDEAS, VISIT
www.saguenaylacsaintjean.net
AND www.bonjourquebec.com

CHEESE PRODUCED

LE PETIT HEIDI
a semi-soft, unripened cheese

LA PETITE PERLE
a crottin-style, soft cheese, available in natural and seasoned flavours

LE PETIT TRÉSOR DU FJORD
a soft, bloomy rind, Camembert-style cheese

LE ROSE DU SAGUENAY
a semi-soft, washed rind cheese
- Plain
- Marinated in olive oil

LE SAINTE-ROSE, LAVÉE AU VIN
a semi-soft cheese washed with a Quebec white wine

TARTINADE LE SAINTE-ROSE
a spreadable soft cheese
- Plain
- Chives
- Chocolate
- Spicy

Sainte-Rose, lavée au vin

AVAILABILITY

STORES
- Onsite store
  June to Labour Day
  Monday to Wednesday
  9 a.m. to 7 p.m.
  Thursday 1 p.m. to 7 p.m.
  Friday 9 a.m. to 2 p.m.
  Weekends
  9 a.m. to 7 p.m.
  Fall and winter
  Monday, Tuesday,
  Thursday and Friday
  10 a.m. to 6 p.m.
  Weekends
  10 a.m. to noon
  Closed Wednesdays
- Ask for their products at fine food shops.

USED AT THE FOLLOWING RESTAURANTS
- Café de la Poste (Sainte-Rose-du-Nord)
- Restaurant Le Doyen, Auberge des 21 (La Baie)
- Restaurant le Privilège (Chicoutimi)
- Restaurant La Galouine (Tadoussac)

For distributor inquiries, please contact Line.

La Baie, Québec

2125, chemin Saint-Joseph
La Baie, QC
1-877-544-2622 OR
418-544-2622

OPERATORS
Pierre, Michel, Jean-Marc, Luc and
Patricia Boivin

MILK TYPE
Pasteurized cow's milk

PRODUCTION LEVEL
Semi-industrial

Provincially licensed

ESTABLISHED BY MARIE BLUTEAU AND HER children Bernadette, Noël, Herman, Patrick and Antonio Boivin in 1939, La Fromagerie Boivin is still a family business. Today the third and fourth generations operate it.

In their own words, their cheese "sings with every mouthful." This must be true, for they produce and deliver their fresh cheese daily to the region's restaurants, grocery and corner stores.

LOCAL ATTRACTIONS AND ACTIVITIES
• Brasserie artisanale La
  Korrigane—artisanal
  microbrewery (La Baie)
• Fjord kayaking excursions
  (La Baie)
• The New France Site—historic
  living history village
  (Saint-Félix d'Otis)

FOR MORE IDEAS, VISIT
www.saguenaylacsaintjean.net
AND www.bonjourquebec.com

CHEESE PRODUCED

CHEDDAR
- Fresh, made into blocks
- Grated
- Medium
- Old
- Extra-Old
- Unsalted

CURDS
- Plain
- BBQ

LE PETIT SAGUENÉEN
a firm, unripened cheese

TORTILLONS
- Plain
- BBQ

Canoe camping in Saguenay-Lac-Saint-Jean Region

AVAILABILITY

STORES
- Onsite store
  Summer
  Daily 8:30 a.m. to 9:30 p.m.
  Winter
  Daily 8:30 a.m. to 6 p.m.
- Boulangerie Val-Jalbert
  (Montreal)
- Regional grocery and corner
  stores
- I.G.A. and Métro grocery
  stores (Montreal and
  Quebec City regions)

For distributor inquiries, please contact the company directly.

Fromagerie St-Laurent

735, R.R. # 6
Saint-Bruno, QC
1-800-463-9141 OR
418-343-3655

THIS THIRD-GENERATION FAMILY ENTER-prise began with Auguste, Maurice's father. He moved the family to the Lac-Saint-Jean region in the 1930s and eventually acquired five small cheese factories. In 1940, Maurice took over the running of the company. Ten years later, he sold the majority of the smaller plants and concentrated his efforts on the largest in Hébertville. Renovations barely completed, a fire destroyed the plant. Mr. Saint-Laurent rebuilt in nearby Saint-Bruno where a better location that provides improved access to water was found. The plant now processes approximately 14 million litres of milk a year. His sons Luc, Yves and François now oversee the company.

Fromagerie St-Laurent is known as being an innovator. It was one of the first companies to sell cheese curds and it created the first commercially produced old cheddar soaked in port wine.

FOUNDER
Maurice Saint-Laurent

MILK TYPE
Pasteurized cow's milk

PRODUCTION LEVEL
Semi-industrial

Federally registered

LOCAL ATTRACTIONS AND ACTIVITIES
- Archealogical and Historical Centre of Métabetchouane (Desbiens)
- Caverne trou à la fée—cave experiences (Desbiens)
- Circuit de la terre à la ferme—farm tours (Alma)
- Public beach (Saint-Gédeon)

FOR MORE IDEAS, VISIT
www.saguenaylacsaintjean.net
AND www.bonjourquebec.com

CHEESE PRODUCED

BRICK

CHEDDAR
- Fresh
- Light
- Medium
- Old
- Old with port wine
- Fine Herbs

CURDS

GOUDA

PARMESAN

SWISS

TORTILLONS

AVAILABILITY

STORES
- Onsite store
  Summer
  Daily 7 a.m. to 9 p.m.
  Winter
  Daily 7 a.m. to 6 p.m.

USED AT THE FOLLOWING RESTAURANTS
- Restaurant Marchand Saint-Bruno (Saint-Bruno)

For distributor inquiries, please contact Alain Royer, 450-655-7575.

THE DEFINITIVE GUIDE TO CANADIAN ARTISANAL AND FINE CHEESE

THE DEFINITIVE GUIDE TO CANADIAN ARTISANAL AND FINE CHEESE

FROMAGERIE
L E H M A N N

291, rang Saint-Isidore
Hébertville, QC
418-344-1414

OWNERS/CHEESEMAKERS
Marie, Jacob, Sem, Isaban and
Lea Lehmann

MILK TYPE
Raw cow's milk

PRODUCTION LEVEL
Artisanal farmstead

Provincially licensed

THE LEHMANNS SELECTED ONE OF THE oldest dairy cow species, Brown Swiss, because it produces a very rich milk. The Lac-Saint-Jean region has high-quality pastures, and the Lehmanns take good care of their animals: every cheesemaker knows that the better the milk, the greater potential the cheese has for unique taste and aroma.

LOCAL ATTRACTIONS AND ACTIVITIES
- Circuit régional de chaloupe à rames—regional rowing competition (Hébertville and region)
- Festivalma—cultural and sports festival (Alma)
- Mont Lac-Vert hiking trails (Hébertville)
- Public beach (Hébertville)

FOR MORE IDEAS, VISIT
www.saguenaylacsaintjean.net
AND www.bonjourquebec.com

CHEESE PRODUCED

LE KÉNOGAMI
a soft, washed rind cheese, aged for 60 days

PIKAUBA
a semi-soft, washed rind cheese

LE VALBERT
a firm, washed rind cheese, aged for 3 to 6 months

1- Le Valbert; 2- Le Pikauba; 3- Le Kénogami

AVAILABILITY

STORES

- Onsite store
  June to October
  Thursday to Sunday
  1 to 5 p.m.
  Winter
  Friday and Saturday
  1 to 5 p.m.
- Corneau Cantin
  (Jonquière and Chicoutimi)
- Charcuterie La Bastille
  (Alma)

USED AT THE FOLLOWING RESTAURANTS

- Hôtellerie Cépal (Jonquière)
- Restaurant Le Doyen,
  Auberge des 21 (La Baie)
- Restaurant Le Privilège
  (Chicoutimi)
- Restaurant Spag
  (Chicoutimti)

For distributor inquiries, please contact Marie for regional inquiries or Plaisir Gourmets, 418-876-3814 for province-wide inquiries.

68

156, avenue Albert-Perron
Saint-Prime, QC
418-251-3164

FOUNDER
Adélard Perron

MASTER CHEESEMAKER
Patrice Croyeau

MILK TYPE
Raw, thermalized and
pasteurized cow's milk

PRODUCTION LEVEL
Industrial

Federally registered

THIS IS CANADA'S OLDEST FAMILY-OWNED cheesemaking company, with over 115 years of experience between the four generations of Perrons. Their specialty, known internationally, is high-quality cheddar. They remain the only private company to export cheddar to the United Kingdom. Britons have been enjoying Perron cheese since the early 1900s. Until the 1950s, cheddar was the most important source of protein in the British diet.

Next door, the Cheddar Museum demonstrates the important role the cheddar cheese industry played in the Saguenay-Lac-Saint-Jean region.

LOCAL ATTRACTIONS AND ACTIVITIES
- Centre écologique de Saint-Félicien—trout fishing ponds (Saint-Félicien)
- Cycling trails
- Paraskiing (Saint-Prime)
- Boréalium—a boreal wildlife park (Saint-Félicien)

FOR MORE IDEAS, VISIT
www.saguenaylacsaintjean.net
AND www.bonjourquebec.com

THE DEFINITIVE GUIDE TO CANADIAN ARTISANAL AND FINE CHEESE

CHEESE PRODUCED

USING RAW MILK

CHEDDAR (WHITE)
• Special Reserve 115th—18 months old

SWISS

USING THERMALIZED MILK

CHEDDAR (WHITE)
• 1-Year-Old
• 2-Year-Old
• Le Doyen, 4-year-old
• Soaked in 10-year-old port wine

USING PASTEURIZED MILK

BRICK

CHEDDAR (WHITE)
• Fresh
• Medium

COLBY

CURDS
• Plain
• BBQ

GOUDA

MONTEREY JACK

MOZZARELLA

SWISS
• Regular
• Light

TORTILLONS

Swiss

1- Swiss; 2- Four-year-old Cheddar; 3- Aged Cheddar with port wine

AVAILABILITY

STORES
• Onsite store
  8 a.m. to 6 p.m.
• Fromagerie du Marché Atwater (Montreal)
• Regional I.G.A., Loblaws, Métro and Provigo grocery stores

USED AT THE FOLLOWING RESTAURANTS
• Laurie Raphaël (Quebec City)
• Restaurant Yogi-Roberval (Roberval)
• Voodoo Grill (Quebec City)

For distributor inquiries, please contact the company's sales team.

2350, rang Saint-Eusèbe
Saint-Félicien, QC
418-679-5609

FOUNDERS
Rodrique, Gérard and Pierre
Bouchard; Lise Rosa; and Suzie
Brossard

CHEESEMAKERS
Pierre Bouchard and Denis
Gagnon

MILK TYPE
Organic thermalized cow's milk

PRODUCTION LEVEL
Artisanal farmstead

Provincially licensed

WANTING TO RAISE HEALTHIER ANIMALS, the owners of the dairy farm Ferme des chutes began the process of becoming organic in 1978. It took five years to obtain their organic certification, but they gained a new respect for the environment, their herd of Holstein cows was healthier and their veterinary bills were a tenth of their original amount. If an organic diet caused the animals to be healthier, they wondered if it may lead to similar positive results for humans.

In 1993 they built the cheesemaking facility to transform their organic milk into certified organic cheddar. Their organic production is certified by Québec-Vrai.

Their aged cheddars are named after local waterfalls and rapids on the nearby Ashuapmushuan River, a historic route used by the voyageurs during the time of the fur trade.

LOCAL ATTRACTIONS AND ACTIVITIES
- Boréalium—a boreal wildlife park (Saint-Félicien)
- Croisière le Héron bleu—scenic boat cruises
- Mountain biking trails (Saint-Félicien)
- Les Grands Jardins de Normandin—a botanical garden (Normandin)

FOR MORE IDEAS, VISIT
www.saguenaylacsaintjean.net
AND www.bonjourquebec.com

CHEESE PRODUCED

CHEDDAR

- Fresh
- Le Rapide Arcand (6-month-old)
- La Chute à Michel (1-year-old)
- La Chute à l'Ours (2-year-old)
- La Chute Chaudière (3-year-old)

CURDS

LE SAINT-FÉLICIEN
*a Brick/Colby-style firm, rindless
cheese*

1- La Chute à l'Ours; 2- Le Rapide Arcand; 3- Curds; 4- La Chute Chaudière; 5- Mild Cheddar;
6- Le St-Félicien; 7- La Chute à Michel

AVAILABILITY

STORES

- Onsite store
  June to Labour Day
  Monday to Friday
  8 a.m. to 6 p.m.
  Weekends
  8 a.m. to 5 p.m.
  Winter
  Monday to Friday
  8 a.m. to 5 p.m.
- Corneau et Cantin
  (Chicoutimi)
- Le Crac (Quebec City)
- La Giroflee (Quebec City)

USED AT THE FOLLOWING
RESTAURANTS

- Café du Clocher (Alma)
- Café Cambio (Chicoutimi)
- Restaurant Le Bordelais
  (Alma)
- Restaurant Spag
  (Chicoutimi)

For distributor inquiries, please contact the company directly.

Fromagerie
St-Fidèle

THE CHEESE OF FROMAGERIE SAINT-FIDÈLE were available in urban centres as early as 1902. The town of La Malbaie (formerly known as Murray Bay) has been a popular tourist destination for over 200 years, and in the early 20th century, ships of the Canada Steamship Line brought vacationers to the area. The ships would return to their home ports along the St. Lawrence River, delivering wheels of the local cheese to awaiting cheesemongers. With the arrival of the railway to the region in 1918, the cheese was sent overland to Quebec City. Over the years, the company expanded by purchasing other local cheese operations and building newer and larger facilities. In 2001 a consortium of dairy producers and cheese processors from the Lac-Saint-Jean region acquired the company.

❧

I was happy to discover they were soaking their Swiss cheese in apple cider and apple-based mistelle liqueur, produced by Cidredrie et Verger Pedneault. Joanne and I visited Michel Pedneault at his apple orchard on l'Isle-aux-Coudres back in 2003. I love cider, so this was a special treat for me. The 20-minute ferry ride across the St. Lawrence River permitted us to enjoy the beautiful shoreline scenery of the Charlevoix region.

2815, boulevard Malcolm-Fraser
La Malbaie, QC
418-434-2220

MILK TYPE
Pasteurized cow's milk

PRODUCTION LEVEL
Semi-industrial

Federally registered

LOCAL ATTRACTIONS AND ACTIVITIES
- Cidrerie et Verger Pedneault—apple orchard and ciderie (Îles-aux-Coudres)
- Les Jardins du Centre—an organic vegetable grower (Les Éboulements)
- Potterie Port aux Persils—local artisanal potter (Port aux Persils)
- Le Relais des saveurs-Fumoir Charlevoix—a smokehouse and outlet of local products (La Malbaie)

FOR MORE IDEAS, VISIT
www.tourisme-charlevoix.com
AND www.bonjourquebec.com

CHEESE PRODUCED

CHEDDAR
- Fresh, in both white and orange

CURDS (WHITE ONLY)

SWISS
- Light
- Soaked in apple cider
- Soaked in mistelle
- Soaked in port wine

Hautes-Gorges Provincial Park

Light Swiss

AVAILABILITY

STORES
- Onsite store
  Summer
  8 a.m. to 9 p.m.
  Winter
  8 a.m. to 5 p.m.
- Laiterie Charlevoix
  (Baie-Saint-Paul)
- Les Jardins du Centre
  (Les Éboulements)
- Regional I.G.A., Métro and
  Provigo grocery stores

USED AT THE FOLLOWING RESTAURANTS
- Auberge des Peupliers
  (La Malbaie)
- Auberge La Muse
  (Baie-Saint-Paul)
- La Pinsonnière (La Malbaie)

For distributor inquiries, please contact Accès Ingrédients,
450-649-9595.

74

1167, blvd. Monseigneur de Laval
Baie-Saint-Paul, QC
418-435-2184

CHEESEMAKER
Dominique Labbé

MILK TYPE
Raw and pasteurized cow's milk

PRODUCTION LEVEL
Semi-industrial

Federally registered

LOCAL ATTRACTIONS AND ACTIVITIES
• Baie-Saint-Paul's art galleries
• Le Massif ski resort
• La Route des saveurs—
  Charlevoix region culinary
  flavour trail
• Whale-watching tours
  (Tadoussac)

FOR MORE IDEAS, VISIT
www.tourisme-charlevoix.com
AND www.bonjourquebec.com

LAITERIE CHARLEVOIX HAS BEEN IN business since 1948, when Stanislas and Elmina Labbé began making cheese locally. The company's heritage continues with Dominique Labbé as the cheesemaker. Their facility is located on the main highway from Quebec City to Tadoussac. It's a great place to stop and stretch travel weary legs.

As part of the EconoMuseum system, the company offers interpretive displays on cheesemaking.

CHEESE PRODUCED

USING RAW COW'S MILK

CHEDDAR
aged

USING PASTEURIZED COW'S MILK

CURDS

FLEURMIER
a soft, bloomy rind cheese in the Camembert-style

MILD CHEDDAR

1- Fleurmier; 2- Mild Cheddar; 3- Curds; inset: Laiterie Charlevoix sign

AVAILABILITY

STORES

- Onsite store
  Daily 8 a.m. to 7 p.m.
- Local convenience stores
- Maison Moisan
  (Quebec City)
- Fromagerie du Marché
  Atwater (Montreal)

USED AT THE FOLLOWING RESTAURANTS

- La Pinsonnière (La Malbaie)
- Le Pigneron (La Malbaie)
- Fairmont Manoir Richelieu
  (La Malbaie)

For distributor inquiries, please contact the company.

LA MAISON D'AFFINAGE MAURICE DUFOUR INC.

1339, blvd. Monseigneur de Laval
Baie-Saint-Paul, QC
418-435-5692

FOUNDERS
Maurice Dufour and Francine Bouchard

MILK TYPE
Raw and pasteurized cow's milk

PRODUCTION LEVEL
Semi-industrial

Federally registered

LOCAL ATTRACTIONS AND ACTIVITIES
- Croix de Clermont Mountain Regional Lookout Site (Clermont)
- Les Jardins Secrets du Vieux Moulin—a botanical garden (Baie-Saint-Paul)
- La Route des saveurs—Charlevoix region culinary flavour trail
- Maison René Richard Museum and Art Gallery (Baie-Saint-Paul)

FOR MORE IDEAS, VISIT
www.tourisme-charlevoix.com
AND www.bonjourquebec.com

MAURICE DUFOUR HAD A VISION. HE wanted to promote and support regional agriculture by creating an exceptional product derived from a primary ingredient. He chose milk as his primary ingredient and artisanal cheese as his product. Maurice believes the milk produced in the Baie-Saint-Paul region has unique flavours and aromas and is well-suited for cheesemaking.

In 1995 his cheese, Le Migneron de Charlevoix, leapt onto the market. Maurice wanted to produce enough artisanal cheese to supply the entire province. Five years later, Le Ciel de Charlevoix, a raw milk, blue cheese, became their second artisanal cheese. Le Migneron de Charlevoix was named the 2002 Grand Champion at the Canadian Grand Prix Cheese competition. He and his young team like to experiment. They are currently developing a sheep's milk cheese, to be launched in 2006.

For a complete cycle of cheese experiences, begin with a tour of the facility. Next, taste and enjoy the cheese offered. Finally, discover and savour the cheese in prepared dishes. At their onsite restaurant, Joanne was quite impressed with her mouth-watering Tian de légumes estivaux des Jardins du centre, a dish of seasonal, local organic vegetables baked with a layer of cheese. This was her first vegetarian main course in several weeks of travelling in Quebec and she was craving vegetables. I devoured my Soufflé au Migneron, perfumed with cognac. It was appreciated slowly, each spoonful fastidiously cleaned of the flavourful food before going for the next bite of bliss.

CHEESE PRODUCED

USING RAW COW'S MILK

LE CIEL DE CHARLEVOIX
a semi-soft, surface ripened blue cheese

USING PASTEURIZED COW'S MILK

LE MIGNERON DE CHARLEVOIX
a semi-soft, surface ripened, washed rind cheese

Le Ciel de Charlevoix production

1- Le Migneron de Charlevoix; 2- Le Ciel de Charlevoix

AVAILABILITY

STORES

• Onsite store
  Summer
  Daily, 9 a.m. to 4 p.m.
  Off-season
  Call to verify hours of operation
• Available in specialty food shops across Quebec
• Available in good specialty cheesemongers in Ontario and the eastern U.S.

USED AT THE FOLLOWING RESTAURANTS

• Onsite restaurant
• Auberge des Peupliers (La Malbaie)
• Les Saveurs Oubliées (Les Éboulements)

For Quebec distributor inquiries, please contact the company. For Ontario, please call Alain Besré, Fromagerie du Marché Atwater, 1-866-932-4959.

LE BEAUPRÉ

MARQUE   BRAND

STEEVE AND HIS STAFF USE TRADITIONAL techniques and equipment to produce their cheese, believing the older ways allow the flavours of the cheese to develop more fully. Steeve enjoys experimenting and creating new products and was the innovator in producing the first flavoured fresh cheddar-type cheese. His spicy Ganapeño and salty Tortillo would go well with a good Quebec beer. He recently launched his Norvegia and is currently working on the development of two new washed rind cheeses.

9430, blvd. Sainte-Anne,
Sainte-Anne-de-Beaupré, QC
418-827-1771

FOUNDER AND MASTER
CHEESEMAKER
Steeve Fontaine

MILK TYPE
Pasteurized cow's milk

PRODUCTION LEVEL
Semi-industrial

Provincially licensed

LOCAL ATTRACTIONS AND ACTIVITIES
• Basilique
  Sainte-Anne-de-Beaupré—
  catholic shrine
  (Sainte-Anne-de-Beaupré)
• Musée de l'abeille—
  bee Economuseum
  (Château-Richer)
• Musée Edison du
  phonographe—
  phonograph museum
  (Sainte-Anne-de-Beaupré)
• Moulin du Petit Pré—historic
  French grist mill and modern
  winery (Château-Richer)

FOR MORE IDEAS, VISIT
www.cotesdebeaupre.com
AND www.bonjourquebec.com

CHEESE PRODUCED

CHEDDAR

- Fresh (white, orange and marble)
- BBQ
- Fine Herbs
- Three Peppercorns
- Aged 1- and 2-Year-Old

FUMERON
a maple-smoked cheddar

GANAPEÑO
a semi-soft, unripened, Armenian-style braided cheese with red chilis

LE NORVEGIA
a semi-soft, ripened, Norwegian-style cheese

PETIT GOURMET
a semi-soft, rindless, Havarti-style cheese

- Plain
- Fine Herbs
- Garden Vegetables
- Garlic
- Three Peppercorns

TORSABEL
a semi-soft, unripened, Armenian-style braided cheese with black niger seed

TORTILLO
a semi-soft, unripened, fine threads of stretched tortillon cheese

- Plain
- BBQ

YET TO BE NAMED
- two washed rind, semi-soft cheeses

Quebec City's Lower Town

AVAILABILITY

STORES

- Onsite store
  Monday to Wednesday
  8:30 a.m. to 6 p.m.
  Thursday and Friday
  8:30 a.m. to 9 p.m.
  Saturday and Sunday
  8:30 a.m. to 6:30 p.m.
- Available at local I.G.A.,
  Maxi, Métro and Provigo
  grocery stores

USED AT THE FOLLOWING RESTAURANTS

- Ashton (Quebec City)
- Le Montagnais
  (Sainte-Anne-de-Beaupré)
- Normandin (Quebec City)

For distributor inquiries, please contact the company.

4696, chemin Royal
Sainte-Famille
Île d'Orléans, QC
418-829-1077

PRESIDENT AND CHEESEMAKER
Jocelyn Labbé

MILK TYPE
Pasteurized cow's milk

PRODUCTION LEVEL
Artisanal

Provincially licensed

LOCAL ATTRACTIONS AND ACTIVITIES
- La Chocolaterie de l'Île d'Orléans (Sainte-Pétronille, Île d'Orléans)
- Maison Drouin— historical habitant house (Sainte-Famille, Île d'Orléans)
- Seigneurie Mauvide-Genest— historical seigneurial manor (Saint-Jean, Île d'Orléans)
- Wineries, cideries and producers of black currant cassis liqueur (Île d'Orléans)

La Chocolaterie de l'Île d'Orléans offers the best chocolate-dipped, soft ice cream cone Joanne and I have ever enjoyed! The Belgian chocolate coating is so thick that you can bite the top off and use a spoon to eat the ice cream centre.

FOR MORE IDEAS, VISIT
www.iledorleans.com
AND www.bonjourquebec.com

WHEN JOANNE AND I VISITED L'ÎLE D'ORLÉans in 2003, we were told that cheese had been produced on the island since approximately 1635. Local legend has it that Anne Aubin used to make the cheese and sell it regularly at the Quebec City farmers' market. This unique island cheese was the first cheese produced in North America. It continued to be made in people's homes until 1970.

For nearly 40 years it has not been available in stores, but the technique of making the cheese was not lost. Gérard Aubin, a master cheesemaker, continued to make it for his own personal enjoyment. Through Jocelyn Labbé's perseverance, Mr. Aubin came out of retirement at the age of 88 to show him how to make the cheese. With modern scientific methods and patience, Mr. Labbé was able to reproduce the cheese. Milk from the island's dairy farmers is used to give the cheese its distinctive local flavour. The cheese is produced in very small quantities, by the bucket. The curds are ladled into the moulds, as per Mr. Aubin's instructions.

The facility is located next door to Maison Drouin, a restored habitant house (circa 1675). During the summer months, a terrace is open and visitors can grill their cheese themselves and enjoy it with a salad or other snack. When you taste this cheese, you experience the island's cultural and culinary heritage.

CHEESE PRODUCED

LA FAISELLE
a fresh, unripened cheese

LE PAILLASSON
a soft grilling cheese, aged for 3 days

LE RAFFINÉ
a soft, washed rind cheese, aged for 28 days

Fromages de l'Isle d'Orléans' historical technique; Fromages de l'isle d'Orleans sign

Le Paillasson

AVAILABILITY

STORES

- Onsite store
  June to Labour Day
  Daily 10 a.m. to 6 p.m.
  September and October
  Weekends
  10 a.m. to 6 p.m.
- Buffet Maison (Île d'Orléans)
- Maison Moisan
  (Quebec City)
- Fromagerie du Marché
  Atwater (Montreal)
- Marché du Vieux-Port
  (Quebec City)

USED AT THE FOLLOWING RESTAURANTS

- Auberge La Goéliche
  (Sainte-Pétronille, Île
  d'Orléans)
- Le Relais des Pins
  (Sainte-Famille, Île
  d'Orléans)
- Resto Bistro L'Ardoise
  (Quebec City)

For distributor inquiries, please contact Jocelyn.

G. PRETTY

**Ferme
S·M·A·**
La ferme en ville

2222, rue d'Estimauville
Beauport, QC
418-667-0478

OWNERS
Les Soeurs de la charité de
Québec

CHEESEMAKER
Christian Lavoie

MILK TYPE
Pasteurized cow's milk

PRODUCTION LEVEL
Semi-industrial

Provincially licensed

LOCAL ATTRACTIONS AND ACTIVITIES
• Baie de Beauport—a riverfront
  park
• Le Chemin du Roy—a scenic
  and historic drive
• Grands Feux Loto-Québec—
  fireworks festival (Beauport)
• Maison Girardin—
  18th-century restored home
  (Beauport)
• Montmorency Falls (Beauport)

FOR MORE IDEAS, VISIT
www.quebecregion.com
AND www.bonjourquebec.com

THIS FARM WAS ESTABLISHED IN 1893 BY the religious order on rural land between Quebec City and Beauport. Now it is surrounded on all sides by development, hence its designation as *la ferme en ville*, the farm within the city. The farm consists of 600 acres (243 hectares) of crop land, 200 Holstein cows, a cheesemaking facility and greenhouses for growing flowers.

The mission of the farm is to provide rehabilitation and training for individuals. Many work on the farm as apprentices, learning new career skills from experts and gaining valuable personal and social experiences.

Its present cheesemaking operation began in 1988. The company has almost complete control of all the various stages involved in the production and sale of their cheese. The farm grows the feed for their cows and 90 percent of their milk requirements are supplied by their own herd. They produce the cheese onsite and distribute 50 percent to their retail clients; the remaining 50 percent is sold at their farm store. It is the only cheesemaking establishment I have ever seen with a drive-through sales window.

The farm enterprise has become such a part of the local community, many people do not know Ferme S.M.A.'s real name is Ferme Saint-Michel l'Archange.

CHEESE PRODUCED

CHEDDAR
- Fresh cheddar in blocks
- Plain
- Le P'tit Piquant (with chili flakes)
- Le P'tit Potager (with herbs)
- Three Peppers
- Aged cheddar (6- to 12-month-old)

CURDS
- Plain
- Le P'tit Piquant (with chili flakes)
- Le P'tit Potager (with herbs)

TORTILLONS

1- Le P'tit Piquant Cheddar; 2- Le P'tit Piquant Curds; 3- Le P'tit Potager Cheddar; 4- Three Peppers Cheddar; 5- Tortillons; 6- Fresh Cheddar; 7- Plain Curds

AVAILABILITY

STORES
- Onsite store
  Monday to Wednesday
  8 a.m. to 6 p.m.
  Thursday and Friday
  8 a.m. to 8 p.m.
  Saturday 8 a.m. to 6 p.m.
  Sunday 10 a.m. to 5 p.m.
- Local I.G.A., Métro and Provigo grocery stores
- Local corner stores

USED AT THE FOLLOWING RESTAURANTS
- Auberge Le Canard Huppé (Saint-Laurent, Île d'Orléans)

For distributor inquiries, please contact the company.

84

Fromagerie des Amériques

JEAN-PIERRE OPERATES A CHEESEMAKING facility within the city limits. A third-generation cheesemaker with experience working in Alberta and Quebec cheese plants, he knew the expense involved in establishing such a facility. To reduce capital expenditures, he obtains his pressed cheese from other producers. He and his staff complete the cheesemaking process, creating the finished products. Jean-Pierre is training the next generation, his daughter, in the craft of cheesemaking.

903, boulevard Charest
Quebec City, QC
418-684-2345

FOUNDER
Jean-Pierre Baribeau

MILK TYPE
Pasteurized cow's milk

PRODUCTION LEVEL
Semi-industrial

Federally registered

LOCAL ATTRACTIONS AND ACTIVITIES
- Old Quebec City—a UNESCO World Heritage Site
- Marché du Vieux-Port—indoor farmers' market
- Maison Moisan—an amazing fine food shop
- Odyssey Canada and The National Battlefield Park—site of the 1759 Battle of The Plains of Abraham
- The Citadelle and the city's historic fortifications

FOR MORE IDEAS, VISIT
www.quebecregion.com
AND www.bonjourquebec.com

CHEESE PRODUCED

ANOUBLIE
a grilling cheese

BLUDZ
a finely shredded tortillons cheese

CHEDDAR
- 2-Year-Old cured in 15-year-old port wine

TORTILLONS
- Plain
- BBQ

Maison Moisan

Fromagerie des Amériques

1- Port marinated Cheddar; 2- Anoublie; 3- Plain Tortillons; 4- BBQ Tortillons

AVAILABILITY

STORES
- Onsite store
  Monday to Friday
  8 a.m. to 3:30 p.m.
- Local I.G.A. and Métro grocery stores

For distributor inquiries, please contact Jean-Pierre.

Ferme
Tourilli
Artisan Fromager

1541, rang Notre-Dame
Saint-Raymond-de-Portneuf, QC
418-337-2876

OWNER/CHEESEMAKER
Eric Proulx

MILK TYPE
Pasteurized goat's milk

PRODUCTION LEVEL
Artisanal farmstead

Provincially licensed

LOCAL ATTRACTIONS AND ACTIVITIES
- Cycling trails
- Les blés sont murs—
  artisanal bakery
  (Deschambault-Grondines)
- La Vallée secrète—
  nature adventures
  (Saint-Raymond-de-Portneuf)
- River canoeing and kayaking

FOR MORE IDEAS, VISIT
www.tourisme.portneuf.com
(French only) AND
www.bonjourquebec.com

ERIC, RAISED ON A FARM IN THE EASTERN Townships of Quebec, wanted to enjoy a country lifestyle with his young family. After a brief career as a geographer, he decided to raise Alpine goats and make cheese with their milk. It took two years of full-time commitment to the project before he began commercial production in 2002. Eric now wants to motivate other young cheesemakers to establish this comfortable lifestyle for themselves.

Eric is constantly experimenting, creating new cheese. In cooperation with Pascal Cothet, chef at L'Auberge La Bastide, they created Le Bastidou, a basil pesto-flavoured cheese.

THE DEFINITIVE GUIDE TO CANADIAN ARTISANAL AND FINE CHEESE

CHEESE PRODUCED

BARRE À BOULARD
a semi-soft cheese

LE BASTIDOU
a semi-soft, natural rind cheese with a layer of basil pesto in the middle; aged for 25 days

LE BOUQUETIN DE PORTNEUF
a semi-soft to firm, naturally ripened crottin-style cheese; aged for 10 to 15 days

LE CAP-ROND
a semi-soft, natural ripened Selles-sur-Cher style cheese, coated with crushed oak ashes

Ferme Tourilli goats; Cheesemaker Eric Proulx

1- Barre à Boulard; 2- Le Cap Rond; 3- Le Bouquetin de Portneuf; 4- Le Bastidou

AVAILABILITY

STORES

- Onsite store
  May to December
  Thursday to Sunday
  1 to 4 p.m.
- La Trappe à Fromage (Gatineau)
- Maison Moisan (Quebec City)
- Le Marché des Saveurs (Montreal)
- Trois-Rivières public market

USED AT THE FOLLOWING RESTAURANTS

- Auberge La Bastide (Saint-Raymond-de-Portneuf)
- Café du Clocher Penché (Quebec City)
- Restaurant Panache (Quebec City)
- Restaurant Toast (Quebec City)

Joanne and I were blown away by the delicious and innovative dishes served to us at Toast. We loved sitting in the private courtyard, under a canvas awning. It is our favourite restaurant in Quebec City.

For distributor inquiries, please contact Plaisirs Gourmets, 418-876-3814.

OVER 150 YEARS AGO, ALEXIS CAYER settled onto virgin land and helped develop what would become the Portneuf region of Quebec. His descendants have continued working on his vision, contributing character and identity to the region with their artisan skills as landscapers, builders, farmers and, eventually, cheesemakers.

La Fromagerie Alexis de Portneuf produces a large variety of cheese, fashioned in the French-style.

71, avenue Saint-Jacques
Saint-Raymond-de-Portneuf, QC
1-866-901-3312

MILK TYPE
Pasteurized cow's and goat's milk

PRODUCTION LEVEL
Industrial

Federally registered

LOCAL ATTRACTIONS AND ACTIVITIES
- Ferme d'élevage de wapitis J.L. Bédard—wapiti (elk) ranch (Saint-Raymond)
- La Ferme l'Émeulienne—emu ranch and B & B (Petit Capsa)
- Les Chemins des arts—artist studio tour (Portneuf region)
- Outdoor adventures (hiking, canoeing/kayaking, horseback riding, snowshoeing) at Vallée Bras du Nord (Saint-Raymond)

FOR MORE IDEAS, VISIT
www.tourisme.portneuf.com
(French only) AND
www.bonjourquebec.com

CHEESE PRODUCED

USING PASTEURIZED COW'S MILK

BELLE CRÈME
a triple cream brie-style, soft, bloomy rind cheese

BLEUBRY
a soft, bloomy rind, blue cheese

BONAPARTE
a double cream brie-style, soft, bloomy rind cheese

BRIE DE PORTNEUF
a soft, bloomy rind cheese

BRIE DOUBLE CRÈME DE PORTNEUF
a soft, bloomy rind cheese with added cream

BRISE DU MATIN
a soft, double cream brie-style, bloomy rind cheese

CAMEMBERT CAMPAGNARD
a soft, bloomy rind cheese

CAMEMBERT DE PORTNEUF
a soft, bloomy rind cheese

LE CALENDOS
a soft, Camembert-style, bloomy rind cheese

LA RUMEUR
a double cream brie-style, soft, bloomy rind cheese

SAINT-HONORÉ
a triple cream brie-style, soft, bloomy rind cheese

LE SAINT-RAYMOND
a soft, mixed rind (bloomy and washed) cheese

LA SAUVAGINE
a soft, washed rind cheese

USING GOAT'S MILK

AGED CAPRANO
a firm, natural rind cheese, aged for 18 months

CAPRANO
a firm, natural rind cheese, aged for 6 months

CAPRINY
a soft, unripened cheese
- Plain
- Herbs
- Pepper

LE CENDRILLON
a soft, surface ripened, ash-coated cheese

CHÈVRE D'ART
a soft, surface ripened cheese

PAILLOT DE CHÈVRE
a soft, surface ripened cheese, created according to traditional techniques

USING COW'S AND GOAT'S MILK

CHÈVRE DES NEIGES
a soft, unripened cheese

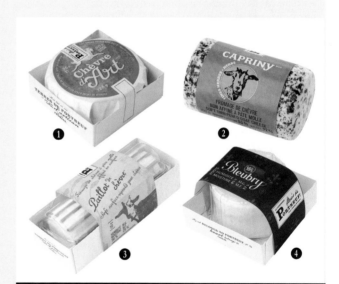

1- Chèvre d'Art; 2- Capriny; 3- Paillot de Chèvre; 4- Bleubry

AVAILABILITY

STORES

- Onsite store
  Monday to Wednesday and Saturday
  8:30 a.m. to 5 p.m.
  Thursday and Friday
  8:30 a.m. to 9 p.m.
  Sunday 9 a.m. to 5 p.m.
- National grocery store chains

For distributor inquiries, please contact their sales team.

THE DEFINITIVE GUIDE TO CANADIAN ARTISANAL AND FINE CHEESE

THE FIRST DAY OF PRODUCTION FOR Fromageries Jonathan was October 29, 2003, but the preliminary planning and preparations had begun years before. Jonathan Portelance had worked on the establishment of other cheese-making operations in both the Portneuf region and the Magdalen Islands of Quebec and wanted to bring a European cheesemaking concept to the Mauricie region. He and his business partners created a premium, organic, raw milk cheese, with the cheesemaking facility and its ripening/ageing room right on Michel Pichet's dairy farm.

In January 2004 Le Baluchon hit the market for all to experience and enjoy.

400, de Lanaudière
Sainte-Anne-de-la-Pérade, QC
418-325-3536

PRESIDENT
Jonathan Portelance

MILK TYPE
Organic raw cow's milk

PRODUCTION LEVEL
Artisanal farmstead

Federally registered

LOCAL ATTRACTIONS AND ACTIVITIES
• Centre thématique sur le poulamon—Tommycod icefishing site (Sainte-Anne-de-la-Pérade)
• Chemin du Roy—a scenic drive along the St. Lawrence River
• La Mauricie National Park
• Les Bières de la Nouvelle-France— microbrewery (Saint-Paulin)

FOR MORE IDEAS, VISIT
www.tourismemauricie.com
(French only) AND
www.bonjourquebec.com

CHEESE PRODUCED

Le Baluchon
a semi-soft, washed rind cheese

Le Baluchon

AVAILABILITY

STORES

- Onsite store
  Daily 9 a.m. to noon and
  1 p.m. to 5 p.m.
- La Laiterie Charlevoix
  (Baie-Saint-Paul)
- La Trappe à Fromage
  (Gatineau)
- Maître Affineur Maître
  Corbeau (Montreal)
- Marché du Vieux-Port
  (Quebec City)
- Whole Foods Market
  (Toronto)

**USED AT THE FOLLOWING
RESTAURANTS**

- L'Arrêt du Temps (Sainte-
  Anne-de-la-Pérade)
- Bistro H20 (Batiscan)
- Le Saint-Amour
  (Quebec City)
- Maison Deschambault
  (Deschambault)

*For distributor inquiries, please contact Le Choix du Fromager,
1-877-328-2207 or Plaisirs Gourmets, 418-876-3814.*

G. PRETTY

1303, rang Bayonne S.
Berthierville, QC
Office: 418-328-8788,
Cheese plant: 450-836-7979

OWNERS
Lise Mercier and Guy Dessureault

CHEESEMAKER
Guy Dessureault

MILK TYPE
Raw and pasteurized cow's milk

PRODUCTION LEVEL
Artisanal

Federally registered

LOCAL ATTRACTIONS AND ACTIVITIES
- Arbraska—aerial treetop experiences (Rawdon)
- Chapelle des Cuthbert—Quebec's oldest Protestant church (circa 1786) (Berthierville)
- Domaine de l'Île Ronde—winery (Saint-Sulpice)
- Musée Gilles-Villeneuve—dedicated to Gilles Villeneuve and his son Jacques, both Canadian Formula One race car drivers (Berthierville)

FOR MORE IDEAS, VISIT
www.lanaudiere.ca AND
www.bonjourquebec.com

GUY DESSUREAULT OWNS AN ORGANIC dairy farm and wanted to create a value-added product. Using Ayrshire milk from a neighbouring dairy farm, he and Dany Bizier began experimenting in making cheese. They opted for Ayrshire milk due to its high fat and protein content. In 2001 their first raw-milk cheese, Le Cendré des prés, was available for the public to taste. This unique soft cheese has a layer of maple ash in the centre, more common in semi-soft cheese than soft, brie-type cheese. They are currently working on the development of a blue cheese.

When you visit their facility, stop at their onsite food service venue, and enjoy a plate of their cheese with other food of the region and a glass of Quebec wine or port. This was the first cheese establishment to be licensed in the province. Wine and cheese right at the plant? Now that's an epicurean experience!

CHEESE PRODUCED

USING RAW MILK

LE CENDRÉ DES PRÉS
*a soft, bloomy rind, brie-style cheese
with a layer of maple ash in the
centre*

LE PRÉ-CIEUX
a semi-soft, washed rind cheese

LES PRÉS DE BAYONNE
a soft, bloomy rind, brie-style cheese

USING PASTEURIZED MILK

LE FETA DU DOMAINE

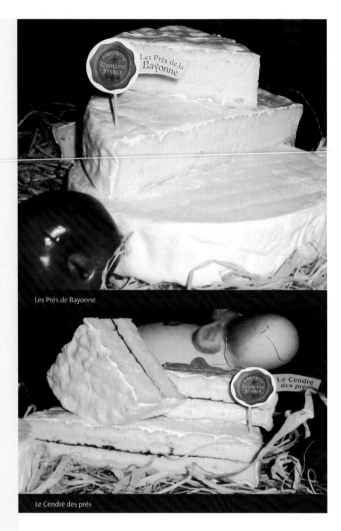

Les Prés de Bayonne

Le Cendré des prés

AVAILABILITY

STORES

- Onsite store
  Monday to Friday
  8:30 a.m. to 4:30 p.m.
  Saturday 10 a.m. to 5 p.m.
  June to end of September
  Sundays 10 a.m. to 5 p.m.
- Regional specialty shops and
  fine food stores
- Regional I.G.A. and Métro
  grocery stores

USED AT THE FOLLOWING
RESTAURANTS

- Their own relais gourmand
- Auberge du Lac Taureau
  (Saint-Michel-des-Saints)
- La table de mes rêves
  (Sainte-Béatrix)

*For distributor inquiries, please contact Le Choix du Fromager,
514-328-2207.*

MARTIN GUILBAULT BUILT HIS CHEESE-making facility on his family's ancestral farm. Le Victor et Berthold is named after his grandfather and his uncle. His delicious raw-milk cheese caught the attention of Quebecers. His Le Fêtard is soaked and washed in one of my favourite brands of beer, Unibroue's La Maudite. YUM! Le Laracam is named after the next potential cheesemaker in the family, his son.

3601, rue Principale
Notre-Dames-de-Lourdes, QC
450-753-9217

OWNER/CHEESEMAKER
Martin Guilbault

MILK TYPE
Raw cow's milk

PRODUCTION LEVEL
Artisanal

Provincially licensed

LOCAL ATTRACTIONS AND ACTIVITIES
- Festival mémoire et racines—an outdoor folk festival (Saint-Charles-Borromée)
- La Courgerie—Les Trouvailles de Potiron—a farm specializing in growing over 200 varieties of squash, pumpkins, gourds and marrow (Sainte-Élisabeth)
- La Bergerie des Neiges—a sheep farm, B & B and restaurant (Saint-Ambroise-de-Kildare)

FOR MORE IDEAS, VISIT
www.lanaudiere.ca AND
www.bonjourquebec.com

CHEESE PRODUCED

Le Fêtard
a semi-soft to firm cheese, soaked and washed with Unibroue's La Maudite beer, offered as Classic (aged 90 days) and Reserve (aged 1 year)

Le Laracam
a soft, washed rind cheese

Le Victor et Berthold
a semi-soft, washed rind cheese, offered as Classic (aged 75 to 90 days) and Reserve (aged 100 to 150 days)

Le Fêtard

AVAILABILITY

Stores
- Onsite store
  Monday to Thursday
  9 a.m. to 3:30 p.m.
  Friday and Saturday
  9 a.m. to 5 p.m.
- Fromagerie du Marché
  Atwater (Montreal)
- Marché du Vieux-Port
  (Quebec City)
- Fromagerie Hamel
  (Montreal)

Used at the following Restaurants
- Auberge de la
  Montagne Coupée
  (Saint-Jean-de-Matha)
- Restaurant Leméac
  (Montreal)

For distributor inquiries, please contact Martin.

LUC LIVERNOCHE, A CHEESEMAKER FOR 25 years, trained at a young age in his native town. He desired to establish an enterprise where he could work with his wife and four children. As there was no cheesemaking facility in the Lanaudière region in 1996, he established Fromagerie Champêtre.

Fromagerie Champêtre is well known for its high-quality fresh cheddar. They have created several other fine cheese, including Le Grand Chouffe—a semi-soft cheese washed with McChouffe, a Belgian brown beer of the Ardennes region.

415, rue Des Industries
Le Gardeur, QC
450-654-1308

OWNERS
Denise and Luc Livernoche

FOUNDING CHEESEMAKER
Luc Livernoche

MILK TYPE
Pasteurized cow's milk

PRODUCTION LEVEL
Semi-industrial

Federally registered

LOCAL ATTRACTIONS AND ACTIVITIES
• Church of the Purification-de-la-Bienvenue-Vierge-Marie de Repentigny — the oldest church in the Montreal diocese (circa 1727) (Repentigny)
• Festival Gospel de Repentigny
• Île Lebel Regional Park (Repentigny)

FOR MORE IDEAS, VISIT
www.lanaudiere.ca AND
www.bonjourquebec.com

CHEESE PRODUCED

CHEDDAR
- Fresh (white, orange and marble)

CURDS

LE GRAND CHOUFFE
a semi-soft cheese washed with Belgian beer

LE PRESQU'ÎLE
a semi-soft, mixed rind (bloomy and washed) cheese

LA RACLETTE CHAMPÊTRE
a semi-soft, washed rind cheese

1- Marble Cheddar; 2- Fresh orange-coloured Cheddar; 3- Fresh white Cheddar; 4- La Raclette Champêtre; 5- Presqu'île; 6- Le Grand Chouffe; 7- Curds

AVAILABILITY

STORES
- Regional bakeries
- Regional specialty food shops
- Regional grocery stores

For distributor inquiries, please contact J.L. Freeman, 514-522-2355.

FABIENNE IS ORIGINALLY FROM SWITZER-land and Frédéric is from Normandy. Their company is named after their native homelands. Upon settling in Canada, they raised cows and goats.

Frédéric and Fabienne found it difficult to sell all the milk produced by their Alpine, Saanen and Toggenburg goats to local milk processors, so they began producing cheese. In 1995 their first cheese were available to the public. Since then they have received rave reviews from the most discerning judges, their returning customers.

When stopping at their shop, visit the goats or see the cheese being made.

985, rang Rivière Nord
Saint-Roch-de-L'Achigan, QC
450-588-6508

OWNERS/CHEESEMAKERS
Frédéric and Fabienne Guitel

MILK TYPE
Raw and pasteurized cow's and goat's milk

PRODUCTION LEVEL
Artisanal farmstead

Provincially licensed

LOCAL ATTRACTIONS AND ACTIVITIES
• Dorwin Falls Park (Rawdon)
• Festival Lanaudière—a classical music festival (Joliette)
• Sir Wilfrid Laurier National Historic Site—the birthplace of Canada's seventh prime minister (Saint-Lin-Laurentide)

FOR MORE IDEAS, VISIT
www.bonjourquebec.com

CHEESE PRODUCED

USING RAW COW'S MILK

LE FREDDO
a firm, washed rind cheese

LA TOME
a firm to hard, washed rind cheese

USING PASTEURIZED COW'S MILK

LE PETIT NORMAND
a Camembert-style, soft, bloomy rind cheese

LE PIZY
a soft, bloomy rind cheese

USING RAW GOAT'S MILK

LE CAPRA
a firm, washed rind cheese

USING PASTEURIZED GOAT'S MILK

LE BARBU
a crottin-style, soft, bloomy rind cheese

CHÈVRE FRAIS
a fresh cheese made with garlic flowers

LE CAPRICE
a fresh cheese
• Plain
• Fine Herbs

LE CROTTIN
a fresh, unripened cheese
• Plain
• Marinated in olive oil

LE PETIT POITOU
a Camembert-style, soft, bloomy rind cheese

LE SABOT DE BLANCHETTE
a pyramid-shaped, soft, natural rind cheese with possible natural blue mould spots

Saint-Jérôme's Foire Vin Fromage

AVAILABILITY

STORES
• Onsite store
   May to Christmas
   Monday to Friday
   10 a.m. to 6 p.m.
   Saturday
   10 a.m. to 5 p.m.
   Sunday noon to 5 p.m.
   January to May
   same as above except
   closed on Sundays
• S. Bourassa Ltée.
  (Saint-Sauveur)
• Fromagerie du Marché
  (Saint-Jérôme)
• Le Marché des Saveurs
  (Montreal)
• La Trappe à Fromage
  (Gatineau)
• Marché du Vieux-Port
  (Quebec City)

USED AT THE FOLLOWING RESTAURANTS
• Le Dialogue
  (Saint-Jean-de-Matha)
• Le Prieurié (L'Assomption)
• Le Relais Champêtre
  (Saint-Alexis-de-Montcalm)

For distributor inquiries, please contact Fabienne or Plaisirs Gourmets, 418-876-3814.

THE DEFINITIVE GUIDE TO CANADIAN ARTISANAL AND FINE CHEESE

1921, Lionel-Bertrand
Boisbriand, QC
450-419-4477

FOUNDER/CHEESEMAKER
Marie Kadé

MILK TYPE
Pasteurized cow's milk

PRODUCTION LEVEL
Semi-industrial

Federally registered

LOCAL ATTRACTIONS AND ACTIVITIES
• Blainville Equestrian Park
• Nid'Otruche—ostrich farm
  (Saint-Eustache)
• Le Petit Théâtre du Nord—
  theatre company (Boisbriand)
• Pick-your-own berry farms

FOR MORE IDEAS, VISIT
www.laurentides.com AND
www.bonjourquebec.com

CHEESEMAKING IN THE HOME WAS A family tradition for Marie Kadé, who learned the technique during her childhood in Syria. After more than 10 years of experience making cheese for friends and family in Quebec, Marie opened her own commercial facility. Her Tressé cheese was so popular amongst her friends that they wanted to buy it. First rule of entrepreneurship: one must supply a demand. To increase her knowledge and skills, Marie attended cheese-making courses at the Institut de technologie agroalimentaire (Sainte-Hyacinthe). Then she began modifying her small-batch recipes to produce larger quantities of cheese.

Fromagerie Marie Kadé is one of the few cheese-making companies in Canada specializing in the production of Arabic-style cheese.

CHEESE PRODUCED

AKAWI
a soft, unripened cheese

BALADI
a soft, unripened cheese

DOMIATI
a cheese aged to various stages, fresh, soft, and firm

ESPAGNOLE
a soft cheese

HALLOOM
a semi-soft, unripened cheese

ISTAMBULI
a semi-soft, unripened cheese

KOBROSSI
a semi-soft, unripened cheese

LABNEH
a fresh, unripened cheese
- Plain
- In vegetable oil

MIXES MAISON
a house blend of 4 to 5 different cheese

MOUJADALÉ
a firm, rindless cheese

MOZZARELLA

NABULSI
a semi-soft, unripened cheese

SHINGLISH
a semi-soft, unripened cheese

SYRIEN
a semi-soft, unripened cheese

TRESSÉ
a firm, unripened cheese

VACHEKAVAL
a firm, rindless, cheddar-style cheese

1- Baladi; 2- Halloom; 3- Tressé

AVAILABILITY

STORES
- Marché Le Ruisseau

USED AT THE FOLLOWING RESTAURANTS
- Boulangerie Andalos (Montreal)
- Boulangerie Haddad (Montreal)

For distributor inquiries, please contact Phoenicia Products Inc., 514-389-6363.

317, Highway 158
Sainte-Sophie, QC
450-530-2436

FOUNDERS
Ronald and Serges Alary

CHEESEMAKER
Gabriel Alary

MILK TYPE
Organic raw cow's milk

PRODUCTION LEVEL
Artisanal farmstead

Provincially licensed

LOCAL ATTRACTIONS AND ACTIVITIES
- Local cideries and wineries
- Le P'tit Train du Nord Linear Park—a 200 km cycling trail
- Musée de Poupées—doll interpretation centre (Sainte-Sophie)

FOR MORE IDEAS, VISIT
www.laurentides.com AND
www.bonjourquebec.com

THE FARM WAS ESTABLISHED IN 1922 BY Joseph Alary and Marie-Joseph Latour. It was passed from one generation to another, evolving from a subsistence farm to a Holstein dairy farm that is certified organic by Quebec Vrai. In 2001 Ronald, grandson of Joseph and Marie-Joseph, had the idea of establishing a cheese-making facility on the property that would use their own raw milk. He was unsure how the organic milk was being used when it left the farm. Was it mixed with conventional milk? He and his son Gabriel worked together and their facility opened to the public in 2003.

Les Fromagiers de la Table Ronde is the only organic cheesemaking facility in the vicinity of Saint-Jérôme. Their Rassembleu cheese won the 2004 Prix Caseus in the Best New Cheese category at the Warwick Cheese Festival.

CHEESE PRODUCED

FOU DU ROY
a semi-soft, washed rind cheese

LE RASSEMBLEU
a firm, blue, bloomy rind cheese

TROUBADOUR
a cheddar-style cheese, aged 60 days to 2 years.

1- Fou du Roy; 2- Troubadour; 3- Le Rassembleu

AVAILABILITY

STORES
- Onsite store
  Monday to Friday
  9 a.m. to 5 p.m.
  Weekends
  11 a.m. to 5 p.m.
- Fromagerie du Marché
  (Saint-Jérôme)
- La Trappe à Fromage
  (Gatineau)
- Fromagerie du Marché
  Atwater (Montreal)
- Marché du Vieux-Port
  (Quebec City)

USED AT THE FOLLOWING RESTAURANTS
- L'Eau à la Bouche
  (Sainte-Adèle)

For distributor inquiries, please contact Plaisirs Gourmets, 418 -876-3814.

THE DEFINITIVE GUIDE TO CANADIAN ARTISANAL AND FINE CHEESE

104

624, boulevard A.-Paquette
Mont-Laurier, QC
866-816-4957 OR
819-623-2250

OWNERS
Christian Pilon and Francine
Beauséjour

CHEESEMAKER
Francine Beauséjour

MILK TYPE
Pasteurized cow's, goat's and
sheep's milk

PRODUCTION LEVEL
Artisanal

Provincially licensed

FRANCINE BEGAN WORKING AT THE COMpany under the tutelage of founder Gérald Brisebois. She and her husband, Christian, invested in the company, becoming majority shareholders in 2001. They divided the responsibilities—Francine making the cheese and Christian overseeing its distribution. Theirs is one of a few cheese companies that use all three different kinds of milk. Their innovative cheeses are flavoured with European chilis and washed with locally produced jalapeño beer and mead.

They named their cheeses after local historic personalities or legends. Curé Labelle, a mid 19th-century local priest, convinced the provincial government to open the Laurentians region to settlement. He wanted to staunch the flow of French Canadians seeking land and new opportunities in the United States. Originating from a First Nations legend, Windigo is a cannibalistic monster inhabiting the nearby Windigo Falls. Go for a dip—I dare you!

LOCAL ATTRACTIONS & ACTIVITIES
- Le P'tit Train du Nord Linear Park—a scenic cycling trail (Annonciation to Mont-Laurier)
- Call of the Wolf wildlife adventures (Rivière Rouge)
- Notre-Dame Cathedral (Mont-Laurier)
- Windigo Falls (Ferme-Neuve)

FOR MORE IDEAS, VISIT
www.hautes-laurentides.com
AND www.bonjourquebec.com

CHEESE PRODUCED

USING COW'S MILK

CHEDDAR
- White
- Orange
- Marble
- Medium, veined with port wine

CURDS
- Plain
- BBQ
- Chef's Secret
- Garlic and Dill
- Sun-dried Tomatoes and Basil

LE CURÉ LABELLE
a Reblochon-style, soft, surface ripened, washed rind cheese

TORTILLARD
a semi-soft, pasta filata–style, salty cheese

LE WABASSE
a semi-soft cheese, washed with a locally brewed ginger beer

LE WINDIGO
an Emmental-style, firm cheese, washed for 60 days with locally produced mead

USING GOAT'S MILK

LA BARRE DU JOUR
a Morbier-style, semi-soft, washed rind cheese with a layer of European Espelette chili in the middle, instead of the traditional vegetable ash; washed with a locally made jalapeño-flavoured beer

BRIE DE CHÈVRE
a soft, bloomy rind cheese, made only in the summer

CHEDDAR

LA FÉE DES BOIS
a raclette-style, semi-soft cheese washed with a locally made jalapeño-flavoured beer.

FETA

USING SHEEP'S MILK

BRIE DE BREBIS
a soft, bloomy rind cheese, made only in the summer

USING COW'S AND SHEEP'S MILK

DUO DU PARADIS
a semi-soft, washed rind cheese, named for using both cow's and sheep's milk, and after Mme. Paradis, who raises the sheep in the Outaouais region

Making Tortillard

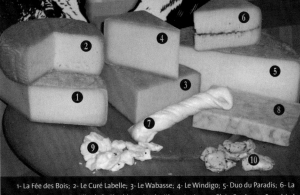

1- La Fée des Bois; 2- Le Curé Labelle; 3- Le Wabasse; 4- Le Windigo; 5- Duo du Paradis; 6- La Barre du Jour; 7- Tortillard; 8- Cheddar veined with port wine; 9- Plain Curds; 10- Sun-dried Tomato and Basil Curds

AVAILABILITY

STORES
- Onsite store
  Monday to Wednesday
  8:30 a.m. to 6 p.m.
  Thursday & Friday
  8:30 a.m. to 8 p.m.
  Saturday 8:30 a.m. to 5 p.m.
- Le Marché des Saveurs (Montreal)
- Maniwaki Farmers' Market
- Mont-Tremblant Farmers' Market
- Val David Farmers' Market
- Saint-Adolphe Farmers' Market

USED AT THE FOLLOWING RESTAURANTS
- Faim Gourmet (Mont-Laurier)

For distributor inquiries, please contact Alain Allard at Le Choix du Fromager, 877-328-2207 or 514-328-2207.

THE DEFINITIVE GUIDE TO CANADIAN ARTISANAL AND FINE CHEESE

IN 2000 GÉRALD DECIDED TO OPEN HIS second cheesemaking facility in the Mont-Laurier region. He built his enterprise in the family's maple sugar shanty, surrounded by a maple forest. Le Cru des érables, with its maple-liqueur washed rind, reflects the terroir of the area. Gérald named Le Casimir after his grandfather, who produced cheese from the milk of his small herd of cows. Perhaps this herd grazed at the foot of nearby Devil's Mountain, hence the naming of another cheese: Le Diable aux vaches (devil to the cows). Le Sieur Corbeau des Laurentides was developed for the local population. The cheese has a similar texture and flavour to their favoured cheddar. Gérald's products were quickly adopted by the cheese lovers of Quebec. He produces approximately 400 kg of each cheese per week.

1580, boulevard Eugène-Trinquier
Mont-Laurier, QC
819-623-3459

OWNERS
Gisèle Guindon and Gérald Brisebois

CHEESEMAKER
Étienne Richer

MILK TYPE
Thermalized cow's milk

PRODUCTION LEVEL
Artisanal farmstead

Provincially licensed

LOCAL ATTRACTIONS & ACTIVITIES
- La montagne du Diable—Devil's Mountain (Ferme-Neuve)
- Wild mushroom picking (Rivière Rouge)
- Muskeg Motorized Excursions (Nominingue)
- The twin covered bridges of Kamika

FOR MORE IDEAS, VISIT
www.hautes-laurentides.com
AND www.bonjourquebec.com

CHEESE PRODUCED

LE CASIMIR
a soft, Camembert-style, bloomy rind cheese

LE CRU DES ÉRABLES
a soft, Münster-type cheese, washed with Charles-Aimé Robert, a Quebec maple sap liqueur

LE DIABLE AUX VACHES
a soft, Maroilles-type, washed rind cheese

LE SIEUR CORBEAU DES LAURENTIDES
a tomme-style, semi-soft, bloomy rind cheese

1- Le Diable aux vaches; 2- Le Sieur Corbeau des Laurentides; 3- Le Cru des érables;
4- Le Casimir

AVAILABILITY

STORES
- Onsite store
  Monday to Saturday
  9 a.m. to 5 p.m.
- Le Marché des Saveurs
  (Montreal)
- Fromagerie du Marché
  Atwater (Montreal)
- La Trappe à Fromage
  (Gatineau)
- Val David Farmers' Market

USED AT THE FOLLOWING RESTAURANTS
- Menu Plaisir (Laval)
- Tocqué (Montreal)

For distributor inquiries, please contact Gérald.

THE DEFINITIVE GUIDE TO CANADIAN ARTISANAL AND FINE CHEESE

827, chemin de la Carrière
Brownsburg-Chatham, QC
450-533-4313

MILK TYPE
Pasteurized goat's and sheep's
milk

PRODUCTION LEVEL
Artisanal farmstead

Provincially licensed

LOCAL ATTRACTIONS AND ACTIVITIES
- La Clef des champs equestrian
  centre (Brownsburg-Chatham)
- New World Rafting
  (Grenville-sur-la-Rouge)
- Simon's Sales Gigantic Flea
  Market (Lachute)
- Tam Bao Son Buddhist
  Monastery (Harrington)

FOR MORE IDEAS, VISIT
www.argenteuil.qc.ca
(French only) AND
www.bonjourquebec.com

IN 2001 THIS SMALL GREEK ORTHODOX religious community of sisters was established on an old farm. They finance their endeavours by raising chickens and growing grapes, other fruit and vegetables. The sisters manage their own herd of goats and sheep, which they have named Le Troupeau Bénit, the blessed herd.

They initially began making Greek-style cheese for their own consumption but demand for their cheese from the local Greek-Canadian community prompted them to commercialize production. The sisters believe that making their cheese with prayers ensures the grace of God. Blessed are the cheesemakers!

❧

Visiting their community, located in the tranquil woods of Argenteuil county, was very interesting. The sisters all wear the traditional black gowns and follow the traditions of the Greek Orthodox religion. Their gift store also sells pastries, chocolates, religious texts and icons. Joanne and our friends Joseph and Marilyn found the experience fascinating.

CHEESE PRODUCED

USING GOAT'S MILK

ATHONITE
a firm, rindless, Gouda-style cheese, coated in red wax

BON BERGER
a semi-soft, rindless, Havarti-style cheese, coated in yellow wax

FETA
• Goat's milk only
• Goat's and sheep's milk mix

GRAVIERA
a firm, Gruyère-style cheese, coated in clear wax
• Goat's milk
• Sheep's milk
• Goat's and sheep's milk mix

MYTZITHRA
a fresh, unripened, unsalted, Greek-style ricotta cheese

LES PETITES SOEURS
a fresh, unripened cheese, stored in grapeseed oil
• Chives
• Herbes de Provence
• Garden Herbs
• Mint
• Pepper and Onion

SYMANDRE
a semi-soft, rindless, Havarti-style cheese, coated in yellow wax
• Herbs
• Pepper and Onion
• Pepper mixture

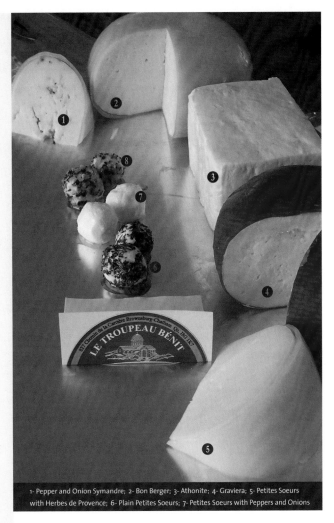

1- Pepper and Onion Symandre; 2- Bon Berger; 3- Athonite; 4- Graviera; 5- Petites Soeurs with Herbes de Provence; 6- Plain Petites Soeurs; 7- Petites Soeurs with Peppers and Onions

AVAILABILITY

STORES
• Onsite store
   Daily 9 a.m. to 6 p.m.
• Fromagerie du Marché
   (Saint-Jérôme)
• La Croûte et le Fromage
   (Lachute)
• Le Marché des Saveurs
   (Montreal)
• Le Quai du Lait Cru
   (Montreal)

USED AT THE FOLLOWING RESTAURANTS
• Hôtel Lac Carling
   (Carling Lake)
• Spaggio's (Montreal)

For distributor inquiries, please contact Sister Mireille at the monastery.

THE DEFINITIVE GUIDE TO CANADIAN ARTISANAL AND FINE CHEESE

SUZANNE HAS A PASSION FOR GOATS. SHE manages a herd of 120 Saanen goats on her farm, Au Claire de Lune in the Saint-François district. In 1996 she began using the milk to make cheese in a facility built next to her barn. Suzanne wanted the structures to be close together so the milk used for the cheese would be as fresh as possible. Her Bouchées d'Amour won a Caseus Prize at the 2002 and 2003 Warwick Cheese festivals.

High-quality cheese and excellent customer service make a visit to her facility an unforgettable experience.

4740, boulevard Mille-Îles
Laval, QC
450-666-6810

OWNER/CHEESEMAKER
Suzanne Latour Ouimet

MILK TYPE
Raw and pasteurized goat's milk

PRODUCTION LEVEL
Artisanal farmstead

Provincially licensed

LOCAL ATTRACTIONS AND ACTIVITIES
- Amikayak—kayaking experiences (Sainte-Rose)
- Cosmosdome Space Camp and Science Centre (Laval)
- Intermiel Inc.—producer of honey, mead and maple products (Mirabel-Saint-Benoît)
- Local wineries (Vignoble de la Rivière-du-Chêne and Vignoble de Negondos)

FOR MORE IDEAS, VISIT
www.tourismelaval.com AND
www.bonjourquebec.com

CHEESE PRODUCED

USING RAW GOAT'S MILK

LA TOUR SAINT-FRANÇOIS
a firm, washed rind cheese with small holes

USING PASTEURIZED GOAT'S MILK

BOUCHÉES D'AMOUR
a fresh, unripened cheese, marinated in grapeseed oil
- Plain
- Chives
- Garlic and Parsley
- Herbes de Provence

FLEUR DES NEIGES
a soft, feta-like cheese

LE LAVALLOIS
a soft, bloomy rind cheese

LE PETIT PRINCE
a fresh, unripened cheese
- Plain
- Chives
- Garlic and Parsley
- Herbes de Provence
- Peppercorn

LE PRÉ DES MILLE-ÎLES
a soft, washed rind cheese

SAMUEL ET JÉREMIE
a firm, unripened cheese named after Suzanne's two boys

SIEUR COLOMBAN
a firm, ripened cheddar-style cheese, named after Suzanne's father; is coated in wax, permitting it to age slowly from a minimum of three months to two years; the longer it is aged; the more character it develops

TI-LOU
a salty firm cheese with a natural rind

1- La Tour St-François; 2- Fleur de Neige; 3- L'Avalanche—a yogurt; 4- Maman Chèvre—goat's milk; 5- Samuel et Jérémi; 6- Sieur Colomban; 7- Le Pré des Milles-Îles; 8- Le Petit Prince; 9- Bouchées d'Amour; 10- Ti-Lou; 11- Le Lavallois

AVAILABILITY

STORES
- Onsite store
  Tuesday and Wednesday
  10 a.m. to 6 p.m.
  Thursday and Friday
  10 a.m. to 8 p.m.
  Saturday and Sunday
  10 a.m. to 5 p.m.
- Fromagerie Hamel
  (Montreal)
- Le Marché des Saveurs
  (Montreal)
- La Moisson Sainte-Thérèse
  (Sainte-Thérèse)
- Olifruits Ltée. (Laval)

USED AT THE FOLLOWING RESTAURANTS
- L'Escargot Fou
  (Saint-Vincent-de-Paul)
- Les Menus Plaisirs
  (Sainte-Rose)
- Derrière Les Fagots
  (Sainte-Rose)

For distributor inquiries, please contact Suzanne.

6500, blvd. Henri Bourassa E.
Montreal, QC
1-800-361-3868 OR
514-321-6100

MILK TYPE
Thermalized and pasteurized
cow's milk

PRODUCTION LEVEL
Industrial

Federally registered.

AGROPUR IS CANADA'S LARGEST CHEESE co-operative. It was established in 1938, originally as the Coopérative Agricole de Granby. Over the years, the co-op grew and acquired other dairy enterprises, increasing its production levels. When I lived in Montreal as a child, my dad would often go to Granby on business and return with a 2.3 kg block of their Crino mozzarella. For days afterwards, I would eat grilled cheese sandwiches, dripping long strings of delicious gooey cheese. Yum!

In 1974 Agropur bought the rights to produce the venerable Oka cheese from the Trappist monks of Oka. This semi-soft, washed rind, Port-Salut–style cheese had been made by the monks since 1893. It's one of the best known Canadian cheeses, both domestically and internationally. This cheese and other varieties are made down the street from the monastery.

❦

My great-aunt Lucienne would always buy a wheel of Oka for the annual family reunion on New Year's Day. Myself and my 80 or more Boyer relatives looked forward to the desert buffet, featuring a wheel of the delicious, locally made cheese.

THE DEFINITIVE GUIDE TO CANADIAN ARTISANAL AND FINE CHEESE

CHEESE PRODUCED

USING THERMALIZED COW'S MILK

OKA CLASSIQUE ·
*a semi-soft, washed rind, Port-Salut–
style cheese*

USING PASTEURIZED COW'S MILK

ALLÉGRO
- 4% milk fat content cheese
  made with skim milk
- 7% milk fat content cheddar
  cheese (white, orange and with
  peppercorns)
- 15% milk fat content Swiss-style
  cheese
- 17% milk fat content, soft,
  surface ripened cheese

BRICK

BRIE-STYLE
a soft, bloomy rind cheese
- Brie Anco Double Cream
- Brie Chevalier Double Cream
- Regular
- Fine Herbs
- Peppercorn
- Brie Chevalier Triple Cream
- Brie L'Extra
- Brie L'Extra Double Cream
- Brie Normandie Double Cream
- Brie Notre-Dame
- Brie Vaudreuil
- Brie Vaudreuil Double Cream

CAMEMBERT-STYLE
a soft, bloomy rind cheese
- Camembert Gourmet
- Grand Camembert L'Extra
- Grand Camembert Vaudreuil

BRITANNIA CHEDDAR
- Mild (white, orange and marble)
- Medium (white and orange)
- Old (white and orange)
- Extra-Old (white and orange)
- Premier Selection (1-year-old
  white)

(CONTINUED ON PAGE 115)

1- Britannia Cheddar; 2- Danesborg Havarti; 3- Brie Chevalier Triple Crème; 4- Oka

Cheesemonger at Montreal's Atwater Public Market

LOCAL ATTRACTIONS AND ACTIVITIES
- Historic Old Montreal
- Montreal's Festival juste pour rire—a comedy festival
- Montreal's International Jazz Festival
- Mount-Royal Park
- Public markets in the Atwater, Jean-Talon and Maisonneuve districts (Montreal)
- St. Joseph's Shrine (Montreal)

FOR MORE IDEAS, VISIT
www.tourisme-montreal.org
AND www.bonjourquebec.com

CHEESE PRODUCED
(cont'd)

- Fine Réserve (2-year-old white)
- Late Vintage (3-year-old white)

COLBY

DÉLICRÈME
a fresh, cream cheese
- Basil and Tomato
- Dill
- Garden Vegetable
- Garlic and Herbs
- 5 Peppers
- Herbs and Spices
- Jalapeño
- Pacific Smoked Salmon
- Peach
- Pineapple
- Strawberry

DANESBORG FETA
- Regular
- Diced
- Light

DANESBORG HAVARTI
- Plain
- Basil and Tomato
- Caraway
- Creamy
- Dill
- Fine Herbs
- Garden Vegetables
- Jalapeño
- Lactose-free
- Light
- Olives and Oregano
- Sour Cream and Chives

DANESBORG MÜNSTER
a semi-soft, interior ripened cheese

GOUDA ANCO
- Mild
- Smoked
- Spiced

MONTEREY JACK

MOZZARELLA

OKA
a semi-soft, washed rind, Port-Salut–style cheese
- Regular
- Light

PRESTIGIO RICOTTA

PROVIDENCE OKA
a soft, washed rind cheese

RACLETTE OKA
a semi-soft, washed rind cheese

SAINT-PAULIN ANCO
a semi-soft, washed rind cheese

SWISS GRUBEC
- Regular
- Light

AVAILABILITY

STORES
- Onsite stores
- La Trappe (1400 chemin Oka, Oka)
    Monday to Friday
    9 a.m. to 5 p.m.
- Saint-Hyacinthe plant (995 rue Johnson, Saint-Hyacinthe)
    Monday to Friday
    9 a.m. to 5 p.m.
- Fine cheese shops
- National grocery store chains

For distributor inquiries, please contact their sales team.

THE DEFINITIVE GUIDE TO CANADIAN ARTISANAL AND FINE CHEESE

6869, boulevard Métropolitain E.
Saint-Léonard, QC
1-800-672-8866 OR
514-328-6662

FOUNDERS
Lino Saputo and his parents,
Giuseppe and Maria

MILK TYPE
Raw and pasteurized cow's and
thermalized sheep's milk

PRODUCTION LEVEL
Industrial

Federally registered

IN 1954, A FEW YEARS AFTER THEIR ARRIVAL
from Italy, Lino Saputo convinced his father, a
master cheesemaker, to start producing cheese
under their own company name. Giuseppe
Saputo was well versed in the craft from his experiences working in Italy. With $500 dollars in
hand to purchase manufacturing equipment and
a bicycle for deliveries, Giuseppe Saputo & Figli
Ltée. was launched.

Over the next 50 years, the company grew and
became Saputo Inc. They are one of the largest
cheesemaking companies in Canada, with national distribution of their products.

Their cheese are known under the brands of
Saputo, Armstrong, Alexis de Portneuf, Kingsey and Dairyland. The company has expanded
into the American market, producing and selling
cheese south of the border.

LOCAL ATTRACTIONS AND ACTIVITIES
- Cycling or walking along the
  Lachine Canal (Montreal)
- Montreal's Festival en
  lumière—a gastronomy
  festival
- Notre-Dame Basilica
  (Montreal)
- McCord Museum at McGill
  University (Montreal)

FOR MORE IDEAS, VISIT
www.tourisme-montreal.org
AND www.bonjourquebec.com

CHEESE PRODUCED

SAPUTO, STELLA OR BARI BRANDS

USING RAW COW'S MILK

BELLA LODI
a hard, natural, black rind cheese

PARMIGIANO REGGIANO
a hard, natural rind cheese, ripened for 24 months

USING PASTEURIZED COW'S MILK

ASIAGO

BOCCONCINI

CACIOCAVALLO
• Plain
• Smoked

FETA

FRIULANO

GRANA PADANO

MOZZARELLA

MOZZARELLISSIMA
a semi-soft, pasta filata–style cheese

MOZZARINA MEDITERRANEO
a soft cheese, similar to the imported Italian Mozzarella di buffala

PARMESAN

PASTORELLA
a firm, natural rind cheese

PROVOLONE

RICOTTA

TRECCE

TUMA

USING THERMALIZED SHEEP'S MILK

ROMANO

ARMSTRONG BRAND

USING PASTEURIZED COW'S MILK

BRICK

CHEDDAR
• Mild
• Medium

• Old
• Extra-Old
• Light
• Marble

COLBY

FARMERS

MONTEREY JACK

1- Parmigiano Reggiano; 2- Bella Lodi; 3- Grana Padano

AVAILABILITY

STORES
• National grocery store chains

For distributor inquiries, please contact their sales team.

THE DEFINITIVE GUIDE TO CANADIAN ARTISANAL AND FINE CHEESE

Ferme Floralpe Enr.

1700, Highway 148
Papineauville, QC
819-427-5700

OWNER
Eliette Lavoie

MILK TYPE
Thermalized goat's milk

PRODUCTION LEVEL
Artisanal farmstead

Federally registered

NESTLED ON THE SHORES OF THE OTTAWA River between Montreal and Gatineau, Ferme Floralpe is a treasure of the Outaouais region. Their cheese have been distinguished for their excellence: L'Heidi won a Prix Caseus at the Warwick Cheese Festival in the category of goat/sheep, surface ripened, soft cheeses.

LOCAL ATTRACTIONS AND ACTIVITIES
- Fairmont Château Montebello—an enormous log cabin style hotel (Montebello)
- Manoir Papineau—seigneurial manor of Joseph Papineau, leader of the failed 1837 Lower Canada rebellion (Montebello)
- Omega Zoological Park

FOR MORE IDEAS, VISIT
www.outaouais-tourism.ca
AND www.bonjourquebec.com

CHEESE PRODUCED

LA BUCHEVRETTE
a bloomy rind, soft cheese, in the form of a small log

FETA

L'HEIDI
a surface ripened soft cheese, named after the literary character

LE MICHA
an unripened soft cheese, named after a past staff member

LE MONTAGNARD
a firm, cheddar-style cheese, named after Heidi's grandfather

LE PETER
a washed rind, surface ripened soft cheese, named after Heidi's friend

Ferme Floraple sign

1- Le Montagnard; 2- Le Peter; 3- L'Heidi; 4- Le Micha; 5- La Buchevrette

AVAILABILITY

STORES
- Onsite store
  Monday to Friday
  8 a.m. to 4:30 p.m.
  Saturday
  10 a.m. to 4 p.m.
- ByWard Market (Ottawa)
- La Trappe à Fromage
  (Gatineau)

USED AT THE FOLLOWING RESTAURANTS
- Le Panaché (Gatineau)
- L'Indocile (Gatineau)

For distributor inquiries, please contact the company.

470, Highway 315
Chénéville, QC
819-428-3061

OWNER
Colette Duhaime

CHEESEMAKERS
Ginette Crevier and Diane de Montigny

MILK TYPE
Pasteurized cow's and goat's milk

PRODUCTION LEVEL
Artisanal farmstead

Provincially licensed

AFTER A 30-YEAR CAREER AS A JOURNALIST, Colette found a new employment opportunity in the region. Her late husband, Normand Gamache, followed her and together they established a hobby farm. He fell in love with goats and eventually their herd grew to 30 animals. Colette and Normand decided to start making cheese to help defray the cost of feeding all their goats.

La Biquetterie's cheeses are handmade in small batches. The curds are placed in the moulds using the ladle technique. This gives a great texture to the cheese. To reflect the region's atmosphere, the cheeses are named after the local communities.

LOCAL ATTRACTIONS AND ACTIVITIES
• Laflêche Adventures—cave and aerial park (Val-des-Monts)
• Les Créateurs de la Petite-Nation studio tours
• Musée des pionniers—pioneer museum (Saint-André-Avellin)

FOR MORE IDEAS, VISIT
www.outaouais-tourism.ca
AND www.bonjourquebec.com

THE DEFINITIVE GUIDE TO CANADIAN ARTISANAL AND FINE CHEESE

CHEESE PRODUCED

USING COW'S MILK

FROMAGE EN GRAIN DE LA PETITE NATION
fresh cheese curds

LE CHÉNÉVILLE
a fresh cheddar

LE MONTPELLIER
a fresh, unripened cheese

USING GOAT'S MILK

LE PETIT VINOY
a fresh, unripened cheese
- Chives
- Fine Herbs
- Peppercorn

Montgolfière Festival

1- Le Montpellier; 2- Le Petit Vinoy with Chives; 3- Le Chénéville; 4- Le Prit Vinoy with Fine Herbs; 5- Le Petit Vinoy with Peppercorn; 6- Fromage en Grain de la Petite Nation

AVAILABILITY

STORES
- Onsite store
  9 a.m. to 6 p.m.
  Ring doorbell for service
- Local Métro grocery stores

USED AT THE FOLLOWING RESTAURANTS
- Le Chialeux (Montebello)

For distributor inquiries, please contact the sales team of Saputo Inc.

CHRISTIAN BECAME THE FOURTH GENERA-tion of Barrettes to operate the family farm. He and Hélène wondered how their herd's milk was used and decided to establish a cheesemaking facility after evaluating several dairy processing options. Hélène enrolled in distance education courses to learn the techniques of cheesemaking and gained hands-on experience working at other cheese plants. A master cheesemaker came to their new facility to teach her a few more tricks of the trade. From 1996 to 1998, curds were made and sold within the region. In 1998, after a year of testing, they launched the Cru du Clocher, their raw-milk cheddar. Disaster struck in December 1999, when a fire destroyed the barn and part of the herd, but they carried on with milk from other farmers who met their standards for care and feeding of the cows and milk quality.

Hélène believes the climate of northern Quebec produces sweeter pastures for cows to graze on. Their milk reflects this difference and is concentrated in the cheese of Le Fromage au Village.

45, rue Notre-Dame Ouest
Lorrainville, QC
819-625-2255

OWNERS
Christian Barrette and Hélène Lessard

CHEESEMAKER
Hélène Lessard

MILK TYPE
Raw and pasteurized cow's milk

PRODUCTION LEVEL
Artisanal

Federally registered

LOCAL ATTRACTIONS AND ACTIVITIES
• Chantier Gédéon—a reconstructed lumber camp (Angliers)
• Domaine des Ducs—Quebec's most northern winery (Ville-Marie)
• Fishing camps
• Fort Témiscamingue National Historic Site—fur-trading post amongst the Algonquin First Nation (Ville-Marie)

FOR MORE IDEAS, VISIT
www.temiscamingue.net/vacances/english/bienvenue.html
AND www.bonjourquebec.com

CHEESE PRODUCED

USING RAW MILK

LE CRU DU CLOCHER
a 6-month- to 2-year-old cheddar

USING PASTEURIZED MILK

CURDS

Barn & Sunflowers

AVAILABILITY

STORES
- Onsite store
  Monday to Friday
  9 a.m. to 5 p.m.
  Saturday
  9 a.m. to 3 p.m.
- Fromagerie du Marché
  Atwater (Montreal)
- Le Marché des Saveurs
  (Montreal)
- Marché du Vieux-Port
  (Quebec City)
- S. Bourassa Ltée.
  (Saint-Sauveur)

USED AT THE FOLLOWING
RESTAURANTS
- Chez Eugène (Ville-Marie)
- Delta Hôtel Centre-Ville
  (Montreal)

For distributor inquiries, please contact Hélène.

124

128, Highway 101
Montbeillard, QC
819-797-8999

OWNERS/CHEESEMAKERS
The Dion family

MILK TYPE
Raw and pasteurized goat's milk

PRODUCTION LEVEL
Artisanal farmstead

Provincially licensed

MR. AND MRS. DION BOUGHT THEIR FIRST goat in 1982 to help feed the family. Now 60 Alpines, Saanens and Nubians graze on their farm's pastures. In 1986 Gilberte Dion began making cheese after attending several cheese-making courses. Three-quarters of their herd's milk is used to make cheese. Many regional stores sell their products as well as fine cheese shops in Montreal, Saint-Jérôme and Quebec City.

Guided visits are available upon request from Wednesday to Sunday.

LOCAL ATTRACTIONS AND ACTIVITIES
• Gourmet fair of the Abitibi-Témiscamingue (Ville-Marie)
• Lake Joannes Forestry Education Centre—walking and mountain biking trails (McWatters)
• Maison Dumulon—a collection of historic buildings including a restored general store, a post office and a Russian orthodox church (Rouyn-Noranda)

FOR MORE IDEAS, VISIT
www.48nord.qc.ca
(French only) AND
www.bonjourquebec.com

CHEESE PRODUCED

LE BRIN DE CHÈVRE
goat curds

LE DÉLICE
a fresh, unripened cheese
- Plain
- Chives
- Fine Herbs
- Garlic
- Peppercorn

LE MONTBEIL
a cheddar-style goat cheese
- Mild
- Medium
- Old
- Medium, made with raw milk

PARMESAN

LE P'TIT FETA

LE ROULÉ
a soft, unripened cheese in a log shape
- Plain
- Chives
- Fine Herbs
- Garlic
- Peppercorn

Goats at Chèvrerie Dion

AVAILABILITY

STORES
- Onsite store
  Daily 9 a.m. to 5 p.m.
- Fromagerie du Marché
  (Saint-Jérôme)
- Fromagerie du Marché
  Atwater (Montreal)
- Le Marché des Saveurs
  (Montreal)
- Marché du Vieux Port
  (Quebec City)
- Regional Loblaws, Maxi,
  Métro and Provigo grocery
  stores

USED AT THE FOLLOWING
RESTAURANTS
- Auberge des Gouverneurs
  (Noranda)
- Centre des Congrès
  (Noranda)
- Pizza Pizzédelic (Rouyn)

For distributor inquiries, please contact the Dions.

THE DEFINITIVE GUIDE TO CANADIAN ARTISANAL AND FINE CHEESE

E. DALLAIRE-CLOUTIER

604, Deuxième rue E.
La Sarre, QC
1-866-333-1156 OR
819-333-1121

FOUNDERS
Réal Bérubé, Léon Poirier and
Pierre Vachon

CHEESEMAKERS
France Daigel and Michel
Lévesque

MILK TYPE
Raw and pasteurized cow's and
thermalized sheep's milk

PRODUCTION LEVEL
Semi-industrial

Federally registered

LOCAL ATTRACTIONS AND ACTIVITIES
- Paradis du Nord—a musical
  saga (La Sarre)
- Aiguebelle Provincial Park
  (Taschereau)
- Red-painted covered bridges
- Water activities on Lac Abitibi

FOR MORE IDEAS, VISIT
www.abitibi-ouest.net
AND www.bonjourquebec.com

FROMAGERIE LA VACHE À MAILLOTTE'S mission is to create cheese of the terroir. Jacquelin Sevigny, the director of operations, believes there is a higher sugar content in local plants because of their northern location, with its shorter growing season. Cows and sheep grazing on these sweeter pastures produce distinctive milk, and different flavours are present in the cheese. The best way to verify this is by tasting their cheese.

CHEESE PRODUCED

USING RAW COW'S MILK

FARANDOLE
a semi-soft, washed rind cheese

USING PASTEURIZED COW'S MILK

CHEDDAR
- Fresh in blocks (white, orange and marble)

CURDS
- Plain
- BBQ
- Garlic and Dill

FREDONDAINE
a semi-soft, washed rind, Port-Salut–style cheese

FROMAGE À POUTINE

GRATED CHEESE

SONATINE
a firm, natural, brushed rind cheese

TORTILLONS

USING THERMALIZED SHEEP'S MILK

ALLÉGRETTO
a firm, washed rind cheese in a pyramid shape

Allégretto cheese

AVAILABILITY

STORES
- Onsite store
  Monday to Saturday
  8 a.m. to 6 p.m.
- Fromagerie du Marché Atwater (Montreal)
- Le Marché des Saveurs (Montreal)
- Marché du Vieux-Port (Quebec City)
- S. Bourassa Ltée. (Saint-Sauveur)

USED AT THE FOLLOWING RESTAURANTS
- Auberge des Gouverneurs (Rouyn-Noranda)
- Fairmont Château Frontenac (Quebec City)
- L'Escale (Val d'Or)
- Meule et Caquelon (Rouyn-Noranda)
- Tocqué (Montreal)

For distributor inquiries, please contact the company directly.

128

FROMAGERIE FINE - SAINTE-LUCE

MICHEL ENJOYS PLAYING IN THE KITCHEN and considers himself a good home cook and amateur winemaker. His love of food made him want to introduce his neighbours to raw-milk cheese, but none were produced locally. Michel began experimenting and eventually learned how to make cheese commercially. He uses local milk, from cows grazing on the pastures along the St. Lawrence River. In 2003 the facility opened its doors to the public, permitting others to experience locally made raw-milk cheese.

224, Highway 132 W.
Sainte-Luce, QC
418-739-4116

OWNER/CHEESEMAKER
Michel Lavoie

MILK TYPE
Raw and pasteurized cow's milk

PRODUCTION LEVEL
Artisanal

Provincially licensed

LOCAL ATTRACTIONS AND ACTIVITIES
- Les Halles Saint-Germain—
  a public market (Rimouski)
- Musée de bateaux
  miniatures—miniature ships
  museum (Rivière-du-Loup)
- Sainte-Luce sandcastle
  competition
- Promenade of Wooden
  Sculptures (Sainte-Luce)

FOR MORE IDEAS, VISIT
www.tourismebas-st-laurent.com
AND www.bonjourquebec.com

CHEESE PRODUCED

USING RAW COW'S MILK

SAINT-BARNABÉ
a semi-soft, washed rind cheese,
named after a local island in the St.
Lawrence River

USING PASTEURIZED COW'S MILK

SIEUR DE LAVOYE
a soft, bloomy rind cheese, named
after one of Michel's ancestors

TARTIGO
a fresh, unripened, fromage frais-style
cheese, named after a river near the
Quebec city of Matane

TARTIGOUTEUX
a fresh, spreadable cheese
- Mon P'tit Basile (basil-flavoured)
- Ma P'tite Lucie
  (cayenne-flavoured)
- Ma P'tite Julie (Cajun-flavoured),
  named after his daughter
- Mon Pote (garden vegetables)

Historic home

1- Saint-Barnabé; 2- Tartigouteux; 3- Sieur de Lavoye

AVAILABILITY

STORES
- Onsite store
  June to Labour Day
  Tuesday to Sunday
  10 a.m. to 6 p.m.
  September
  Friday to Sunday
  10 a.m. to 6 p.m.
  October to June,
  closed to the public
- Regional I.G.A. and Métro
  grocery stores

USED AT THE FOLLOWING RESTAURANTS
- 360 (Rimouski)
- Auberge Sainte-Luce
  (Sainte-Luce)
- Gîte du Mont-Albert (New
  Richmond)
- Auberge du Mange
  Grenouille (Le Bic)

For distributor inquiries, please contact Michel.

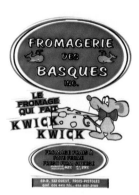

67, Highway 132 W.
Trois-Pistoles, QC
418-851-2189

FOUNDERS
Madelaine Rioux, Germain and
Yves Pettigrew

CHEESEMAKERS
Michel and Yves Levesque

MILK TYPE
Pasteurized cow's milk

PRODUCTION LEVEL
Semi-industrial

Provincially licensed

LOCAL ATTRACTIONS AND ACTIVITIES
• Cycling trails
• Marché des 3 fumoirs—fish
  market and smokehouse
  (L'Isle-Verte)
• Notre-Dame-des-Neiges
  church (Trois-Pistoles)
• Parc de l'aventure basque
  en Amérique—Basques
  historical interpretation site
  (Trois-Pistoles)

FOR MORE IDEAS, VISIT
www.tourismebas-st-laurent.com
AND www.bonjourquebec.com.

THE PETTIGREW FAMILY BEGAN PRODUCING cheeses in 1994, using the milk from their herd. They began by making fresh pressed cheeses. They became so popular that the Pettigrews had to find other sources of milk. For two years, they experimented in making aged and ripened cheese.

Their Notre-Dame-des-Neiges, a soft, bloomy rind cheese, is named after the local church. Legend has it that the location of the church was chosen by a freak August storm that dumped snow on the precise site. Their Héritage and Swiss cheese are washed with Unibroue's Trois-Pistoles beer. This makes me happy—Unibroue is my favourite brewery in Canada.

Their store is located on the Trans-Canada Highway linking New Brunswick with Quebec. It's open very early in the morning (3:30 a.m.) for those driving to and from the Maritimes. The cheesemakers work late at night to produce fresh cheese for travelers; curds or tortillons are a great snack while driving. Their summer dairy bar sells ice cream cones and is a popular stop for both locals and tourists.

CHEESE PRODUCED

CHEDDAR
- Fresh
- White
- Orange
- Marble
- Peppercorn
- Medium
- Strong
- Extra-Strong
- 2-Year-Old
- 3-Year-Old
- 4-Year-Old
- Maple-smoked

CURDS
- Plain
- Bacon
- BBQ
- Peppercorn
- Tomato and Basil

L'HÉRITAGE
a semi-soft, surface ripened, washed rind cheese, based on a Basques recipe
- Traditional
- Washed with Unibroue's Trois-Pistoles beer

LE NOTRE-DAME-DES-NEIGES
a soft, bloomy rind cheese, named after the local church

LE P'TIT BASQUE
a fresh cheese cured briefly in brine

SWISS
- Traditional
- Washed with Unibroue's Trois-Pistoles beer

TORTILLONS
- Plain
- BBQ
- Fine Herbs

Fromagerie des Basques outdoor mural

1- Fresh Orange Cheddar; 2- Marble; 3- Fresh White Cheddar; 4- Peppercorn Cheddar; 5- Herb Cheddar; 6- L'Héritage; 7- Notre-Dame-des-Neiges; 8- Swiss washed with Trois-Pistoles Beer; 9- Regular Swiss; 10- BBQ Curds; 11- Bacon Curds; 12- Tomato and Basil Curds; 13- Plain; 14- Plain Tortillons; 15- BBQ Tortillons; 16- Fine Herbs Tortillons

AVAILABILITY

STORES
- Onsite store
  Monday to Wednesday
  3:30 a.m. to 6 p.m.
  Thursday to Saturday
  3:30 a.m. to 8 p.m.
  Sunday 8 a.m. to 6 p.m.
- Fromagerie du Marché Atwater (Montreal)
- Marché du Vieux-Port (Quebec City)
- Regional I.G.A. and Métro grocery stores

USED AT THE FOLLOWING RESTAURANTS
- L'Estra (Trois-Pistoles)

For distributor inquiries, please contact the company's sales team.

MARIO QUIRION LEFT THE CHAUDIÈRE-Appalaches region as a trained cheesemaker. He settled down in Notre-Dame-du-Lac and discovered there was no commercial cheesemaking in the area. Fromagerie le Détour was the first cheesemaking facility to produce cheese using cow's, goat's and sheep's milk in the province. It was also the first to make raw-milk cheese in the Bas-Saint-Laurent region. Over 20 different kinds of cheese are produced at the plant.

Travelers driving to and from New Brunswick enjoy stopping to purchase good cheese and an ice cream cone at their dairy bar.

100, Route Transcanadienne
Notre-Dame-du-Lac, QC
418-899-7000

CHEESEMAKER
Mario Quirion

MILK TYPE
Raw and pasteurized cow's, goat's and sheep's milk

PRODUCTION LEVEL
Artisanal

Federally registered

LOCAL ATTRACTIONS AND ACTIVITIES
• Cycling trails
• Domaine Acer—maple Economuseum (Auclair)
• Pohénégamook Natural Holiday Resort (Pohénégamook)

FOR MORE IDEAS, VISIT
www.tourismebas-st-laurent.com
AND www.bonjourquebec.com

CHEESE PRODUCED

USING RAW COW'S MILK

CHEDDAR LAIT CRU (WHITE)

USING PASTEURIZED COW'S MILK

CHEDDAR
- Fresh (white, orange and marble)
- Mild (white, orange and marble)
- Medium (white, orange and marble)
- Old (white and orange)
- Black Peppercorn
- Fine Herbs
- Light
- Maple-smoked

COLBY

CURDS

DAME DU LAC
a semi-soft, mixed rind cheese

FROMAGE FRAIS
a fresh, unripened cheese flavoured with maple

FROMAGE EN SAUMURE
a fresh cheese washed in brine
- Bâtonnets
- Knots

MARQUIS DE TÉMISCOAUATA
a soft, bloomy rind cheese made with Jersey cow's milk

MONTEREY JACK

TORTILLONS FILOCHE
a semi-soft, unripened, stretched, salty, string cheese

USING PASTEURIZED GOAT'S MILK

SENTINEL
a soft, runny, washed rind cheese

USING PASTEURIZED SHEEP'S MILK

a Camembert-style, soft, bloomy rind cheese

USING COW'S AND SHEEP'S MILK

CLANDESTIN
a soft, washed rind cheese

1- Maple-Smoked Cheddar; 2- Marquis de Témiscouata; 3- Dame du Lac; 4- Sentinelle; 5- Clandestin; 6- Colby; 7- Curds; 8- Old-Tyme Butter

AVAILABILITY

STORES
- Onsite store
  Daily 6 a.m. to 6 p.m.
- Aux Petits Délices (Sainte-Foy)
- Fromagerie du Marché Atwater (Montreal)
- Maison Moisan (Quebec City)

USED AT THE FOLLOWING RESTAURANTS
- Auberge du Mange Grenouille (Le Bic)
- Restaurant l'Artisan (New York City)

For distributor inquiries, please contact the company.

fromagerie le Mouton Blanc
le vrai goût du Kamouraska

176, Highway 230 W.
La Pocatière, QC
418-856-6627

OWNERS
Rachel White and Pascal-André Bisson

SHEPHERDESS
Rachel White

CHEESEMAKER
Pascal-André Bisson

MILK TYPE
Raw sheep's milk

PRODUCTION LEVEL
Artisanal farmstead

Provincially licensed

AFTER SEVERAL TRIPS TO EUROPE, RACHEL and Pascal-André decided to begin making cheese to increase the value of their farm. Rachel worked with French shepherds in the Pyrenees Mountains and Pascal-André returned to the south of France to learn traditional sheep's milk cheesemaking techniques.

Their herd of 450 Lacaune and East Friesian dairy sheep provide them with the necessary milk to produce their cheese. In the summer of 2004, Pascal-André produced his first cheese. The cheese are aged naturally in ripening caves built into the foot of the local Monadnock Mountains.

Visits to the farm and the sheep are available upon request.

LOCAL ATTRACTIONS AND ACTIVITIES
- Cycling trails of Kamouraska
- Eel fishing interpretation centre of Kamouraska
- La Seigneurie des Aulnaies—19th-century seigneurial manor (Saint-Roch-des-Aulnaies)
- Zodiac Adventure Cruises (Kamouraska)

For more ideas, visit
www.tourismebas-st-laurent.com
AND www.bonjourquebec.com

CHEESE PRODUCED

La Tomme du Kamouraska
a semi-soft, washed rind cheese

Sun setting over shoreline

La Tomme du Kamouraska

AVAILABILITY

STORES

- Onsite store
  Daily 1 to 5 p.m.
- Fromagerie du Marché
  (Saint-Jérôme)
- Fromagerie Hamel
  (Montreal)
- Marché du Vieux-Port
  (Quebec City)

USED AT THE FOLLOWING
RESTAURANTS

- Auberge des Glacis
  (Saint-Eugène)
- Auberge du Mange
  Grenouille (Le Bic)
- Pub-Azimut (La Pocatière)

For distributor inquiries, please contact Plaisirs Gourmets, 418-876-3814.

136

16, rue Sociétaires
Saint-Jean-Port-Joli, QC
418-598-9840

OWNER/CHEESEMAKER
Robert Tremblay

MILK TYPE
Pasteurized cow's milk

PRODUCTION LEVEL
Artisanal

Provincially licensed

ORIGINALLY A DAIRY FARMER, ROBERT thought that becoming a cheesemaker was the next logical step. In 1993 he began making cheese commercially. He's a strong believer in producing a product of the terroir and uses milk from nearby dairy farms.

The day I visited Fromagerie Port-Joli, la Fromagerie du Terroir de Belle-chasse and la Société Coopérative Agricole de L'Île-aux-Grues, Hurricane Katrina (September 2005) was making her presence known in the region, with torrential downpours and very stong winds. Joanne was snug as a bug that day at La Maison de L'Ermitage, our B & B. She was reading an English version of Aux Anciens Canadiens, a historical novel written by Philippe Aubert de Gaspé, one of Saint-Jean-Port-Joli's famous citizens.

I had never seen my windshield wipers work so fast for so long. I could only see 10 metres in front of my car. The hot news on the radio talk shows was the increase in gas prices. Due to Katrina, the price at the pumps jumped up $0.25 that morning, from $1.09 to $1.34 a litre. Whoa! I found the first gas station and filled up at the lower price. Obviously the gas station attendant had not yet received the phone call advising him to hike up the price.

LOCAL ATTRACTIONS AND ACTIVITIES
- Galleries of woodcarvers' art (Saint-Jean-Port-Joli)
- Historic town of Saint-Jean-Port-Joli
- L'Épopée de la moto— motorcycle museum (Saint-Jean-Port-Joli)

FOR MORE IDEAS, VISIT
www.cotedusud.com
(French only),
www.chaudieresappalaches.com
AND www.bonjourquebec.com

CHEESE PRODUCED

CHEDDAR
- Fresh
- Mild
- Fine Herbs
- Medium
- Old
- Extra-Old
- 3-Year-Old
- 5-Year-Old
- 5-Year-Old in port wine

CURDS
- Plain
- BBQ
- Fine Herbs

PARTLY-SKIM MILK CHEESE

TORTILLONS
- Plain
- BBQ

TRESSES
a braided version of Tortillons

1- Cheddar marinated in Port Wine; 2- Aged Cheddar; 3- Fine Herbs Cheddar; 4- Tresses; 5- Tortillons; 6- Plain Curds; 7- BBQ Curds

AVAILABILITY

STORES
- Onsite store
  Monday to Friday
  9 a.m. to 5 p.m.
- Regional I.G.A. and Métro
  grocery stores

USED AT THE FOLLOWING RESTAURANTS
- L'Entre Jean (Montmagny)
- Cap Martin (La Pocatière)

For distributor inquiries, please contact Robert.

210, chemin du Roi
Île-aux-Grues, QC
418-248-5842

CHEESEMAKERS
Gilbert Lavoie and
Christian Vinet

MILK TYPE
Raw, thermalized and
pasteurized cow's milk

PRODUCTION LEVEL
Artisanal

Federally registered

LOCAL ATTRACTIONS AND ACTIVITIES
- Centre de la Volière—local
  art gallery and museum
  displaying Mi-Carême
  costumes (Île-aux-Grues)
- Le Grenier de l'Île—art gallery
  exhibiting work of local artists
  such as Jean-Paul Riopelle
  (Île-aux-Grues)
- Ornitour—bird watching tours
  (Île-aux-Grues)
- Walking and cycling trails

FOR MORE IDEAS, VISIT
www.isle-aux-grues.com
(French only),
www.chaudiereappalaches.com
AND www.bonjourquebec.com

ON THIS SMALL ISLAND OF 156 RESIDENTS,
10 dairy producers pooled their milk to create
a dairy co-operative, then built a cheesemaking
plant. By limiting themselves to the milk produced on the island, the cheesemakers are certain to have fresh milk that displays the unique
flavours of the terroir of l'Île-aux-Grues.

ᗭᗡ

*I had quite the experience getting to the island. The day was very
stormy, as the remains of Hurricane Katrina (September 2005) were
sweeping through the region. Upon my arrival at the Montmagny
wharf, I called Christian to verify my appointment with him. He
doubted he could see me. The next opportunity would be the following
morning. No go! I had appointments scheduled the next day in Quebec City. Christian informed me I could hitch a ride with Jean-Marc
in the delivery truck, which was heading to the cheese plant. In the
gale-force winds, I found the truck and yelled to Jean-Marc so he
could hear me. He invited me into the truck's dry cab.*

*The ferry was running late because of the rough seas and strong
winds. The captain performed some fancy manoeuvres to get his ves-
sel turned in the right direction. The spray was flying over the bow
of the ferry, hitting all vehicles on board, as the ferry crossed the St.
Lawrence River.*

*Officially the ferry would be docked at the island's wharf for less
than 30 minutes before its return trip to the mainland. Jean-Marc
was not worried. He and the captain knew the importance of his
delivering the cheese to the mainland. The ferry would not leave without us. Knowing we had little time, I photographed the cheese quickly.
Some of the cheeses were destined for Toronto's The Cheese Boutique,
owned by Mr. Fatos Pristine, my neighbourhood cheesemonger. I was
tempted to write "Hello Mr. Pristine, from Gurth Pretty" on a box
of cheese.*

*Photos taken, cheese loaded on the truck, Jean-Marc and I were ready
to return to the wharf. Would the ferry still be there? Would I have to
call Joanne at the B & B and tell her I was marooned on an island?
This was not even a three-hour tour! The ferry was not called the S.S.
Minnow and Jean-Marc did not look like the Skipper. Nothing to
worry about—the ferry was still there. Phew! I made it back to Joanne
with time to spare before our dinner reservation.*

CHEESE PRODUCED

USING RAW MILK

CHEDDAR
- Medium
- Old (1-year-old)
- Extra-Old (2-year-old)

USING THERMALIZED MILK

LE MI-CARÊME
a soft, bloomy rind cheese, named after a traditional masquerade still practised on the island during the second week of Lent

LE RIOPELLE DE L'ISLE
a soft, bloomy rind cheese, similar to a triple cream. (Jean-Paul Riopelle, famous painter and long-term resident of the island, lent his name and one of his paintings to assist in the promotion of this cheese.)

USING PASTEURIZED MILK

LE SAINT-ANTOINE
a mild cheddar
- Blocks
- Curds
- Fine herbs in both blocks and curds

1- Tomme de Grosse-Île; 2- Mi-Carême; 3- Riopelle de l'Isle; 4- Cheddar; 5- Saint-Antoine with Fines Herbs

AVAILABILITY

STORES
- Onsite store
  Call ahead for availability
- Aux Petites Délices (Sainte-Foy)
- Fromagerie du Marché Atwater (Montreal)
- Fromagerie Hamel (Montreal)
- Le Petit Quartier (Quebec City)

USED AT THE FOLLOWING RESTAURANTS
- Laurie Raphaël (Quebec City)
- Manoir des Érables (Montmagny)

For distributor inquiries, please contact Plaisirs Gourmets, 418-876-3814.

THE DEFINITIVE GUIDE TO CANADIAN ARTISANAL AND FINE CHEESE

585, chemin Saint-Vallier
Saint-Vallier, QC
1-866-884-4027 OR
418-884-4027

OWNERS
Raymond Girard and Hélène
Guillemette

MILK TYPE
Pasteurized cow's and goat's milk

PRODUCTION LEVEL
Semi-industrial

Provincially licensed

IN 2001 RAYMOND AND HÉLÈNE BOUGHT this company from the local dairy producers co-operative. They continued producing cheese using milk and other flavour-enhancing ingredients from the Bellechasse region. Only pure milk with no additives goes into the production of their cheese. Le Saint-Vallier, Fleur Saint-Michel, Honfleur and le Saint-Charles are named after local towns. The Fines herbes de la Boyer is named after the nearby Boyer River. (My paternal grandmother was a Boyer. Perhaps my ancestors lived in this region of Quebec.)

Many cheesemaking facilities in Quebec also offer soft ice cream for sale. Anne-Marie Girard, the owners' daughter, had a surprise for me. Their dairy bar offers soft maple-flavoured ice cream, which I had never seen before. I am a great fan of anything maple flavoured! But before she would hand the cone to me, she dipped it in dark Belgian chocolate. Quebecers know how to enjoy life. Even with the non-stop downpour of rain, several people came in specifically for an ice cream cone. If one has a craving, one must fulfill it!

LOCAL ATTRACTIONS AND ACTIVITIES
• Centre des migrations—snow goose migration centre (Montmagny)
• Cycling and walking trails
• Grosse Île and the Irish Memorial National Historic Site—former immigration and quarantine station
• Musée des voitures à chevaux—horse carriage and sleigh museum (Saint-Vallier)

FOR MORE IDEAS, VISIT
www.chaudieresappalaches.com
AND www.bonjourquebec.com

CHEESE PRODUCED

USING PASTEURIZED COW'S MILK

BEL TWIST
a semi-soft, unripened, stretched, tortillons-style cheese
- Plain
- BBQ
- Dill Pickle
- Sour Cream and Onion

LE CANTONNIER
a hard, natural rind, Parmesan-style cheese

CHEDDAR (YELLOW AND ORANGE)
- Old
- Extra-Old
- Honfleur, a fresh cheddar with fine herbs
- Le P'tit bronzé, a maple-smoked fresh cheddar
- Le Saint-Charles, 2-year-old cheddar in port wine

CURDS
- Plain
- BBQ
- Fine Herbs

FLEUR SAINT-MICHEL
a semi-soft grilling cheese made with garlic flowers

LE SAINT-VALLIER
a semi-soft grilling cheese

TRESSE
a semi-soft, unripened, stretched Armenian-style cheese with black niger seed

VILLAGEOIS
a soft, feta-style cheese

USING PASTEURIZED GOAT'S MILK

FINES HERBES DE LA BOYER
a cheddar with fine herbs

SAINT-GERVAIS
an old cheddar

SAINT-RAPHAËL
an Italian-style, firm cheese

Snow geese migration near Montmagny; Grosse-Île National Historic Site

1- Tresse; 2- Le Cantonnier; 3- P'tit Bronzé; 4- Honfleur; 5- Cheddar; 6- Saint-Charles; 7- Fleur Saint-Michel; 8- Saint-Raphaël; 9- Fines Herbes de la Boyer; 10- Feta; 11- BBQ Tortillons; 12- Plain Curds; 13- Fine Herbs Curds; 14- BBQ Curds

AVAILABILITY

STORES
- Onsite store
  June to Labour Day
  Daily 9 a.m. to 9 p.m.
  Off-season
  Daily 9 a.m. to 5 p.m.
- Local Maxi and Métro grocery stores
- Local dépanneurs—convenience stores

For distributor inquiries, please contact the company.

La Chèvrerie du Buckland
Fromage Fermier inc.

MARC AND BARBARA LOVE ANIMALS AND they changed their careers to follow their passion. With the assistance of their children, they now manage a herd of 45 Alpine goats on their farm.

Their goats are pasture-fed and eat a diverse selection of wild plants. Marc and Barbara believe this is why their milk tastes so good. The cheese is made from high-quality milk, with no additives.

4416, rue Principale
Notre-Dame-Auxiliatrice-
de-Buckland, QC
418-789-2760

OWNERS/CHEESEMAKERS
Marc Bruneau and Barbara Brunet

MILK TYPE
Raw goat's milk

PRODUCTION LEVEL
Artisanal farmstead

Provincially licensed

LOCAL ATTRACTIONS AND ACTIVITIES
• Massif du Sud Provincial Park
• Village des défricheurs—a historic village (Saint-Prosper)
• Saint-Luc Historic Lumber Camp (Saint-Luc)

FOR MORE IDEAS, VISIT
www.chaudiereappalaches.com
AND www.bonjourquebec.com

CHEESE PRODUCED

TOMME DE MARÉCHAL
a firm, natural rind cheese, aged for 3 months

Warwick Cheese Festival

AVAILABILITY

STORES

- Onsite store
  Knock at the farmhouse door during daytime hours for service
- They operate a booth on Saturdays during spring and summer at the Marché Jean-Talon (Montreal)
- Fromagerie Hamel (Montreal)
- Marché du Vieux-Port (Quebec City)

For distributor inquiries, please contact them directly.

USED AT THE FOLLOWING RESTAURANTS

- Manoir des Érables (Montmagny)
- Manoir de Tilly (Saint-Antoine)
- Le Saint-Amour (Quebec City)

144

FROMAGERIE GILBERT INC

Depuis 1921!

BACK IN 1921, 18 DAIRY FARMERS GOT TOgether to establish a buttermaking facility on the Gilbert farm. To distinguish it from other local companies, it was named after the farm. Soon after, cheese production began. In their 84-year history, the plant burnt down four times. The owners were persistent and rebuilt.

Fromagerie Gilbert is an autonomous enterprise. Every second day, their milk truck picks up the milk from the same dairy farmers, who guarantee the quality of the milk. Whole milk is used for producing the cheese in the traditional cheddar way. Most of their cheeses are available fresh and are sold at the company store and other grocery stores.

263, chemin Kennedy
Saint-Joseph-de-Beauce, QC
1-800-797-5622 OR
418-397-5622

MILK TYPE
Pasteurized cow's milk

PRODUCTION LEVEL
Semi-industrial

Provincially licensed

LOCAL ATTRACTIONS AND ACTIVITIES
- La cache à Maxime—winery (Scott)
- La route des deux vallées— scenic route
- Organ music festival (Sainte-Marie)

FOR MORE IDEAS, VISIT
www.chaudiereappalaches.com
AND www.bonjourquebec.com

THE DEFINITIVE GUIDE TO CANADIAN ARTISANAL AND FINE CHEESE

CHEESE PRODUCED

FRESH CHEDDAR MADE DAILY
- White, produced year-round
- Orange and marble, made during the festive season

CURDS
- Plain
- BBQ
- Fine Herbs

LA CUVÉE DU MAÎTRE
a firm, unripened cheese with 27% milk fat

LIGHT
- 6% milk fat
- 12% milk fat

MOZZABO
a blend of grated mozzarella and cheddar

TORTILLONS
- Cut
- Filaments
- Knots

Carrefour Mondial de l'Accordéon

1- Mild Cheddar; 2- Plain Curds; 3- BBQ Curds; 4- Tortillons with Peppercorn; 5- BBQ Tortillons; 6- Plain Tortillons

AVAILABILITY

STORES
- Onsite store
  Daily 6 a.m. to 8 p.m.
- Marché du Vieux-Port (Quebec City)
- Regional I.G.A. and Provigo grocery stores

USED AT THE FOLLOWING RESTAURANTS
- La cache à Maxine (Scott)
- Père Nature (Saint-Georges)

For distributor inquiries, please contact the company.

146

THE DEFINITIVE GUIDE TO CANADIAN ARTISANAL AND FINE CHEESE

17520, boulevard Lacroix
Saint-Georges-de-Beauce, QC
418-228-2184

MILK TYPE
Raw and pasteurized cow's milk

PRODUCTION LEVEL
Semi-industrial

Provincially licensed

AUGUST 30, 1995, MARKED THE OFFICIAL opening of La Fromagerie La Pépite d'Or, with the release of their first cheddar. Within a few months, flavoured cheeses were launched. One year later, the nine partners acquired Fromages Sainte-Marie, permitting them access to equipment to produce stretched cheese. One of their newest creations is Le Grand Cahill, a 60-day-old raw-milk cheddar named after Michael Cahill, an Irish entrepreneur (1828-1890). He assisted in the early development of Saint-Georges and the Beauce region of Quebec.

Their store also sells regional food products.

LOCAL ATTRACTIONS AND ACTIVITIES
• Maison J.A. Vachon—home of the founder of the little Vachon snack cakes, a Quebec institution (Sainte-Marie)
• Véloroute de la Chaudière—45 km cycling trail (Sainte-Marie)
• Scenic train excursions of the Chaudière-Appalaches region (Thetford Mines)
• Woodstock en Beauce—a huge outdoor music festival; past performers include April Wine, The Box, Bad Religion and the Violent Femmes (Saint-Éphrème-de-Beauce)

FOR MORE IDEAS, VISIT
www.destinationbeauce.com
AND www.bonjourquebec.com

CHEESE PRODUCED

USING RAW MILK

LE GRAND CAHILL
a cheddar cheese

USING PASTEURIZED MILK

BRINED CHEESES
- Balls
- Bâtonnets
- Cubes
- Filaments

CURDS
- Plain
- Poutine
- Bacon
- BBQ
- Fine Herbs
- Garlic
- Maple
- Onion
- Souvlaki
- 3 Pepper

FRESH CHEDDAR
- Plain
- Fine Herbs
- Jalapeño
- Marble
- Orange
- Unsalted

GRATED
- Mozzarella
- White cheddar
- Orange cheddar
- House mix (two colours)

TWIST FILAMENTÉ
a semi-soft, unripened, stretched cheese
- Plain
- BBQ
- Garlic and Herbs
- Souvlaki
- Armenian-style with black niger seed
    In knots
    In balls

AVAILABILITY

STORES
- Onsite store
  Summer
  Daily 5 a.m. to 9 p.m.
  Off season:
  Monday to Wednesday
  5 a.m. to 6 p.m.
  Thursday and Friday
  5 a.m. to 9 p.m.
  Saturday 5 a.m. to 6 p.m.
  Sunday 8 a.m. to 6 p.m.
- Regional I.G.A. and Métro grocery stores

For distributor inquiries, please contact their sales team.

USED AT THE FOLLOWING RESTAURANTS
- Auberge Benedict Arnold (Saint-Georges-de-Beauce)

THE DEFINITIVE GUIDE TO CANADIAN ARTISANAL AND FINE CHEESE

Moisture 42% · M.F. 27%

Fabriqué et emballé par · Made and packed by
Fromagerie La Bourgade Inc.
16, boulevard Caouette Nord, Thetford Mines, Qc, G6G 2B8 · (418) 335-3313

STEEVE AND HIS STAFF MAKE CHEESE THE old-fashioned way, pasteurizing the milk and making cheese in small batches. His love of cheese led him to establish his own cheese-making company in 1994. Seventy percent of his cheese is sold locally. The onsite family-style restaurant offers a full menu, including seafood and Italian dishes.

16, boulevard Caouette N.
Thetford Mines, QC
418-335-3313

OWNER/ORIGINAL CHEESEMAKER
Steeve Vallée

MILK TYPE
Pasteurized cow's milk

PRODUCTION LEVEL
Semi-industrial

Provincially licensed

LOCAL ATTRACTIONS AND ACTIVITIES
- Domaine du Bison—a bison ranch (Lambton)
- O'Brien Historic General Store (Thetford Mines)
- Thetford Mines Mineralogical & Mines Museum
- Open pit and underground mine experiences (Thetford Mines)

FOR MORE IDEAS, VISIT
www.tourisme-amiante.com (French only),
www.chaudiereappalaches.com
AND www.bonjourquebec.com.

CHEESE PRODUCED

CURDS

FRESH CHEDDAR
- White
- Hot Pepper
- Sun-dried Tomato and Basil

TWIST
a semi-soft, unripened, stretched cheese
- Armenian-style
  with black niger seed
  plain

AVAILABILITY

STORES
- Onsite store
  Monday to Saturday
  7 a.m. to 8 p.m.
  Sunday 10 a.m. to 9 p.m.
- Regional I.G.A., Loblaws
  and Métro grocery stores

For distributor inquiries, please contact their sales team.

USED AT THE FOLLOWING RESTAURANTS
- Their own Resto-Pub
  La Bourgade

CHEESEMAKING HAS BEEN IN THE BLOOD of the Bergeron family for three generations. Grandfather Edmond Bergeron produced cheddar in the Lac-Saint-Jean community of Saint-Bruno. His sons Raymond and Égide established themselves in Saint-Antoine-de-Tilly, making cheddar from the local milk. Now the third generation, consisting of Chantal, Mario, Roger and Sylvain, are continuing the family tradition of cheesemaking. No longer making cheddar, they are specializing in the production of Gouda.

In 1989 Fromagerie Bergeron began operation. Their pledge is to produce top-of-the-line cheese known and appreciated across North America for its consistent good taste.

3837, route Marie-Victorin
Saint-Antoine-de-Tilly, QC
418-886-2234

FOUNDERS
Chantal, Mario, Roger and Sylvain Bergeron

MILK TYPE
Pasteurized cow's and goat's milk

PRODUCTION LEVEL
Semi-industrial

Federally registered

LOCAL ATTRACTIONS AND ACTIVITIES
- Domaine Joly-De Lotbinière—ancestral seigneurial manor of Sir Henri-Gustave Joly de Lotbinière, former French-Canadian lieutenant-governor of British Columbia (1900-1906); property is renowned for its beautiful gardens (Sainte-Croix)
- Expo de Lotbinière—summer agricultural fair (Sainte-Agapit)
- La Ferme du Platon—game bird farm (Sainte-Croix)

FOR MORE IDEAS, VISIT
www.cldlotbiniere.qc.ca (French only),
www.chaudiereappalaches.com
AND www.bonjourquebec.com

CHEESE PRODUCED

USING COW'S MILK

LE CALUMET
a firm, natural rind, Gouda-style cheese, smoked with cherrywood

LE COUREUR DES BOIS
a firm, natural rind, Gouda-style cheese with cumin seeds, coated in black wax

LE FIN RENARD
a firm, washed rind, Gouda-style cheese

GOUDA CLASSIQUE
a firm, natural rind cheese, coated in red wax

GOUDA CURDS

GOUDA EXTRA DOUX

LE POPULAIRE
aged for one month

LE LOTBINIÈRE
a firm, natural rind, Jarlsberg-style cheese, coated in yellow wax

LE POPULAIRE
freshly pressed Gouda curds

LE P'TIT BONHEUR
a firm, natural rind, Gouda-style cheese, coated in red wax and aged for 6 to 8 months

LE SEIGNEUR DE TILLY
a firm, natural rind, Gouda-style cheese, coated in yellow wax; developed as a light version of Gouda Classique

LE SIX %
a firm, natural rind, Gouda-style cheese with a milk fat content of 6%

USING GOAT'S MILK

PATTE BLANCHE
a firm, natural rind, Gouda-style cheese, coated in black wax

1- Le Fin Renard; 2- Le P'tit Bonheur; 3- Le Seigneur de Tilly; 4- Coureur des Bois; 5- Gouda; 6- Gouda Curds; 7- Fondue Parmesan; 8- Gouda Classique

AVAILABILITY

STORES

- Onsite store
  Summer
  Daily 9 a.m. to 7 p.m.
  Off season
  Daily 10 a.m. to 5 p.m.
- Corneau and Cantin (Chicoutimi)
- Les Fromages d'Ernest (Drummondville)
- Laiterie Charlevoix (Baie-Saint--Paul)
- Marché du Vieux-Port (Quebec City)
- Mayrand (Saint-Léonard)

USED AT THE FOLLOWING RESTAURANTS

- Casse-croûte Chez Lizon (Saint-Appolinaire)
- Manoir de Tilly (Saint-Antoine)

For distributor inquiries, please contact their sales team.

152

766, 9 rang E.
Plessisville, QC
819-362-7472

FOUNDERS
Gérard Dubois and his sons Alain,
Rénald and Richard

CHEESEMAKER
Richard Dubois

MILK TYPE
Pasteurized cow's milk

PRODUCTION LEVEL
Artisanal

Federally registered

LOCAL ATTRACTIONS AND ACTIVITIES
- Cabane à sucre—maple syrup shanties
- The Celtic Way—a heritage drive showcasing the Irish and Scottish settlement of the region (Inverness)
- The Craig and Gosford Discovery Circuit—scenic and historic drive
- Le musée du broze d'Inverness—bronze Economuseum (Inverness)

FOR MORE IDEAS, VISIT
www.tourisme-erable.qc.ca
AND www.bonjourquebec.com

RICHARD AND HIS BROTHERS WANTED TO create a value-added product with the milk from their sixth-generation family farm. For several years in the 1980s, they produced organic yogurt. The market crashed in 1989 so they started making cheese. In 1995 Le Mamirolle, their first savoury cheese, was released.

Their goal was to have their cheese accessible to all, whether living in small towns or big cities. The public paid greater attention after Le Mamirolle and Délices des Appalaches won several awards at the Warwick Cheese Festival. Due to high consumer demand for their cheese, they now purchase high-quality milk from neighbouring dairy farms to increase production.

CHEESE PRODUCED

DÉLICES DES APPALACHES
a semi-soft cheese, washed with Quebec ice cider

LOUIS DUBOIS
a semi-soft, washed rind cheese named in recognition of a pioneer ancestor

LE MAMIROLLE
a semi-soft, washed rind cheese

LA RACLETTE DES APPALACHES
a semi-soft, washed rind cheese

Chesterville Church

AVAILABILITY

STORES

- Onsite store
  Monday to Friday
  8:30 a.m. to 4:30 p.m.
  Closed noon to 1 p.m.
- Fromagerie du Marché
  Atwater (Montreal)
- Local I.G.A., Maxi, Métro
  and Provigo grocery stores
- Maison Moisan
  (Quebec City)
- Marché du Vieux-Port
  (Quebec City)

USED AT THE FOLLOWING RESTAURANTS

- Cochon Dingue
  (Quebec City)
- Manoir du Lac William
  (Saint-Ferdinand)

For distributor inquiries, please contact Saputo Inc., 1-800-672-8866 or 514-328-6662.

THE DEFINITIVE GUIDE TO CANADIAN ARTISANAL AND FINE CHEESE

LUCILLE HAS OWNED SHEEP FOR 28 YEARS. She raised them originally for wool and meat. In 1991 her focus changed to milk and cheese production. The sheep are in the pastures from early spring to the first snowfall, grazing on the local flora and drinking from the natural springs. The milk from their herd of East Friesian sheep is a product of the local terroir. Milk from four selected local sheep milk producers is used on occasion, but the different milks are not mixed together, as each has minute flavour differences. Lucille's cheese are made with care. They are made by hand, aged in a special ripening room in an underground cave, and hand-wrapped.

Lucille was the first sheep cheese producer in Quebec and has received many awards, including first-prize designations at competitions hosted by The American Cheese Society.

3690, rang trois
Sainte-Hélène-de-Chester, QC
819-382-2300

FOUNDER AND CHEESEMAKER
Lucille Giroux

BUSINESS PARTNER
Alastair MacKenzie

MILK TYPE
Raw and pasteurized sheep's milk

PRODUCTION LEVEL
Artisanal

Provincially licensed

LOCAL ATTRACTIONS AND ACTIVITIES
- Appalachian Mountains
- Cranberry Centre (Saint-Louis-de-Blandford)
- Parc Marie-Victorin—botanical garden (Kingsey Falls)
- Warwick Cheese Festival in June

FOR MORE IDEAS, VISIT
www.tourismecentredu-quebec.com AND
www.bonjourquebec.com

CHEESE PRODUCED

USING RAW MILK

LE CLOS VERT
a semi-soft, tomme-style cheese

USING PASTEURIZED MILK

LE BERCAIL
a soft, surface ripened cheese

LE BLEU DE LA MOUTONNIÈRE
a semi-soft, blue cheese

LE CABANON
a soft cheese wrapped in a maple leaf and soaked in eau-de-vie alcoholic spirits

FETA
marinated in olive oil and herbs

LA FLEUR DES MONTS
a firm, natural rind cheese, inspired by the sheep cheese of the Pyrenees

LE FOIN D'ODEUR
a soft, mixed bloomy rind, brie-style cheese

LE NEIGE DE BREBIS
a fresh, unripened cheese made in the Corsican Broccio-style

RICOTTA

LE SOUPÇON DE BLEU
a semi-soft blue cheese

Alastair walking behind the sheep

1- Le Bleu de la Moutonnière; 2- Le Soupçon de Bleu; 3- La Fleur des Monts; 4- Clos Vert; 5- La Fleur des Monts; 6- Le Cabanon; 7- Bercail; 8- Le Foin d'Odeur; 9-Feta; 10- Ricotta

AVAILABILITY

STORES
- Onsite store
  Tuesday to Thursday
  10 a.m. to 3 p.m.
  Friday and Saturday
  11 a.m. to 1 p.m.
- They operate a booth daily at the Marché Jean-Talon (Montreal)
- Fromagerie du Marché Atwater (Montreal)
- Gourmet des Oliviers (Trois-Rivières)
- Marché du Vieux-Port (Quebec City)

USED AT THE FOLLOWING RESTAURANTS
- Manoir du Lac William (Saint-Ferdinand d'Halifax)
- Le P'tit Extra (Montreal)
- Laurie Raphaël (Quebec City)
- Le Saint-Amour (Quebec City)

For distributor inquiries, please contact Lucille or Alastair.

156

FROMAGERIE TOURNEVENT BEGAN AS A goat dairy back in the 1970s. Renée and Lucie left their city jobs to return to the land and dedicate themselves to raising goats. Due to a glut in the goat milk market in 1979, they began to experiment with creating cheese. Seven years later, cheesemaking became their main focus. Care of the goats was taken over by a local agricultural co-operative. Experimenting with raw milk led to the creation of their Chèvre Noir. Their latest cheese, Petite Brise, is an organic cow's milk cheese, certified by Québec Vrai.

Fromagerie Tournevent was the first cheesemaking company in Quebec to produce pure goat's milk cheeses for wide distribution. Their cheeses have won several Prix Caseus at the Warwick Cheese Festival and European awards. In 2005 the company was acquired by Damafro Inc.

7004, rang Hince
Chesterville, QC
1-800-363-2017
(Damafro Inc.)

FOUNDERS
Renée Marceau and Lucie Chartier

ORIGINAL CHEESEMAKER
Lucie Chartier

MILK TYPE
Raw and pasteurized goat's and organic cow's milk

PRODUCTION LEVEL
Semi-industrial

Federally registered

LOCAL ATTRACTIONS AND ACTIVITIES
- Cranberry Interpretation Centre (Saint-Louis-de-Blandford)
- Cycling trails
- Village Québécois d'Antan—an historic village (Drummondville)
- Quatre Vents Equestrian Centre (Saint-Fortunat)

FOR MORE IDEAS, VISIT
www.tourismecentreduquebec.com AND
www.bonjourquebec.com

CHEESE PRODUCED

USING RAW GOAT'S MILK

LE CHÈVRE NOIR
a firm, ripened cheese aged for a minimum of 6 months

USING PASTEURIZED GOAT'S MILK

LE BIQUET
a soft, unripened cheese
- Plain
- Herbs
- Black Peppercorn

CAPRIATI
a semi-soft, unripened cheese
- Plain
- Marinated in sunflower and olive oils

CHÈVRE DE CAMPAGNE
a fresh, unripened cheese

CHÈVRE DOUX
a soft, unripened cheese

CHÈVRE FIN
a soft, bloomy rind cheese
- Plain
- Ash-coated

CHÈVRE NOIR
a firm, ripened cheese

CHEVRINO
a firm, unripened cheese

FETA TRADITION
aged in brine for 3 months with no lipase added
- Plain
- Marinated in sunflower and olive oils with sun-dried tomatoes

LE TOURNEVENT
a soft, unripened cheese

LE VELOUTIN
a fresh, unripened, cream cheese
- Garlic and Herbs
- Sweet Red Pepper

USING ORGANIC PASTEURIZED COW'S MILK

PETITE BRISE
a fresh, spreadable cheese
- Plain
- Garlic Flowers
- 3 Pepper

1- Marinated Feta; 2- Chèvre Noir; 3- Le Tournevent

AVAILABILITY

STORES
- Onsite store
  Monday to Friday
  9 a.m. to 5 p.m.
- Regional Loblaws, Métro & Provigo grocery stores

USED AT THE FOLLOWING RESTAURANTS
- Temps des Cerises (Danville)

For distributor inquiries, please contact Damafro Inc., 1-800-363-2017 or 450-797-3301.

LA FROMAGERIE VICTORIA WAS ESTAB-lished in 1988 when Youville Rousseau and Florian Gosselin bought the existing Fromage Victoria company. They added a restaurant to the facilities and transformed the large chee-semaking facility into a performance hall and micro-cheese plant. A video presentation on the making of cheese is offered to groups who call ahead. Dinner theatre packages and folk music are scheduled regularly. The restaurant offers breakfasts, quick meals and an à la carte menu featuring their cheese. The dairy bar offers a wide range of hard and soft ice cream, including one with no fat or cholesterol.

The Centre-du-Québec region is known as the birthplace of poutine, a gooey plate of French fries with fresh, squeaky cheese curds and brown chicken gravy. Sounds disgusting, does not look great, but tastes delicious! Even just looking at the image of the dish on their website made my mouth water. It is a tradition for my wife, Joanne, and I to make a big plate of poutine after completing our half-marathon races. The expectation of eating this rich and cheesy dish empowers both of us to run those last grueling kilometres. Why are we running this 21-km race? Oh yeah, to eat poutine after we cross the finish line!

101, rue de l'Aqueduc
Victoriaville, QC
819-752-6821

OWNERS
Youville Rousseau and Florian Gosselin

MILK TYPE
Pasteurized cow's milk

PRODUCTION LEVEL
Semi-industrial

Provincially licensed

LOCAL ATTRACTIONS AND ACTIVITIES
• Golf courses
• Leather Economuseum (Victoriaville)
• Maison Wilfrid-Laurier National Historic Site—home of Canada's eigth prime minister and the first of French-Canadian ancestry (Victoriaville)
• Pépinière Bonsai—Japanese miniature tree nursery (Tingwick)

FOR MORE IDEAS, VISIT
www.tourismecentredu-quebec.com AND
www.bonjourquebec.com

CHEESE PRODUCED

CURDS, WHITE ONLY

FROMAGE NON-SALÉ
a firm, unripened, unsalted cheese

FROMAGE VICTORIA
a fresh, white cheddar available in different shapes

LE PETIT LAIT
a fresh, unripened cheese

TORTILLONS

AVAILABILITY

STORES
- Onsite store
  Spring and summer
  Daily 6 a.m. to 11 p.m.
  Fall and winter
  Daily 6 a.m. to 9 p.m.

USED AT THE FOLLOWING RESTAURANTS
- Their onsite restaurant
- Jardin des Bois-Francs
  (Victoriaville)
- Restaurant Princesse
  (Princeville)

For distributor inquiries, please contact their sales team.

GEORGES AND YVON CÔTÉ ENTERED THE cheesemaking industry in 1976 upon the purchase of a small cheese plant in Kingsey Falls. High demand for their products precipitated a move to a larger facility in nearby Warwick in 1979. The plant was enlarged four times to keep up with demand. In 1996 a new ripening and distribution centre was built to store, cut and package their cheese according to retailers' specifications. In April 2005 Saputo Inc. acquired Fromage Côté.

The company produces several brands of cheese: Kingsey, Princesse, Héritage Jules Roiseux (available in Quebec only) and DuVillage de Warwick (available across Canada).

80, rue Hôtel de Ville
Warwick, QC
819-358-3331

FOUNDERS
Georges and Yvon Côté

MILK TYPE
Pasteurized cow's milk

PRODUCTION LEVEL
Industrial

Federally registered

LOCAL ATTRACTIONS AND ATTACTIONS
- Parc linéaire des Bois-Francs—a cycling trail
- Les Fêtes Victoriennes—a Victorian-era street festival (Victoriaville)
- Mont Gleason Ski Resort
- Warwick Cheese Festival in June

FOR MORE IDEAS, VISIT www.tourismecentreduquebec.com (French only) AND www.bonjourquebec.com

CHEESE PRODUCED

KINGSEY AND PRINCESSE BRANDS USING COW'S MILK

COGRUET
a firm, cooked, rindless, Swiss-style cheese

CURDS

KINGSBERG
a firm, rindless, Jarlsberg-style cheese

PRESSED CHEESE
a firm, unripened cheese

RACLETTE

TORTILLONS

DUVILLAGE DE WARWICK BRAND USING COW'S MILK

BRIE DU MARCHÉ
a soft, bloomy rind cheese

BRIE PLEINE SAVEUR
a soft, bloomy rind cheese

CANTONNIER
a semi-soft, washed rind, Port-Salut-style cheese

LE CENDRÉ
a semi-soft, pressed, washed rind, Morbier-style cheese

DOUBLE CRÈME
a soft, bloomy rind cheese

GRAND CAMEMBERT
a soft, bloomy rind cheese

MONT GLEASON
a firm cheese

PETIT BRIE
a soft, bloomy rind cheese

SAINT-MÉDARD
a semi-soft cheese

SAINT-PAULIN
a semi-soft, washed rind cheese

SIR LAURIER D'ARTHABASKA
a soft, washed rind, Reblochon-style cheese

SUBLIME DOUBLE CRÈME
a soft, bloomy rind cheese

TRIPLE CRÈME
a soft, bloomy rind cheese

VACHERIN
a semi-soft, washed rind cheese

HÉRITAGE JULES ROISEUX BRAND USING COW'S MILK

L'ÉVANJULES
a soft, bloomy rind, Camembert-style cheese

Warwick Cheese Festival sculpture

AVAILABILITY

STORES
- Onsite stores
- Warwick plant (80 rue Hôtel de Ville, Warwick)
  Summer
  Daily 8 a.m. to 10 p.m.
  Off season
  Daily 8 a.m. to 9 p.m.
- Plessisville plant (1245 avenue Forand, Plessisville)
  Summer
  Daily 9 a.m. to 9 p.m.
  Off season
  Monday to Wednesday and weekends
  9 a.m. to 7 p.m.
  Thursday and Friday
  9 a.m. to 8 p.m.
- National grocery store chains

For distributor inquiries, please contact their sales team.

WITH A VISION OF RETURNING TO TRADI-tional farming and a greater stewardship of the environment in mind, 10 dairy farmers joined together to form Fromagerie L'Ancêtre in 1992. Organic practices, they believe, allow the true natural taste of milk to emerge.

In 1995 raw-milk cheddar became their signature product. They were pioneers in the production of raw-milk organic cheese. Since the opening of their own cheesemaking facility, they have added other cheese to their product line. While enjoying a light meal or an artisanal ice cream at their location, you can observe the cheese-making process through windows that look into the plant.

1615, boulevard Port-Royal
Bécancour, QC
819-233-9157

MILK TYPE
Organic raw and pasteurized cow's milk

PRODUCTION LEVEL
Artisanal

Federally registered.

LOCAL ATTRACTIONS AND ACTIVITIES
- Centre de la biodiversité—an ecology centre (Bécancour)
- Moulin Michel de Gentilly—an historic seigneurial grist mill (Bécancour)
- Auberge Godefroy—spa and golf resort (Bécancour)

FOR MORE IDEAS, VISIT
www.becancour.net
(French only),
www.tourismecentredu-quebec.com AND
www.bonjourquebec.com

CHEESE PRODUCED

USING RAW MILK

CHEDDAR
- Mild (white, orange and marble)
- Medium
- Old
- Extra-Old
- 3-Year-Old

EMMENTAL
aged for 2 months

PARMESAN
aged for 12 months

USING PASTEURIZED MILK

FRESH CHEDDAR

CURDS

LE FRUGAL
a firm, ripened cheese with 7% milk fat content

MOZZARELLA
- 15% milk fat content, made with partially skimmed milk
- 20% milk fat content

RICOTTA

1- Cheddar; 2- Emmental; 3- Marble

AVAILABILITY

STORES
- Onsite store
  May to mid-September
  Daily 9 a.m. to 8 p.m.
  Mid-September to May
  Saturday to Wednesday
  9 a.m. to 6 p.m.
  Thursday and Friday
  9 a.m. to 8 p.m.
- Natural and health food stores
- Regional I.G.A., Loblaws and Métro grocery stores

USED AT THE FOLLOWING RESTAURANTS
- Onsite restaurant offering light, healthy meals and artisanal ice cream

For distributor inquiries, please contact them directly.

THE DEFINITIVE GUIDE TO CANADIAN ARTISANAL AND FINE CHEESE

MARCEL LEMAIRE BEGAN MAKING CHEESE back in 1956, and his legacy continues with his five children, who took over the operation of the company after his death in 1978. The enterprise has tripled its business and now employs 41 people.

While dining in their onsite restaurant, you can watch their cheesemakers process the fresh cheddar and curds made daily. Fresh cheese on grilled hamburgers and poutine is an extra reason to stop by for a visit.

2095, highway 122
Saint-Cyrille-de-Wendover, QC
819-478-0601

FOUNDER
Marcel Lemaire

MILK TYPE
Pasteurized cow's milk

PRODUCTION LEVEL
Semi-industrial

Federally registered

LOCAL ATTRACTIONS AND ACTIVITIES
- Golf courses
- Les légendes fantastiques—an outdoor multi-media presentation of Quebec's legends (Drummondville)
- Mondial des cultures de Drummondville—an international multicultural festival of music, dance and costumes in July
- Parc du Mont Arthabaska (Victoriaville)

FOR MORE IDEAS, VISIT
www.tourismecentredu-quebec.com,
www.tourismeboisfrancs.com
AND www.bonjourquebec.com

CHEESE PRODUCED

CHEDDAR
- Fresh
  Garlic
  Fine Herbs
- Grated
- Old
- Extra-Old

CURDS, WHITE ONLY

SWISS

VOLTIGEUR
a semi-soft, rindless, light Monterey Jack-type cheese

Warwick Cheese Festival welcoming statue

AVAILABILITY

STORES
- Onsite store
  Daily 7 a.m. to 8 p.m.
- Regional corner stores
- Regional grocery stores

USED AT THE FOLLOWING
RESTAURANTS
- Onsite restaurant, Resto
  Chez Lemaire

For distributor inquiries, please contact their sales team.

73, route de l'Église
Saint-Guillaume, QC
819-396-2022

CHEESEMAKERS
Claude, Jean-François, Mario,
Michel, Renaud and Roger

MILK TYPE
Raw and pasteurized cow's milk

PRODUCTION LEVEL
Semi-industrial

Federally registered

LOCAL ATTRACTIONS AND ACTIVITIES
• Choco-Bec—artisan chocolates
  (Drummondville)
• Local artists' studios and art
  galleries
• Ulverton Wool Mill

FOR MORE IDEAS, VISIT
www.tourisme-drummond.com
AND www.bonjourquebec.com

AFTER AN ECONOMIC CRISIS LASTING over 10 years, 50 local dairy farmers joined together to establish the Société Coopérative Agricole de Beurrerie de Saint-Guillaume. Their goal was to take control of the distribution and processing of their milk to obtain better benefits from their efforts. In 1940 they renamed the co-operative Agrilait with the opening of their new plant. The co-op continues to operate as an independent and autonomous business, serving the agricultural needs of its 250 members.

Agrilait's six cheesemakers are proud of their efforts and enjoy seeing customers appreciate the cheese. Their Swiss cheese was chosen as a finalist by the public at the 2004 and 2005 Warwick Cheese festivals. For their cheesemakers, making cheese is more than work—it's an artform.

CHEESE PRODUCED

USING RAW COW'S MILK

CHEDDAR
- 1-Year-Old
- 2-Year-Old

USING PASTEURIZED MILK

BRICK

CHEDDAR
- Fresh (white, orange and marble)
- Medium
- Old
- Extra-Old

CURDS

SWISS

TORTILLONS

AVAILABILITY

STORES
- Onsite store
  Daily 7 a.m. to 10 p.m.
- Fromagerie Hamel (Montreal)
- Regional I.G.A., Métro and Sobey's grocery stores
- Regional convenience stores

For distributor inquiries, please contact their sales team.

LAC-MÉGANTIC IS LOCATED IN A BEAUTIFUL natural setting. The community is far enough from large urban centres to be unaffected by their pollution, but close enough to be able to service the grocery stores. Local dairy farms produce high-quality milk.

In 1976 Vianney Choquette, a trained cheesemaker, saw an opportunity to start his own establishment. A local facility had been damaged by a fire and was for sale. Vianney rebuilt the plant and began making cheese. The family enterprise is now in its second generation with his son Mario working for the company. Several of their cheeses are certified organic by Québec Vrai.

Visitors driving the scenic routes over the rounded hills of the Appalachian Mountains can stop by the plant for cheese or ice cream. Guided tours are offered if you make reservations ahead, or you can see the cheesemaking process through the store's window.

3226, rue Laval Nord
Lac-Mégantic, QC
819-583-4664

FOUNDER
Vianney Choquette

MILK TYPE
Pasteurized organic and conventional cow's milk

PRODUCTION LEVEL
Artisanal

Federally registered

LOCAL ATTRACTIONS AND ACTIVITIES
• Mont Gosford's hiking trails and cliff climbing
• Mont Mégantic Observatory
• Winter snowmobiling

FOR MORE IDEAS, VISIT
www.tourisme-megantic.com
AND www.bonjourquebec.com

CHEESE PRODUCED

USING ORGANIC PASTEURIZED
COW'S MILK

CHEDDAR
white only
- Medium
- Old
- Extra-Old

GOUDA

MOZZARELLA

SWISS

USING CONVENTIONAL
PASTEURIZED COW'S MILK

BRICK

CHEDDAR
white and orange
- Medium
- Old
- Extra-Old, white only

FONDU
a spreadable cheese

LE GOUTÉ LÉGER
a block cheese

TORTILLONS TWIST

UNRIPENED, FIRM CHEESE
white and orange
- Blocks
- Curds

AVAILABILITY

STORES
- Onsite store
  Spring and summer
  Daily 8 a.m. to 10 p.m.
  Fall and winter
  Monday to Wednesday
  8 a.m. to 6 p.m.
  Thursday and Friday
  8 a.m. to 9 p.m.
  Weekends
  8 a.m. to 6 p.m.
- Regional I.G.A., Maxi, Métro
  and Provigo grocery stores

For distributor inquiries, please contact the company's sales team.

USED AT THE FOLLOWING
RESTAURANTS
- Restaurant Louis
  (Sherbrooke)
- Restaurant Valentin
  (throughout Quebec)
- Village Grecque
  (Lennoxville)

THE DEFINITIVE GUIDE TO CANADIAN ARTISANAL AND FINE CHEESE

WHAT BEGAN AS A DAUGHTER'S PROJECT to produce cheese for her family became a business. Mélanie, who studied cheesemaking at the Saint-Hyacinthe school of agriculture, wanted to make cheese using milk from her father's herd of Holstein cows. Gaétan takes good care of his herd: their feed includes flax seeds, producing a milk high in good omega-3 fatty acids.

In 1997 they began producing Mélanie's artisanal cheese commercially. Guided tours of the farm and a video presentation are available for organized groups. Please call ahead to make reservations.

503, rue de la Carrière
Weedon, QC
819-877-5435

FOUNDER
Gaétan Grenier

CHEESEMAKER
Mélanie Grenier

MILK TYPE
Pasteurized cow's milk

PRODUCTION LEVEL
Artisanal farmstead

Provincially licensed

LOCAL ATTRACTIONS AND ACTIVITIES
- Lac-Mégantic outdoor public market
- Le Tour du lac en Arts—studio art tour (Lac-Mégantic)
- Pavillon de la faune-wildlife park (Stratford)
- Torchlight snowshoeing at Baie-des-Sables (Lac-Mégantic)

FOR MORE IDEAS, VISIT
www.tourisme-megantic.com
AND www.bonjourquebec.com

CHEESE PRODUCED

CHEDDAR
white only
- Fresh
- Mild
- 1-Year-Old
- 2-Year-Old

CURDS
- Plain
- Seasonings offered to flavour them: Bacon, BBQ and Fines Herbes

MEULE DU BARRAGE
a special cheddar made with a different bacterial culture

TORTILLONS

AVAILABILITY

STORES
- Onsite store
  Daily 6 a.m. to 9 p.m.
- Fromagerie Hamel (Montreal)
- Local corner stores
- Regional I.G.A. and Sobeys grocery stores
- S. Bourassa Ltée. (Saint-Sauveur)

For distributor inquiries, please contact Céline or Gaétan.

USED AT THE FOLLOWING RESTAURANTS
- Onsite restaurant and dairy bar

DENISE WANTED TO USE THE MILK OF their grass-fed Holstein cows to make a specialty product. She and Réjean agreed to use the milk to produce artisanal raw-milk cheese. Since 2001, their cheeses have been available to the public.

72, chemin Cordon
Saint-Edwige-de-Clifton, QC
819-849-3238

OWNERS/CHEESEMAKERS
Denise Duhaime and Réjean Théroux

MILK TYPE
Raw cow's milk

PRODUCTION LEVEL
Artisanal farmstead

Provincially licensed

LOCAL ATTRACTIONS AND ACTIVITIES
• Bishop's University Art Gallery and Centennial Theatre (Lennoxville)
• Mount Orford Provincial Park
• Scenic community of North Hatley

FOR MORE IDEAS, VISIT
www.cantonsdelest.com
AND www.bonjourquebec.com

CHEESE PRODUCED

CAPRICE DES CANTONS
a soft, washed rind cheese

CAPRICE DES SAISONS
a soft, bloomy rind, Camembert-style cheese

Lake Memphremagog

AVAILABILITY

STORES

- Onsite store
    Daily 9 a.m. to 5 p.m.
    Call to verify
- Ferme Beaulieu
  (Lennoxville)
- Fromagerie du Marché
  Atwater (Montreal)
- Fromagerie Hamel
  (Montreal)
- Marché de chez nous
  (Longueuil)

For distributor inquiries, please contact Denise and Réjean.

THE DEFINITIVE GUIDE TO CANADIAN ARTISANAL AND FINE CHEESE

1000, rue Child
Coaticook, QC
819-849-2272

PRESIDENT
Jean Provencher

VICE-PRESIDENT
Johanne Provencher

MILK TYPE
Thermalized and pasteurized
cow's and goat's milk

PRODUCTION LEVEL
Semi-industrial

Federally registered

PLANNING TO OFFER PASTEURIZED MILK, Arthur Bédard, Arthur Saint-Cyr and Henri Guérin founded the dairy in 1940. Their main activities were processing and bottling natural milk, cream and chocolate milk. The bottles were delivered locally by horse-drawn wagons. Mr. Bédard bought out his partners in 1942 and began to make ice cream and cheddar cheese. Forty-seven years, later new owners have expanded the range to include aged cheddars and goat cheese.

At the store you can see Mr. Pellequin, their master cheesemaker, at work with his staff. When his cheese curds are ready, a lineup of hungry customers quickly appears for the salty and squeaky treats.

LOCAL ATTRACTIONS AND ACTIVITIES
- Festival du Lait—milk festival (Coaticook)
- Louis S. Saint-Laurent National Historic Site—boyhood home of Canada's 17th prime minister (Coaticook)
- Mountain biking at Circuits Frontières (East Hereford)
- Parc de la Gorge de Coaticook—a 50-metre-deep gorge with the world's longest suspended footbridge

FOR MORE IDEAS, VISIT
www.cantonsdelest.com
AND www.bonjourquebec.com

CHEESE PRODUCED

USING THERMALIZED COW'S MILK

CHEDDAR
- Coaticook Vielli, aged for 15 months

USING PASTEURIZED COW'S MILK

CHEDDAR
- Fresh (white, orange and marble)

CURDS

MOZZARELLA

SAUMURÉ
a firm, rindless cheese soaked in salt brine

USING PASTEURIZED GOAT'S MILK

CAPRICOOK
a firm, unripened cheese
- Mild, aged for up to 4 months
- Old, aged for more than 9 months

Coaticook Gorge Pedestrian Suspension Bridge

AVAILABILITY

STORES
- Onsite store
  Summer
  Daily 8 a.m. to 10 p.m.
  Off-season
  Monday to Saturday
  8 a.m. to 6 p.m.
- Regional I.G.A., Maxi and Provigo grocery stores

USED AT THE FOLLOWING RESTAURANTS
- Café Central (Coaticook)
- Coffret d'Imagination (Parc de la Gorge, Coaticook)

For distributor inquiries, please contact the company sales team.

Saint-Benoît-du-Lac, QC
1-877-343-4336 OR
819-843-4336

DIRECTOR OF CHEESEMAKING
OPERATIONS
Frère André Blanchet

MILK TYPE
Pasteurized cow's, goat's and
sheep's milk

PRODUCTION LEVEL
Artisanal

Federally registered

LOCAL ATTRACTIONS AND ACTIVITIES
• Boating on Lake
  Memphrémagog
• Domaine Bleu Lavande—
  a lavender farm (Fitch Bay)
• Underground visits of the
  Capelton Mines (North Hatley)
• Owl's Head Ski Resort

FOR MORE IDEAS, VISIT
www.cantonsdelest.com,
www.tourisme-memphrema-
gog.com AND
www.bonjourquebec.com

THE RELIGIOUS COMMUNITY OF BENEDIC-tine monks was established on the shores of Lake Memphrémagog in 1912. Its infancy was tenuous due to slow recruitment and the accidental drowning of its elected leader, but with time, the community began to prosper. In 1943 the monks began making Bleu Ermite cheese. The line of products now consists of 14 cheeses, made with the assistance of professional lay people.

At Abbaye de Saint-Benoît-du-Lac, visitors are welcome to walk the grounds, hear Gregorian chants at a religious service or participate in a monastic retreat. Separate accommodations for men and women are available. A university friend used to go on retreats at the abbey. He said the guaranteed peace and quiet made studying for his final exams easier. The requirement is that the monks' daily prayers and work not be disturbed. The meals are eaten in silence, while scriptures are read aloud.

☙

I have a family connection with the abbaye. My father helped build its chapel when he was a teenager.

CHEESE PRODUCED

USING COW'S MILK

BLEU BÉNÉDICTIN
a semi-soft, blue cheese, aged for 3 months

BLEU ERMITE
a semi-soft, blue cheese, aged for 5 to 6 weeks

CRÈME DE BLEU
a mixture of Bleu Bénédictin and crème fraîche

FONTINA
a firm, rindless cheese

FRÈRE JACQUES
a firm, natural rind, Swiss-style cheese

LE MOINE
a firm, natural rind, Gruyère-style cheese

MONT SAINT-BENOÎT
a semi-soft to firm, rindless, Swiss-style cheese

RICOTTA SAINT-BENOÎT

LE SAINT-AUGUSTIN
a firm, rindless, orange Swiss-style cheese

USING GOAT'S MILK

L'ARCHANGE
a firm, rindless, Gruyère-style cheese

CHÈVRE-NOIT BLEU DE CHÈVRE
a firm, blue cheese

RICOTTA DE CHÈVRE

USING SHEEP'S MILK

CHANOINE BLEU DE BREBIS
a semi-soft, blue cheese

LE MEMPHRÉ
a firm, rindless cheese

Abbaye de Saint-Benoît-du-Lac

1- Bleu Bénédictine; 2- Saint Augustine; 3- Frère Jacques; 4- Ermite

AVAILABILITY

STORES
- Onsite store
  Monday to Saturday
  9 to 10:45 a.m.
  11:45 a.m. to 4:30 p.m.
  June 24 to Labour Day
  9 to 10:45 a.m.
  11:45 a.m. to 6 p.m.
- Fine cheese shops
  nation-wide
- The Cheese Boutique
  (Toronto)

USED AT THE FOLLOWING RESTAURANTS
- Auberge Georgeville
  (Georgeville)

For distributor inquiries, please contact Le Choix du Fromager, 1-877-328-2207.

235, rue Saint-Robert
Saint-Robert, QC
450-782-2111

DIRECTOR
Jean-Pierre Salva

CHEESEMAKER
Gilles Vallée

MILK TYPE
Pasteurized cow's milk

PRODUCTION LEVEL
Semi-industrial

Federally registered

LOCAL ATTRACTIONS AND ACTIVITIES
- Canoeing and guided cruises along the St. Lawrence River
- La Route des épouvantails— with an informational flyer in hand, discover the colourful scarecrows of the region
- Le Musée des Abénakis—a First Nations museum (Odanak)
- Cycling trails

FOR MORE IDEAS, VISIT
www.tourismesoreltracy-region.qc.ca AND
www.bonjourquebec.com

A GROUP OF FORWARD-THINKING MILK producers and a distributor got together in 1992 to create a value-added product with their milk and find a market for it. Cheese, of course, was the product.

Their targeted market was the Arabic-Canadian population of Montreal and Toronto. Arabic cheeses are traditionally made in the home by the women. To offer such authentic cheese, Fromagerie Polyethnique invited women of the local Arabic community to come and make their cheese at the plant. At the same time, they shared their recipes and techniques with Gilles Vallée, the cheesemaker. Already knowledgeable in the production of cheddar, Gilles wanted to learn how to make other styles of cheese.

An important goal of the company is to establish good relationships with the Canadian Arabic community. All their cheese are hallal (approved by Muslim dietary laws).

The managers emphasize their belief in having happy staff who look forward to coming to work every day. Happy workers make good cheese and have pride in their work.

༄

I discovered Nabulsi cheese when I worked at Point Pelee National Park in southwestern Ontario, a region with a fair-sized Lebanese population. The cheese was a yummy snack while birdwatching in the park.

CHEESE PRODUCED

AKAAWI
a semi-soft, unripened, pressed cheese

BALADI
similar to Akawi, but less salty and less pressed

HALLOUMI
a semi-soft, pressed cheese, good for frying

LABNEH
a fresh, yogurt-pressed cream cheese
- Light
- Tzatziki

NABULSI
a semi-soft, unripened, stretched cheese, incorporating niger seed

Cycling uphill

1- Baladi; 2- Haloumi; 3- Akaawi; 4- Labneh; 5- Labneh in oil; 6- Flavoured Haloumi; 7- Nabulsi

AVAILABILITY

STORES
- Onsite store
  Monday to Friday
  8 a.m. to 4 p.m.
- Marché Adonis (several locations in Montreal)

USED AT THE FOLLOWING RESTAURANTS
- L'Auberge de la Rive (Sorel-Tracy)
- Relais Gastronomique Philippe de Lyon (Sorel-Tracy)

For distributor inquiries, please contact the company's sales team.

THE DEFINITIVE GUIDE TO CANADIAN ARTISANAL AND FINE CHEESE

THE DEFINITIVE GUIDE TO CANADIAN ARTISANAL AND FINE CHEESE

THE HISTORY OF LAITERIE CHALIFOUX goes back to 1920, when Alexandrina Chalifoux, an enterprising farmer, sold her surplus milk in neighbouring villages. Her son, Jean-Paul, assisted his mother as soon as he was old enough and later acquired the milk from several local dairy farms. In 1959 their first cheeses, under the brand name Fromages Riviera, were offered for sale. With the acquisition of Fort Richelieu Cooperative in 1978, the company was able to expand.

They were the first in North America to treat their milk using the European process of ultra-filtration. The milk sugar is removed, making the cheese digestible for people who are lactose intolerant. This technique is used with milk designated for their specialty cheeses.

The next generation of the Chalifoux family is continuing the expansion of the company, looking into the development of new national and international markets. Keep an eye out for their products at a cheese counter near you.

1093, boulevard Fiset
(rue Marie-Victorin)
Sorel-Tracy, QC
1-800-363-0092 OR
450-743-4439

FOUNDERS
Alexandrina and Jean-Paul Chalifoux

MILK TYPE
Pasteurized cow's milk

PRODUCTION LEVEL
Semi-industrial

Provincially licensed

LOCAL ATTRACTIONS AND ACTIVITIES
- Festival de la gibelotte—a family-oriented and contemporary music festival (Sorel-Tracy)
- Excursions en calèche—horse-drawn carriage rides (Sorel-Tracy)
- Le Rendez-vous des saveurs—a two-day tasting fair of regional food products (Sorel-Tracy)
- Sorel-Tracy Agricultural Fair

FOR MORE IDEAS, VISIT
www.tourismesoreltracy-region.qc.ca AND
www.bonjourquebec.com

CHEESE PRODUCED

L'ALPINOIS
an Emmental-style, firm, rindless cheese

LE CHALIBERG
a Swiss-style, firm, rindless cheese
- Regular
- Light (17% milk fat content)

CHEDDAR (WHITE AND ORANGE)
- Mild (also available as marble)
- Medium
- Old
- Extra-Old

CURDS

ÉLAN
a semi-soft, rindless cheese made with skim milk

LE FINBOURGEOIS
a Havarti-style, semi-soft, rindless cheese

ST-PIERRE DE SAUREL
an Esrom-style, semi-soft, washed rind cheese
- Regular
- Light (14% milk fat content)

VENTS DES ÎLES
an Edam-style, firm, rindless cheese

AVAILABILITY

STORES
- Onsite store
  Daily 8 a.m. to 9 p.m.
- Regional I.G.A., Loblaws and Métro grocery stores

USED AT THE FOLLOWING RESTAURANTS
- Auberge de la Rive (Sorel-Tracy)
- Restaurant L'Aquarelle (Sorel-Tracy)
- Roadside *cantines* and family-owned eateries for their poutine

For distributor inquiries, please contact their sales team.

THE FERME BORD DES ROSIERS PRODUCES old-fashioned milk, meaning it's non-homogenized, creamy and rich. Their herd is fed a mixture of silage and *okara*, a by-product in the production of tofu. Sixty percent of their diet consists of this soy product. My dad, who works in the animal nutrition industry, heard of a few individual farms following this practice. According to André, following this nutritional formula permits the production of cheese with less than 30% milk fat.

509, Rang bord de l'Eau
Saint-Aimé-de-Massueville, QC
450-788-2527

OWNERS
Yves and André Desrosiers

CHEESEMAKER
Réal Saint-Arnaud

MILK TYPE
Raw, thermalized and pasteurized cow's milk

PRODUCTION LEVEL
Artisanal farmstead

Provincially licensed

LOCAL ATTRACTIONS AND ACTIVITIES
- Chocolaterie et Sucre—chocolate and candy shop (Saint-Robert)
- Christ Church Anglican Church—church bells date from the original chapel, Canada's first Anglican church, circa 1784 (Sorel-Tracy)
- Les Îles à la Rame—canoe/kayak festival (Sorel-Tracy)
- L'Ourson Doré—puppet presentations (Sorel-Tracy)

FOR MORE IDEAS, VISIT
www.tourismesoreltracy-region.qc.ca,
www.tourisme-monteregie.qc.ca
AND www.bonjourquebec.com

CHEESE PRODUCED

USING RAW MILK

MASSU
a cheddar-style, aged cheese

USING THERMALIZED MILK

LE BRAISÉ
*a semi-soft, unripened cheese in brine;
good for grilling*

FROMAGE MAROCCAIN
*a semi-soft, unripened, Akawi-style,
Lebanese grilling cheese*

NABULSI
a semi-soft, unripened, grilling cheese

USING PASTEURIZED MILK

CHEDDAR D'ANTAN
*a fresh, cheddar-style cheese (white
only)*

LABNEH—FROMAGE BLANC
*a fresh, unripened cheese with 1%
milk fat content*

Cider experience

AVAILABILITY

STORES

- Onsite store
  Knock at door for service
- Le Végétarien (several
  locations in Quebec)
- Fromagerie Hamel
  (Montreal)
- Maison Moisan
  (Quebec City)
- Le Marché des Saveurs
  (Montreal)

USED AT THE FOLLOWING
RESTAURANTS

- Laurie Raphaël
  (Quebec City)
- Tocqué (Montreal)

For distributor inquiries, please contact Horizon Nature, 514-326-0185.

THE DEFINITIVE GUIDE TO CANADIAN ARTISANAL AND FINE CHEESE

Damafro
FIN FROMAGER
DE TRADITION EUROPÉENNE

54, rue Principale
Saint-Damase, QC
450-797-3301

OWNER AND MASTER
CHEESEMAKER
Claude Bonnet

MILK TYPE
Pasteurized organic and
conventional cow's and goat's
milk

PRODUCTION LEVEL
Industrial

Federally registered

CLAUDE LEARNED HIS TRADE IN HIS NA-
tive region of Brie, France, specializing in soft,
bloomy rind cheese like brie and Camembert.
In 1984 he purchased Fromagerie Clément after
selling his interests in a French cheese company.
Claude settled in Canada to continue his trade.
Knowledge, skill, quality ingredients and a love
for cheese have made Damafro renowned, and it
has become one of Canada's leading cheese companies.

In the fall of 2005 Damafro purchased Fromagerie Tournevent, one of Quebec's most successful goat cheese producers.

LOCAL ATTRACTIONS AND ACTIVITIES
- Apple orchards and cideries
  (Rougemont)
- Mont-Saint-Hilaire Art
  Museum
- Maison des Cultures
  Amérindiennes—First Nations
  museum with exhibits on
  traditional maple syrup
  gathering (Mont-Saint-Hilaire)
- Saint-Damase Corn Festival

FOR MORE IDEAS, VISIT
www.tourism-monteregie.qc.ca
AND www.bonjourquebec.com

Damafro—Fromagerie Clément Inc.

CHEESE PRODUCED

USING ORGANIC COW'S MILK

CAMEMBERT BIO

GOUDA BIO

LE P'TIT SAINT-DAMASE
a soft, washed rind cheese

USING CONVENTIONAL COW'S MILK

AURA

BRIE
a soft, bloomy rind cheese
- Regular
- Fine Herbs
- Peppercorn
- Pesto
- Pesto and Sun-dried Tomatoes
- Le Connaisseur
- Le Petit Connaisseur
- Le Grand Cru, certified kosher
- Madame Clément
- Le Petit Champlain
- Tour de France
- Double Crème Le Trappeur, with added cream
- Triple Crème Le Trappeur, with added cream

CAMEMBERT
- Regular
- Le Connaisseur
- Le Grand Cru, certified kosher
- Madame Clément
- Double Crème Le Trappeur, with added cream

COTTAGE

DAMA-12
a soft, bloomy rind cheese, made with partially skimmed milk

DAMABLANC
a fresh, unripened cheese

FAISELLE
a fresh, unripened cheese

GOUDA

GRAND-DÉLICE
a semi-soft, washed rind cheese

GRAND DUC
a fresh, unripened cheese
- Fine Herbs
- Peppercorn

MASCARPONE

PETIT SUISSE
a fresh, unripened cheese

QUARK

RACLETTE

RICOTTA

LE SAINT-DAMASE
a semi-soft, washed rind cheese

SAINT-PAULIN
a semi-soft, natural rind cheese

USING ORGANIC GOAT'S MILK

CHÈVRE DES ALPES
a soft, unripened cheese

USING CONVENTIONAL GOAT'S MILK

BRIE TOUR DE FRANCE
a soft, bloomy rind cheese

CABRIE
a soft, bloomy rind cheese

CABRIE LA BÛCHE
a soft, bloomy rind cheese, in the shape of a log

CABRIE LA BÛCHETTE
a soft, bloomy rind cheese, in the shape of a small log

CHÈVRE DES ALPES
a soft, unripened cheese
- Regular
- Fine Herbs
- Peppercorn

GOUDA DE CHÈVRE
a firm, natural rind cheese

LE GRAND CRU
a soft, unripened, certified kosher cheese
- Regular
- Fine Herbs
- Peppercorn

TOMME DE CHÈVRE
a semi-soft, washed rind cheese

TOUR DE FRANCE
a soft, unripened cheese
- Regular
- Fine Herbs
- Peppercorn

AVAILABILITY

STORES
- Onsite store
  Monday to Friday
  8:30 a.m. to 5:30 p.m.
  Saturday
  8:30 a.m. to 12:30 p.m.
- National grocery store chains
- Independent fine food shops

For distributor inquiries, please contact their sales team.

DIANNE HAS BEEN WORKING IN THE DAIRY industry for many years. She wanted to make cheese with fresh milk, straight from the herd, so she and Charles started raising their own goats. They began commercial production in 1990 and were the first to make cheese in the Mont-Saint-Hilaire area. Several of their cheeses have won Caseus awards at the Warwick Cheese Festival. Guided tours of the farm are offered to groups; call ahead to make arrangements.

4395, rang des Étangs
Saint-Jean-Baptiste, QC
450-467-3991

FOUNDERS
Charles Boulerice and Dianne Choquette

CHEESEMAKER
Dianne Choquette

MILK TYPE
Thermalized goat's milk

PRODUCTION LEVEL
Artisanal farmstead

Provincially licensed

LOCAL ATTRACTIONS AND ACTIVITIES
- Local maple syrup shanties
- Maison Paul-Émile Borduas—an art foundation dedicated to the Quebec artist (Mont-Saint-Hilaire)
- Porcelaines Bousquet— porcelain Economuseum (Saint-Jean-Baptiste)

FOR MORE IDEAS, VISIT
www.vallee-du-richelieu.ca, www.tourisme-monteregie.com AND www.bonjourquebec.com

CHEESE PRODUCED

CAPRICIEUX
a fresh, rindless cheese
- Plain
- Almond
- Herbs
- Peppercorn

CHÈVRATOUT
a cheddar-style cheese
- Fresh
- Aged for 6 months to 1 year

CLÉ DES CHAMPS
a soft, bloomy rind, Camembert-style cheese

FETA

HILAIREMONTAIS
a semi-soft cheese, washed with cider

MES PETITS CAPRICES
a soft, bloomy rind cheese

MICHEROLE
a semi-soft, rindless cheese displaying characteristics of cheddar and mozzarella

AVAILABILITY

STORES
- Onsite store
  March to December,
  Wednesday to Sunday,
  9 a.m. to 6 p.m.
- Aliments Naturels Eaux
  Vives (Saint-Hilaire)

USED AT THE FOLLOWING RESTAURANTS
- Les Chanterelles du
  Richelieu (Saint-Denis-sur-Richelieu)
- Gîte de par chez nous
  (Saint-Antoine)

For distributor inquiries, please contact Charles and Dianne.

AU GRÉ DES CHAMPS

400, rang Saint-Édouard
Saint-Jean-sur-Richelieu, QC
450-346-8732

OWNERS
Daniel Gosselin and Suzanne Dufresne

CHEESEMAKER
Suzanne Dufresne

MILK TYPE
Organic raw cow's milk

PRODUCTION LEVEL
Artisanal farmstead

Provincially licensed

LOCAL ATTRACTIONS AND ACTIVITIES
- Fort Chambly National Historic Site—restored 17th-century French fort (Chambly)
- Maple syrup "cabane à sucre" establishments—a spring dining experience with pitchers of maple syrup on each table (Mont-Saint-Grégoire)
- Dunham wine route

FOR MORE IDEAS, VISIT
www.tourism-monteregie.qc.ca
AND www.bonjourquebec.com

DANIEL WAS RAISED ON THIS FARM, MILK-ing Holsteins and working the land with his father. He and Suzanne, his partner, wanted to work on the farm together. They changed their herd to Brown Swiss cows and began using their milk to make cheese. Brown Swiss produce milk with a high milk fat content; the higher the fat content, the higher the yield in cheese production per litre of milk.

Daniel feeds his herd a mixture of hay and wild herbs. He believes it gives the milk a unique flavour. The milk from their 25 animals is pumped directly from the barn, twice daily at each milking time, to the cheesemaking facility. Suzanne works carefully with the raw milk to produce her three organic cheeses certified by Garantie Bio-Écocert. You can see Suzanne making the cheese, through a viewing window located in the store. Afterwards enjoy a sample plate of their cheese and those of other regional cheese-makers.

CHEESE PRODUCED

LE D'IBERVILLE
a semi-soft, washed rind cheese

LE GRÉ DES CHAMPS
a firm, mixed rind cheese (bloomy and washed)

LE MONNOIR
a firm, mixed rind cheese (bloomy and washed), aged for a minimum of 6 months

1- Le Gré des Champs; 2- Le D'Iberville; 3- Le Monnoir

AVAILABILITY

STORES

- Onsite store
  Wednesday to Friday
  10:30 a.m. to 5:30 p.m.
  Saturday & Sunday
  10 a.m. to 5 p.m.
- Fromagerie Hamel
  (Montreal)
- Le Marché des Saveurs
  (Montreal)
- Maison Moisan
  (Quebec City)
- S. Bourassa Ltée.
  (Saint-Sauveur)

USED AT THE FOLLOWING RESTAURANTS

- Fourquet Fourchette
  (Chambly)
- Le Samuel
  (Saint-Jean-sur-Richelieu)
- Naeser
  (Saint-Jean-sur-Richelieu)
- Tocqué (Montreal)

For distributor inquiries, please contact Plaisir Gourmets, 418-876-3814.

459, 4 concession
Noyan, QC
450-294-2207

FOUNDER AND ORIGINAL
CHEESEMAKER
Fritz Kaiser

MILK TYPE
Pasteurized cow's and goat's milk

PRODUCTION LEVEL
Semi-industrial

Federally registered

Local attractions and activities
- Fort Lennox National Historic Site—a restored 19th-century British fort located on the historic Richelieu River invasion route (Île-aux-Noix)
- Lake Champlain
- Local wineries along the province's La route des vins

FOR MORE IDEAS, VISIT
www.tourisme-monteregie.qc.ca
AND www.bonjourquebec.com

UPON COMPLETION OF HIS MILITARY service in Switzerland, Fritz studied the craft of cheesemaking. He later moved to Canada, seeking new opportunities in his field of expertise. His specialty is semi-soft and firm cheese with washed rinds. When he began commercial production in 1981, Fritz was the first in Canada to make raclette cheese.

The nearby Canadian-American border inspired him to create Le Douanier: a cheese with a layer of vegetable ash through the centre, dividing it into two sections. (*Douanier* is the French word for customs officer.) His creation was awarded the title of Grand Champion at the 2004 Canadian Cheese Grand Prix.

I remember sampling L'Empereur for the first time at the Royal Agricultural Winter Fair in Toronto several years ago. Joanne and I had to muscle our way through the crowd surrounding the sample booth. It was well worth the physical exertion! I took a second sample to power myself back through the crowd.

CHEESE PRODUCED

USING COW'S MILK

CHENAL DU MOINE
a soft, washed rind cheese

LE CLOS SAINT-AMBROISE
a semi-soft cheese washed with McAuslan Brewery's Saint-Ambroise beer

CRISTALIA
a semi-soft, natural rind cheese
- Fine Herbs
- Garlic and Parsley
- 5 Pepper

LE DOUANIER
a semi-soft, washed rind, Morbier-style cheese with a layer of vegetable ash in the middle

L'EMPEREUR
a soft, washed rind cheese
- Regular
- Light (13% milk fat)

MIRANDA
a firm, washed rind, Swiss-style cheese aged for 8 to 12 months

MOUTON NOIR
a semi-soft, brushed rind, interior ripened cheese

NOYAN
a semi-soft, washed rind cheese named after the local town

PORT-ROYAL
a semi-soft, brushed rind, Saint-Paulin–style cheese with a milk fat content placing it in the family of double creams—a Quebec original!

RACLETTE
- Regular
- Peppercorn
- Washed with McAuslan Brewery's Griffon beer

SAINT-PAULIN
a semi-soft, brushed rind, interior ripened cheese
- Regular

- Light (12% milk fat)

VACHERIN FRI-CHARCO
a semi-soft, washed rind cheese

ZURIGO
a semi-soft, washed rind cheese

USING GOAT'S MILK

CHEVROCHON
a soft, washed rind cheese

TOMME DU HAUT-RICHELIEU
a semi-soft, washed rind cheese

USING A BLEND OF COW'S AND GOAT'S MILK

DOUX PÉCHÉ
a soft, mixed rind cheese (bloomy and washed rind)

TOMME DE MONSIEUR SÉGUIN
a semi-soft, washed rind cheese

1- Raclette; 2- Raclette with Peppercorn; 3- Le Douanier; 4- Miranda; 5- Saint-Paulin; 6- Mouton Noir; 7- Noyan; 8- Port-Royal; 9- La Tomme Haut-Richelieu; 10- Chevrochon; 11- Doux Péché; 12- L'Empereur

AVAILABILITY

STORES
- Onsite store, Monday to Saturday, 8 a.m. to 5 p.m.
- Fine cheese shops nation-wide
- Fromagerie du Marché Atwater (Montreal)
- Fromagerie Hamel (Montreal)

USED AT THE FOLLOWING RESTAURANTS
- Alpen Haus (Montreal)
- Saint-Moritz (Montreal)

For distributor inquiries, please contact Le Choix du Fromager, 1-877-328-2207 or 514-328-2207.

Les Dépendances

L'EXPÉRIENCE DU FROMAGE

JEAN-PHILIPPE BEGAN WORKING IN THE Quebec cheese industry in 1979. He worked for other companies for two decades, but his goal was to make and ripen cheese himself. On extensive travels through Europe, he learned techniques by visiting cheesemakers and asking them questions.

Since 1999 Jean-Philippe has also been ripening cheese for other cheesemakers. Cheese ripening is a very precise craft; the cheese are constantly monitored and handled. His specialty is ripening them in locally produced alcohol.

3330, local 10, 2ième rue
Saint-Hubert, QC
450-656-6661

FOUNDER, CHEESEMAKER AND
CHEESE RIPENER
Jean-Philippe Gosselin

MILK TYPE
Raw and pasteurized cow's,
goat's and sheep's milk

PRODUCTION LEVEL
Semi-industrial

Provincially licensed

LOCAL ATTRACTIONS AND ACTIVITIES
- Cycling or canoeing at Îles-de-Boucherville Provincial Park (Boucherville)
- Hiking in Mont Saint-Bruno Provincial Park (Saint-Bruno-de-Montarville)
- La Ronde amusement park (Île-Sainte-Hélène)
- La route des cidres-the province's apple cider route

FOR MORE IDEAS, VISIT
www.tourisme-monteregie.qc.ca
AND www.bonjourquebec.com

CHEESE PRODUCED

USING RAW COW'S MILK

FEUILLE D'AUTOMNE
a soft, washed rind cheese, ripened for Fromagerie Fritz Kaiser Inc.

GEAI BLEU
a semi-soft blue cheese, ripened for La Bergerie aux 4 Vents

LE GRAND FOIN
a soft, washed rind cheese wrapped by a band of spruce, ripened for Fromages Chaput Inc.

PEAU ROUGE
a semi-soft, washed rind cheese, ripened for Fromagerie Fritz Kaiser Inc.

PETIT SORCIER
a semi-soft, washed rind, Morbier-style cheese, ripened for Fromages Chaput Inc.

PONT COUVERT
a semi-soft, washed rind cheese, ripened for Fromages Chaput Inc.

VACHERIN DE CHÂTEAUGUAY
a soft, washed rind cheese, ripened for Fromages Chaput Inc.

USING PASTEURIZED COW'S MILK

MINI-TOMME AU CIDRE DE POMME
a soft cheese, washed with apple cider

ROUGETTE DE BRIGHAM
a soft cheese, washed with apple brandy, ripened for Fromagerie Fritz Kaiser Inc.

SORCIER DE MISSISQUOI
a semi-soft, washed rind, Morbier-style cheese with a layer of vegetable ash in the centre, ripened for Fromagerie Fritz Kaiser Inc.

TOMME AU CIDRE DE POMME
a soft cheese, washed with apple cider

USING RAW GOAT'S MILK

BOUQ'ÉMISSAIRE
a soft, ash-covered cheese, ripened for Fromages Chaput Inc.

CHAMBLÉ
a soft, washed rind cheese, ripened for Fromages Chaput Inc.

PIC SAINTE-HÉLÈNE
a soft, bloomy rind, pyramid-shaped cheese, ripened for Fromages Chaput Inc.
- Plain
- Covered in olivewood ash

SAINTE-MAURE DU MANOIR
a soft, ash-coated, surface ripened cheese for Fromages Chaput Inc.

TOURELLE DE RICHELIEU
a soft, bloomy rind cheese, ripened for Fromages Chaput Inc.
- Plain
- Covered in olivewood ash

USING PASTEURIZED GOAT'S MILK

BLANCHE DE BRIGHAM
a soft, bloomy rind cheese, ripened for Fromagerie Fritz Kaiser Inc.

CABRIOLE
a soft, washed rind cheese, ripened for Fromagerie Fritz Kaiser Inc.

MINI-CABRIOLE
a soft, washed rind cheese, ripened for Fromagerie Fritz Kaiser Inc.

QUÉBECOU
a fresh, unripened cheese
- Plain
- Blueberry
- Fine Herbs
- Garlic and Chives
- Raspberry

USING RAW SHEEP'S MILK

BLEU D'ACADIE
a semi-soft blue cheese

USING RAW COW'S AND GOAT'S MILK

FLORENCE
a soft, bloomy rind, Camembert-style cheese, ripened for Fromages Chaput Inc.

USING PASTEURIZED COW'S AND GOAT'S MILK

TARAPATAPOM
a fresh, unripened cheese with layers of caramelized apples, ripened for Fromagerie Fritz Kaiser Inc.

AVAILABILITY

STORES
- Fromagerie du Marché Atwater (Montreal)
- Fromagerie Hamel (Montreal)
- Les Ognions (Lévis)
- Les P'tits Délices (Sainte-Foy)
- S. Bourassa Ltée. (Saint-Sauveur)

USED AT THE FOLLOWING RESTAURANTS
- Intercontinental Hotel (Montreal)
- Tocqué (Montreal)

For distributor inquiries, please contact Jean-Philippe.

449, rang Saint-Simon
Saint-Isidore, QC
450-454-4405

OWNER
Caroline Tardif

CHEESEMAKER
Claude de Margerie

FOUNDERS
Jean-Paul Rivard and Denise
Poirier-Rivard

ORIGINAL CHEESEMAKER
Denise Poirier-Rivard

MILK TYPE
Raw and pasteurized goat's milk

PRODUCTION LEVEL
Artisanal farmstead

Provincially licensed

LOCAL ATTRACTIONS AND ACTIVITIES
- Droulers-Tsiionhiakwatha
  Archaeological Site
  Interpretation Centre
  (Saint-Anicet)
- ExpoRail—Canadian Railway
  Museum
  (Saint-Constant)
- Local cideries and wineries
- Parc héritage Saint-Bernard
  (Châteauguay)

FOR MORE IDEAS, VISIT
www.tourisme-monteregie.qc.ca
AND www.bonjourquebec.com

WITH THEIR CHILDREN LEAVING HOME TO live their own lives, Denise and Jean-Pierre decided to establish themselves as hobby farmers. At least that was the plan until their son gave them a goat. They loved that goat so much they entered her at a local agricultural competition and won first prize. The next step they undertook was breeding, and their little hobby farm grew to 70 Toggenburg goats. They needed to start doing something with all that milk! Denise began making cheese. She taught herself and paid attention to the techniques and steps required in producing high-quality cheese. They named the company after the first blue ribbon (Ruban Bleu) their goat won.

Denise trained Claude to make the cheese, passing on her passion and belief that cheese should be made with care and attention. Caroline joined the cheesemaking team last year and fell in love with the goats, the farm and the delicious cheese they were producing. She purchased the business and plans to continue producing cheese with Claude.

Their interpretive centre provides information about goat breeding, milking and cheese-making industries. Cheese plates are offered for a small fee. Special events, including wine-and cheese-matching seminars, mechoui dinners (lamb roasted on a spit) and wedding receptions can be arranged.

CHEESE PRODUCED

USING RAW MILK

CHÈVRE D'OR
a firm, cheddar-style, surface ripened cheese
- 2-month-old
- 4-month-old
- 6-month-old

USING PASTEURIZED MILK

LE BOUTON DE CULOTTE
an uncooked, soft, unpressed cheese

BRIE

CAMEMBERT

CHÈVRE D'OR
a firm, cheddar-style, surface ripened cheese
- Plain
- Barbary Spices
- Peppercorn
- Rosemary

FETA

FROMAGE À LA CRÈME
a fresh, spreadable cheese
- Plain
- Garlic and Parsley
- Herbes de Provence
- Peppercorn
- Seasonal flavours

LA PAMPILLE
a soft, unripened cheese in the shape of a log
- Plain
- Garlic and Parsley
- Herbes de Provence
- Peppercorn

LA P'TITE CHEVRETTE
a soft, ripened, pyramid-shaped cheese

LE SAINT-ISIDORE
a soft, bloomy rind cheese in the style of Camembert or brie
- Plain
- Covered with vegetable ash (cendrée)

Claude, the cheesemaker; Toggenburg goat

1- Choco-Chèvre—a chocolate cup filled with fresh chèvre; 2- La Petite Chèvrette; 3- Chèvre d'Or with Peppercorns; 4- Pampille with Herbes de Provence; 5- Saint-Isidore; 6- Saint-Isidore Cendrée; 7- Le Bouton de Culotte

AVAILABILITY

STORES
- Onsite store
  Monday to Friday
  10 a.m. to 6 p.m.
  Weekends
  10 a.m. to 5 p.m.
- L'Échoppe (Saint-Lambert)
- Fromagerie du Marché (Saint-Jérôme)
- Fromagerie du Marché Atwater (Montreal)

USED AT THE FOLLOWING RESTAURANTS
- Café d'Ailleurs (Saint-Constant)
- Fairmont Queen Elizabeth (Montreal)
- Il Pizico (Saint-Constant)
- Il Vincino (Châteauguay)
- Hôtel InterContinental (Montreal)

For distributor inquiries, please contact the company.

196

830, boulevard Ford, local 422
Châteauguay, QC
450-692-3555

OWNER/CHEESEMAKER
Patrick Chaput

MILK TYPE
Raw cow's and goat's milk

PRODUCTION LEVEL
Artisanal

Federally registered

LOCAL ATTRACTIONS AND ACTIVITIES
- Chocolaterie La Petite
  Grang—a chocolate shop
  (Salaberry-de-Valleyfield)
- Maison Le Pailleur Museum—
  a home built in 1792
  (Châteauguay)
- Battle of Châteauguay
  National Historic Site—a war
  of 1812 battlefield site (Howick)

FOR MORE IDEAS, VISIT
www.tourisme-monteregie.qc.ca
AND www.bonjourquebec.com

PATRICK AND HIS SIBLINGS LEARNED THE appreciation of good food from their parents. His family imported cheese. Patrick joined the family business and travelled through France, seeking new cheese to import to Canada. He discovered he had a passion for the product. For three years, he gained experience by working in several French cheesemaking facilities.

When Patrick returned to Canada, he began adjusting the recipes and techniques he learned in France to Quebec milk. One might think French and Quebec milk are the same, but the terroir (local growing conditions) affects all food ingredients. Climate, amount of sunshine, soil characteristics and type of animal feed are but a few of the variants. Patrick tests every shipment of raw milk he receives, to ensure it complies with the very high Canadian standards.

His son and daughter are now working with him, ensuring Fromages Chaput will remain a family business and continue to produce high-quality cheese.

CHEESE PRODUCED

USING RAW COW'S MILK

FEUILLE D'AUTOMNE
a soft, washed rind cheese

LE GRAND FOIN
a soft, washed rind cheese, wrapped by a band of spruce

MONTÉRÉGIE
a soft, bloomy rind cheese

LE PETIT SORCIER
a soft, washed rind cheese

PONT COUVERT
a semi-soft, washed rind cheese

USING RAW GOAT'S MILK

BOUQ'ÉMISSAIRE
a soft, bloomy rind cheese, covered in olivewood ash

CHAMBLÉ
a soft, washed rind cheese

PIC SAINTE-HÉLÈNE
a soft, bloomy rind, pyramid-shaped cheese
- Plain
- Covered in olivewood ash

SAINTE-MAURE DU MANOIR
a soft, bloomy rind, ash-coated, surface ripened cheese
- Plain
- Covered in olivewood ash

TOURELLE DE RICHELIEU
a soft, bloomy rind cheese
- Plain
- Covered in olivewood ash

USING RAW COW'S AND GOAT'S MILK

FLORENCE
a soft, bloomy rind cheese

1- Pont Couvert; 2- Bouq'Émissaire; 3- Chamblé; 4- Grand Foin

AVAILABILITY

STORES
- Fromagerie du Marché Atwater (Montreal)
- Fromagerie Hamel (Montreal)
- Le Marché des Saveurs (Montreal)
- S. Bourassa Ltée. (Saint-Sauveur)

USED AT THE FOLLOWING RESTAURANTS
- Globe (Montreal)
- Laurie Raphaël (Quebec City)
- Rosalie (Montreal)

For distributor inquiries, please contact Les Dépendances, 1-888-266-4491 or 450-266-0395.

PIERRE-YVES IS AN AVID SUPPORTER AND promoter of raw-milk cheese. He was the first in Quebec to ripen raw-milk cheese and fought successfully against federal legislation to ban raw-milk cheese in 1995.

He and Jean-Pierre have embarked on a project to create high-quality, raw-milk, soft cheese for national distribution.

254, boulevard Industriel
Châteauguay, QC
450-691-2929

FOUNDERS
Jean-Pierre Desrosiers and
Pierre-Yves Chaput

CHEESEMAKER
Pierre-Yves Chaput

MILK TYPE
Raw cow's milk

PRODUCTION LEVEL
Artisanal

Federally registered

LOCAL ATTRACTIONS AND ACTIVITIES
- Fort Débrouillard Outdoor
  Adventure Site (Roxton Falls)
- Parc héritage Saint-Bernard
  river cruises (Châteuguay)
- Mont Saint-Bruno
  Provincial Park
  (Saint-Bruno-de-Montarville)

FOR MORE IDEAS, VISIT
www.tourisme-monteregie.qc.ca
AND www.bonjourquebec.com

CHEESE PRODUCED

LE ROUSILLON
a soft, washed rind, Münster-style cheese

SAINTE-MARTINE
a soft, bloomy rind cheese

Sainte-Martine

AVAILABILITY

STORES
- Fromagerie du Marché Atwater (Montreal)
- Fromagerie Hamel (Montreal)
- Le Marché des Saveurs (Montreal)

USED AT THE FOLLOWING RESTAURANTS
- L'Eau à la Bouche (Sainte-Adèle)

For distributor inquiries, please contact them directly.

ANTONIO AND MARIA ANTONIA HAVE been making cheese in Les Cèdres since 1974. They produce Montefino, an artisanal goat cheese based on a recipe from Maria Antonia's mother. It's similar to a goat cheese traditionally made by shepherds in the Abruzzo region of Italy. The Diodatis offer different variations of the same cheese. They add flavouring to the fresh and soft cheese and allow other wheels to age and dry. This ripening creates semi-soft and firm cheese, each displaying their own unique characteristics.

❧

I discovered this farm with Joanne on our first weekend getaway together. Trying to impress her, we went horseback riding–a first for my soon-to-be fiancée. Trail riding for an hour stirs up the appetite. As we drove toward a restaurant I knew in nearby Hudson, I saw the sign for Ferme Diodati. Goat cheese and goat sausages were for sale. Being curious, we drove into the farmyard. I rang the doorbell and a young man invited us into their small retail outlet to sample the cheese. We were happily surprised with what we tasted: fresh, soft, semi-soft and firm versions of their Montefino cheese. I enjoyed their semi-soft cheese the most. Joanne and I bought several different cheeses as well as some sausages, to share with family later that day. Our nephews Jonathan and Shayne devoured the grilled sausages. Who knew that eight years later Joanne and I would still be so happy together and that I would be writing about the Diodatis for this book.

1329, chemin Saint-Dominique
Les Cèdres, QC
450-452-4249

OWNERS
Antonio and Maria Antonia Diodati

CHEESEMAKER
Maria Antonia Diodati

MILK TYPE
Pasteurized goat's milk

PRODUCTION LEVEL
Artisanal farmstead

Federally registered

LOCAL ACTIVITIES AND ATTRACTIONS
• Côteau-du-Lac National Historic Site—fortified British canal bypassing rapids on the St. Lawrence River (Côteau-du-Lac)
• Hiking Mont-Rigaud (Rigaud)
• Maison-Atelier-Chapelle— artist studio and private dining room (Les Cèdres)

FOR MORE IDEAS, VISIT
www.tourisme-monteregie.ca
AND www.bonjourquebec.com

CHEESE PRODUCED

FETA

MONTEFINO
a rindless cheese
- Fresh
    Plain
    Red Chili Pepper
- Soft
    Plain
    Nuts
    Olives
    Peppercorn
- Semi-soft
- Firm

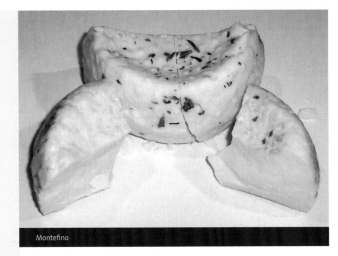

Montefino

AVAILABILITY

STORES
- Onsite store
    Ring doorbell for service
- Le Marché des Saveurs
  (Montreal)

For distributor inquiries, please contact the Diodatis.

THE DEFINITIVE GUIDE TO CANADIAN ARTISANAL AND FINE CHEESE

THE DEFINITIVE GUIDE TO CANADIAN ARTISANAL AND FINE CHEESE

A RECENT NEWCOMER TO THE INDUSTRY, Françis began making cheese commercially in 2004. He says he has a passion for "de la bonne bouffe" (good food) and for sheep. His flock grazes on the flora of the local pastures. Françis believes this contributes to the superior quality of the milk, which has high sugar and protein levels.

Cheese is only made from milk produced when the herd is grazing outdoors, giving the milk the aroma and taste characteristics of the local terroir.

2400, chemin Ridge
Godmanchester, QC
450-601-8083

OWNER/CHEESEMAKER
Françis Jourdain

MILK TYPE
Raw and pasteurized sheep's milk

PRODUCTION LEVEL
Artisanal farmstead

Provincially licensed
Federal registration is pending

LOCAL ATTRACTIONS AND ACTIVITIES
• Five Nations Iroquoian Village (Kahnawake)
• Festival International de Percussions—international percussion festival (Longueuil)
• Hydromiellerie Miel Nature—a honey and mead producer (Melocheville)
• Vignoble du Marathonien—winery (Havelock)

FOR MORE IDEAS, VISIT
www.tourisme-suroit.qc.ca,
www.tourisme-monteregie.qc.ca
AND www.bonjourquebec.com

CHEESE PRODUCED

USING RAW MILK

LE BREBILOUP
a soft, bloomy rind cheese

L'INTONDABLE
Tomme-style cheese, natural rind, aged for 6 months
- Classique
- Nouvelle

USING PASTEURIZED MILK

L'ARTISTE
a fresh, crottin-style cheese

LE PETIT JOURDAIN
a fresh cheese, in between cream cheese and feta in texture

Apple harvest

AVAILABILITY

STORES

- Onsite store
  May to December
  Tuesday to Sunday
  9 a.m. to 4 p.m.
- Boutique Caseus
  (Quebec City)
- Fromagerie du Marché
  Atwater (Montreal)
- Fromagerie Hamel
  (Montreal)
- La Petite Grande
  (Salaberry-de-Valleyfield)

USED AT THE FOLLOWING RESTAURANTS

- Café Mélièze (Montreal)
- Trois Filleuls (Saint-Marc)
- Tournant de la Rivière
  (Chambly)

For distributor inquiries, please contact Françis.

Ontario

If you know of other Ontario commercial cheesemakers,
send details to Gurth@CheeseofCanada.ca for the next edition.

206

PETER SKOTIDAKIS BEGAN HIS FARM WITH 20 goats in 1975. His goal was to make Greek-style feta and supply the large Greek community of nearby Montreal. As demand grew for his cheese, so did the size of his herd, which now numbers over 3,000 goats. Three cheesemakers are employed to process all that milk into two brands of feta products and ricotta.

185 County Rd. #10
St. Eugène, ON
613-674-3183

FOUNDER
Peter Skotidakis

MILK TYPE
Pasteurized cow's and goat's milk

PRODUCTION LEVEL
Industrial

Federally registered

LOCAL ATTRACTIONS AND ACTIVITIES:
- Akwesasne International Powwow (Cornwall Island)
- Glengarry Highland Games—North America's largest gathering of the clans (Maxville)
- Upper Canada Village—This is where I first saw cheddar and curds made—one of the few memories remaining from my grade 5 school trip (Morrisburg)
- Williamstown Fair—Canada's oldest agricultural fair, established in 1811

FOR MORE IDEAS, VISIT
www.cornwalltourism.com
AND www.ontariotravel.net

CHEESE PRODUCED

USING GOAT'S MILK

KADIS FETA

USING GOAT'S AND COW'S MILK

RICOTTA

USING COW'S MILK

SKOTIDAKIS FETA

Hockey on a natural rink

AVAILABILITY

STORES

- Onsite store
    Monday to Friday
    9 a.m. to 6 p.m.
- Costco

USED AT THE FOLLOWING RESTAURANT

- Milos (Montreal)

For distributor inquiries, please contact the company.

P.O. Box 30
St. Albert, ON
1-800-465-1553 OR
613-987-2872

GENERAL MANAGER
Réjéan Ouimet

CHEESEMAKER
Yvan Qathier

MILK TYPE
Pasteurized cow's milk

PRODUCTION LEVEL
Semi-industrial

Federally registered

TO HAVE CHEESE FOR THEIR OWN VILLAGE, local dairy producers established the St-Albert Cheese Co-operative in 1894. With over 112 years of cheesemaking experience, St-Albert is renowned in eastern Ontario for its delicious cheddar, curds and other cheese. Today, 40 dairy producers own the cheese co-operative, employing more than 60 people.

The cheese curds are so highly valued by the community that an annual curds festival is held to honour and devour them each August.

LOCAL ATTRACTIONS AND ACTIVITIES
• Festival de la Curd (St. Albert)
• L'Echo d'un Peuple—historic play (Casselman)
• Ottawa and the National Capital Region
    ByWard Market
    National Aviation Museum
    National Gallery
    Parliament Hill
    Rideau Canal

FOR MORE IDEAS, VISIT
www.ottawatourism.ca
AND www.ontariotravel.net

CHEESE PRODUCED

BRICK

CANADIAN SWISS

CHEDDAR
- Fresh (white, orange and marble)
- Medium, 4 to 8 months old (white and orange)
- Old, 8 to 14 months old (white and orange)
- Extra-Old, over 14 months old (white and orange)
- Fresh unsalted (white only)
- Caraway
- Dill
- Hot Pepper
- Jalapeño
- Onion
- Salsa

COLBY
- Plain
- Hot Pepper

CURDS
- White
- Orange

FARMERS
- Plain
- Garlic

MONTEREY JACK

AVAILABILITY

STORES
- Onsite store
  Daily 9 a.m. to 6 p.m.
- Regional grocery stores in eastern Ontario and western Quebec

USED AT THE FOLLOWING RESTAURANTS
- Brian's Bar and Grill (Casselman)
- Casselman Restaurant (Casselman)

For distributor inquiries, please contact the Co-op's sales team.

HANDCRAFTED CHEESES
- RAW EWE MILK -
LANARK HIGHLANDS, ONTARIO. WWW.ARTISANCHEESE.CA

R.R. # 3
Lanark, ON
613-259-5734

OWNERS/CHEESEMAKERS
James Keith and Elizabeth Harker

MILK TYPE
Raw sheep's milk

PRODUCTION LEVEL
Artisanal farmstead

Municipally certified

LOCAL ATTRACTIONS AND ACTIVITIES
- Dr. James Naismith Museum and Hall of Fame—Canadian inventor of basketball (Almonte)
- Exploring the Bonnechere Caves (Eganville)
- Historic village of Wilno—Canada's first Polish settlement (Madawaska Valley)
- Hiking the Rideau Trail (Kingston to Ottawa)

FOR MORE IDEAS, VISIT
www.lanarkcountytourism.ca
AND www.ontariotravel.net

JAMES AND ELIZABETH BEGAN CHEESE-making as an experiment in self-sufficiency. James had learned how to make goat cheese from his parents.

Their small flock of Icelandic sheep provided enough milk for making cheese for themselves, family and friends. Word spread about their delicious raw cheese and people wanted to purchase them. In 2000 they began commercial production. A small commercial kitchen and an ageing room were built, permitting them to increase production. This expansion created new opportunites to market their cheese at local farmers' markets and health food stores. Their Bonnechere, Madawaska, Dalhousie and Highland Blue cheeses are named after local rivers, lakes and highlands.

Their cheese are made using traditional cheesemaking methods that have evolved through their own experimentation. James created Bonnechere, a Swiss-style mountain cheese where the rind is partially burnt, creating a lightly toasted flavour. Back Forty Artisan Cheese is one of the few producers of raw sheep's milk cheese in Ontario.

CHEESE PRODUCED

BONNECHERE
a firm, burnt rind cheese

DALHOUSIE
a firm, brushed rind cheese

FLOWER STATION FETA

HIGHLAND BLUE
a firm, natural rind, blue cheese

MADAWASKA
a soft, surface ripened, bloomy rind cheese

1- Madawaska; 2- Dalhousie; 3- Highland Blue; 4- Flower Station Feta

Bonnechere

AVAILABILITY

STORES

- All the Best Fine Foods (Toronto)
- Carp Farmers' Market (May to October)
- Foodsmiths (Perth)
- La Botega (Ottawa)
- Pan Chancho (Kingston)
- Whole Foods Market (Oakville and Toronto)

USED AT THE FOLLOWING RESTAURANTS

- Biff's Bistro (Toronto)
- Bistro 115 (Ottawa)

For distributor inquiries, please contact James.

THE DEFINITIVE GUIDE TO CANADIAN ARTISANAL AND FINE CHEESE

THE WORLD'S FINEST AGED CHEDDAR

IN 1881 A SMALL GROUP OF LOCAL DAIRY farmers decided to pool their financial resources and talent to produce premium cheese. The Balderson Corners Cheese Factory was established and began producing cheddar. Rebuilt after a devastating fire in 1928, Balderson Cheese maintains a tradition of making premium aged cheddar. Many of its cheeses, aged over two years, have won Grand Champion status at major cheese competitions. The cheese factory is presently owned by Parmalat Canada.

100 Taylor Rd., R.R. # 2
Lanark, ON
613-259-0202

CHEESEMAKER
Réjean Gallipeau

MILK TYPE
Pasteurized cow's milk

PRODUCTION LEVEL
Industrial

Federally registered

LOCAL ATTRACTIONS AND ACTIVITIES
• Canoeing the Rideau River and Canal
• Hershey Chocolate Plant (Smiths Falls)
• The Diefenbunker—Canada's Cold War Museum (Carp)

FOR MORE IDEAS, VISIT
www.ottawavalley.ca AND
www.ontariotravel.net

CHEESE PRODUCED

CHEDDAR

- Mild, 3 months old (white and orange)
- Medium, 6 months old (white and orange)
- Old, 12 months old (white and orange)
- Extra-Old, 18 months old (white and orange)
- Championship, 12 months old (white only)
- Royal Canadian, 24 months old (white only)
- Vintner's for white wine, 20 months old (white only)
- Vintner's for red wine, 40 months old (white only)
- Heritage, 3-, 4-, 5- and 6-year-old (white only)
- Balderson Double Smoked, 12 months old
- Marble

AVAILABILITY

STORES

- Dussa's Ham and Cheese (Vancouver)
- Farm Boy (Ottawa)
- Fenton's Gourmet Foods (Winnipeg)
- Lakeview Fine Foods (Regina)
- Real Atlantic Superstores (NB, NS and PEI)
- Woldwide Specialty Foods Ltd. (Calgary)

USED AT THE FOLLOWING RESTAURANTS

- Fairmont Château Laurier (Ottawa)
- Luxe Bistro (Ottawa)
- On the Twenty (Jordan)

For distributor inquiries, please contact Galen Shaw, 416-620-3535.

FORFAR DAIRY WAS ESTABLISHED AS A DAIRY co-operative in 1863. For 120 years their main focus was the production of cheddar using local cow's milk. In the 1980s the cheesemakers began to experiment with adding flavours to their cheddar, to provide an edge over their competitors. Not resting on their laurels, the cheesemakers began experimenting with goat's milk, offering their first goat cheeses to the public in 1990. Sheep's milk cheeses were the next to be developed.

In 2001 Forfar Dairy was acquired from the farmer shareholders. The tradition of making fine cheese continues with Murray Campbell and his family at the helm.

1536 County Rd. 42
Portland, ON
1-800-379-1805 OR
613-272-2107

FOUNDER
John Gile

OWNER
Murray Campbell

CHEESEMAKER
Lloyd Steacy

MILK TYPE
Thermalized cow's milk and pasteurized cow's, goat's and sheep's milk

PRODUCTION LEVEL
Semi-industrial

Federally registered

LOCAL ATTRACTIONS AND ACTIVITIES
- Delta Mill (Delta)
- Garlic Festival (Perth)
- Spencerville Fall Fair
- Rideau Canal Museum (Smiths Falls)

FOR MORE IDEAS, VISIT
www.ontariotravel.net

CHEESE PRODUCED

USING THERMALIZED COW'S MILK

CHEDDAR (WHITE AND ORANGE)
- Old
- Regular Extra-Old
- Fine Extra-Old
- Rare Old

USING PASTEURIZED COW'S MILK

CHEDDAR
- Fresh (white and orange)
- Mild (white and orange)
- Medium (white and orange)
- Caraway
- Cranberry
- Garlic
- Green Onion
- Hot Pepper
- Marble
- Olive

CURDS
- White and orange
- Garlic
- Salsa

SKIM MILK CHEESE
- Plain
- Onion

USING PASTEURIZED SHEEP'S MILK

CHEDDAR
- Sun-dried Tomato

FETA

USING PASTEURIZED GOAT'S MILK

CHEDDAR
- Dill
- Flax/Garlic
- Garsley (garlic and parsley)
- Jalapeño

FETA

MOZZARELLA

1- Feta; 2- Hot Pepper Cheddar; 3- Jalapeño Cheddar; 4- Green Onion Cheddar; 5- Mozzarella; 6- Fresh Cheddar

AVAILABILITY

STORES
- Onsite store
  Daily 8:30 a.m. to 5 p.m.
- Online ordering
- Delta Foodmarket (Delta)
- Foodsmiths (Perth)

USED AT THE FOLLOWING RESTAURANT
- Brenda Jane's (Smiths Falls)

For distributor inquiries, please contact Newport Marketing and Sales, 1-800-895-3372.

G. PRETTY

R.R. # 5, 1120 County Rd. # 8
Campbellford, ON
1-800-461-6480 OR
705-653-3187

MILK TYPE
Pasteurized cow's milk

PRODUCTION LEVEL
Semi-industrial

Federally registered

LOCAL ATTRACTIONS AND ACTIVITIES
- Church-Key Brewing
  (Campbellford)
- Indian Motorcycle Museum
  (Campbellford)
- Memorial Military Museum
  (Campbellford)
- Ranney Gorge Pedestrian
  Suspension Bridge
  (Campbellford)

FOR MORE IDEAS, VISIT
www.trenthills.ca AND
www.ontariotravel.net

ESTABLISHED IN THE LATE 1870S TO PROCESS the local milk, the Empire Cheese factory moved three times during its history. In 1953 it amalgamated with the nearby Kimberley Cheese Factory and new facilities were built at the present site. Empire Cheese and Butter is the only remaining cheese co-operative owned by local dairy farmers remaining in Northumberland County. They elect a board of directors, who are responsible for the factory's operation, annually.

The cheese is made as it was 100 years ago, with open vats and no additives. The cheddar is made with full-cream milk and aged naturally.

CHEESE PRODUCED

CHEDDAR
- Mild (white and orange)
- Medium, 6 months old (white and orange)
- Old, 12 months old (white and orange)
- Extra-Old, 24 months old (white and orange)
- Supreme, 3-year-old
- 4-Year-Old

COLBY

COLD PACK
a processed natural cheese
- Salsa

CURDS

MOZZARELLA
- Regular
- Black Pepper
- Caraway
- Dill
- Garlic
- Horseradish
- Jalapeño
- Jalapeño and Red Chilies
- Onion
- Red Chilies

Campbellford fall panorama

AVAILABILITY

STORES
- Onsite store
    Monday to Saturday
    8 a.m. to 5 p.m.
    Sunday 9 a.m. to 5 p.m.
- Burlington Farmers' Market
- Niagara Falls Farmers' Market
- Peterborough Farmers' Market

For distributor inquiries, please contact Newport Marketing and Sales, 1-800-895-3372.

BRUCE GRADUATED IN AGRICULTURAL business and Sharon in food service. In 1985 they purchased a goat farm. In 1989 they decided to combine their knowledge and expertise by establishing Mariposa Dairy, an agricultural food business. With the availability of the raw ingredient, it was a natural step to start processing cheese. The company controls all points of milk production and cheese processing, thus ensuring a high-quality product.

R.R. # 2
Oakwood, ON
705-953-9816

OWNERS
Bruce and Sharon Vandenberg

CHEESEMAKER
Peter McIntyre

MILK TYPE
Pasteurized goat's milk

PRODUCTION LEVEL
Artisanal farmstead

Federally registered

LOCAL ATTRACTIONS AND ACTIVITIES
- Canadian Canoe Museum (Peterborough)
- Cruising on the Trent-Severn Waterway
- Fiesta Buckhorn—an outdoor food and beverage festival (Buckhorn)
- Kawartha Farmfest—multiple food and activities at various locations (Lindsay and surrounding region)
- Serpent Mounds Park—First Nations ancient burial mounds (Keene)

FOR MORE IDEAS, VISIT
www.city.kawarthalakes.on.ca
AND www.ontariotravel.net

CHEESE PRODUCED

MARIPOSA DAIRY CHÈVRE
- Regular
- Black Peppercorns
- Dill
- Herbs and Garlic

MARIPOSA DAIRY FETA

AVAILABILITY

STORES
- Terra Food Co-op (Toronto)
- The Big Carrot (Toronto)

For distributor inquiries, please contact Ontario Natural Food Co-op, 416-503-3663 or 1-800-387-0354.

11301 Highway 62
Ivanhoe, ON
1-800-267-5590 OR
613-473-4269

SENIOR PARTNERS
Bruce Kingston and Paul McKinlay

CHEESEMAKERS
Chris Spencer, Robert Boyle, Matt Foley, Tom Preston

MILK TYPE
Thermalized and pasteurized cow's milk

PRODUCTION LEVEL
Semi-industrial

Federally registered

IVANHOE'S HISTORY BEGINS IN 1870. LOCAL dairy producers followed the industry trend sweeping through the province, and pooled their resources to use their milk for cheesemaking. In the early 20th century, over 1,800 cheese factory co-operatives dotted the Ontario landscape. In 1986 Ivanhoe Cheese was purchased from the producer shareholders and entered a new era in its history.

The new owners put plans for expansion into place, including the development of new cheeses and exploring potential markets. The cheesemakers and staff are passionate about the business. The honoured traditions of cheese-making are followed and many of the cheese are certified kosher and hallal.

For the "Garlic is Great!" Festival several years ago, I planned to demonstrate a recipe using a garlic-flavoured cheese. After researching the Ontario cheesemakers who made such cheese, I went on a road trip to experience and sample them. On a sunny weekend, Joanne and I drove from Toronto to visit Ivanhoe's retail outlet. Wow! What a selection of cheese! We were amazed at the variety and great tastes of those we sampled. I selected the Garlic and Parsley Monterey Jack to use at the festival. I also like their Horseradish Cheddar. Imagine it melted into mashed potatoes. Yum!

LOCAL ATTRACTIONS AND ACTIVITIES
- Loyalist Parkway—scenic drive along the St. Lawrence River
- Prince Edward County's Taste Trail—winery and gourmet route
- Royal Canadian Air Force Memorial Museum (Trenton)

FOR MORE IDEAS, VISIT
www.ontariotravel.net

CHEESE PRODUCED

USING THERMALIZED MILK

ASIAGO

CHEDDAR
- Medium
- Old
- Extra-Old
- Classic 2-year-old
- Vintage 3-year-old

PARMESAN

ROMANO

USING PASTEURIZED MILK

BRICK

CHEDDAR
- Mild
- Horseradish
- Light
- Marble
- Smoked

COLBY

CURDS

FARMERS

FRESH CLASSICS CHEESE SAUCES
for food service operators

GOUDA
- Plain
- Smoked

MONTEREY JACK
- Plain
- Caraway
- Dill
- Garlic and Parsley
- Jalapeño and Red Bell Peppers
- Onion and Chives
- Peppercorn
- Smoked
- Spring Garden Vegetable

MOZZARELLA

MÜNSTER

OLD SHARPE COLD PACK
a processed natural cheese

PROVOLONE

SKIM MILK
- Plain
- Marble

SWISS

Prince Edward County hay bales

AVAILABILITY

STORES
- Onsite store
    Daily 9 a.m. to 5:30 p.m.
    Summer
    Friday until 8 p.m.
    Saturday 8 a.m. to 5 p.m.
- I.G.A., Sobey's, Independent
  and A & P grocery stores
  (Ontario-wide)

For distributor inquiries, please contact the company's sales team.

THE COMPANY WAS FOUNDED BY MICHEL-angelo and Francesca Talarico in 1954 as a small dairy farm, and their three grandsons now manage it. Silani Sweet Cheese creates flavourful products and is acknowledged as the first company in Canada to produce mozzarella and ricotta.

Highway 27 at Second Line,
Schomberg, ON
416-324-3290 OR
905-939-2561

FOUNDERS
Michelangelo and Francesca
Talarico

CHEESEMAKERS
Lazaro Constanza and Kaushik
Master

MILK TYPE
Pasteurized cow's and goat's milk

PRODUCTION LEVEL
Industrial

Federally registered

LOCAL ATTRACTIONS AND ACTIVITIES
• Headwaters Arts Festival
  (Alton)
• Hiking and Mountain biking at
  Albion Hills Conservation Area
  (Palgrave)
• Orangeville Fall Fair

FOR MORE IDEAS, VISIT
www.headwaterstourism.com
AND www.ontariotravel.net

CHEESE PRODUCED

USING COW'S MILK

ASIAGO

BOCCONCINI
- Regular
- Cherry-size

CACCIOCAVALLO

CREAM CHEESE
- Plain
- Dill
- Garlic
- Herb and Spice
- Peach
- Pineapple

FETA
- Regular
- Light
- Crumbled
- Greek
- Macedonian

FRIULANO

MASCARPONE
- Regular
- Light

MOZZARELLA

PARMESAN
- Padano
- Reggiano

PROVOLONE
- Regular
- Light

RICOTTA
- Regular
- Light

USING GOAT'S MILK

FETA

Toronto City Hall

AVAILABILITY

STORES
- Onsite store
  Monday to Friday
  8:30 a.m. to 4 p.m.
  Saturday
  9 a.m. to 3 p.m.
  Sunday 9 a.m. to 2 p.m.
- National grocery store
  chains

For distributor inquiries, please contact their sales team.

"il gusto delle cose buone"

INTERNATIONAL CHEESE WAS ESTABLISHED in 1962 to supply the needs of the Italian-Canadian niche market. Forty-three years later, milk still arrives daily and Mike and Mario make their cheeses with tender loving care. Customers are known to wait in line before the retail outlet opens for freshly made, warm ricotta.

International Cheese Co. is one of Toronto's culinary secrets.

67 Mulock Avenue
Toronto, ON
416-769-3547

CHEESEMAKERS
Mike Salvadore and Mario Pelosi

MILK TYPE
Pasteurized cow's and goat's milk

PRODUCTION LEVEL
Industrial

Federally registered

LOCAL ATTRACTIONS AND ACTIVITIES
- Day excursion to the Toronto Islands
- The Distillery Historic District
- Hockey Hall of Fame
- Historic St. Lawrence Market
- Old Fort York—Canada's largest collection of original War of 1812 military buildings

FOR MORE IDEAS, VISIT
www.tourismtoronto.com
AND www.ontariotravel.net

CHEESE PRODUCED

USING COW'S MILK

BOCCONCINI

BURRINI

CACCIOCAVALLO

FRIULANO

MOZZARELLA

PROVOLONE

RICOTTA

SCAMORZA
a semi-soft, rindless, gourd-shaped, pasta filata–style cheese

USING GOAT'S MILK

SANTA LUCIA
a semi-soft cheese

International Cheese—store interior

AVAILABILITY

STORES
- Onsite store
  Monday 9 a.m. to 3 p.m.
  Tuesday to Friday
  9 a.m. to 5 p.m.
  Saturday 8 a.m. to 5 p.m.
- Fortino's, Galati Foods
  & Longo's grocery stores
  (Toronto region)

USED AT THE FOLLOWING RESTAURANTS
- La Fenice (Toronto)
- Sotto Sotto (Toronto)
- Terone (Toronto)

For distributor inquiries, please contact the company's sales team.

Portuguese Cheese Co.

THE PORTUGUESE CHEESE COMPANY HAS been making artisanal cheese for the Portuguese community of southern Ontario since 1966. In 1999 the DeMelo family purchased the company, with the goal of promoting their cheese to a larger market. Joanne and I first tasted their products at a Toronto food festival in 1999. We were both happy to discover a local cheesemaker.

George is dedicated to continuing the tradition of creating fine Portuguese-style cheese using no animal rennet.

2 Buckingham St.
Toronto, ON
416-259-4349

CO-OWNER/CHEESEMAKER
George DeMelo

MILK TYPE
Pasteurized cow's and goat's milk

PRODUCTION LEVEL
Semi-industrial

Federally registered

LOCAL ATTRACTIONS AND ACTIVITIES
• Bata Shoe Museum
• Toronto's Chinatown
• Kensington Market
• Mackenzie House—home of William Lyon Mackenzie, Toronto's first mayor and leader of the failed 1837 Upper Canada Rebellion
• Royal Ontario Museum

FOR MORE IDEAS, VISIT
www.tourismtoronto.com
AND www.ontariotravel.net

CHEESE PRODUCED

USING COW'S MILK

CORVO
a semi-soft, washed rind, cheddar-style cheese

DURO BLANCO
a firm, natural rind, Latin American-inspired cheese

PICO MOUNTAIN
a semi-soft, washed rind cheese

PICO NOVO
a semi-soft, washed rind cheese

QUESO FRESCO
a fresh, unripened, Spanish-inspired cheese

SÃO MIGUEL
a semi-soft, washed rind, Havarti-style cheese

ST. JOHN'S COW
a fresh, unripened cheese, packaged in its own whey

VAQUINHA
a semi-soft, washed rind cheese

USING GOAT'S MILK

GRACIOSA
a semi-soft, washed rind cheese

ST. JOHN'S GOAT
a fresh, unripened cheese, packaged in its own whey

St. Lawrence Market

AVAILABILITY

STORES

- Cheesemongers at Toronto's Kensington Market
- Galati Foods, Highland Farms and No Frills grocery stores (Toronto region)

USED AT THE FOLLOWING RESTAURANTS

- Chiado (Toronto)
- New Casa Abrilo (Toronto)

For distributor inquiries, please contact the company's sales team.

THE DEFINITIVE GUIDE TO CANADIAN ARTISANAL AND FINE CHEESE

QUALITY CHEESE INC.
makers of fine italian cheese

WHEN ALMERIGO BORGO SR. IMMIGRATED to Canada from the Veneto region of Italy in 1954, he had already learned the craft of cheese-making. The first cheese he had learned to make was the local Asiago, both fresh and aged.

He started his own company in 1957, which grew as demand for his cheese increased. His mozzarella helped supply cheese for the pizza craze of the 50s to 70s. In 1988 he left the initial company to establish Quality Cheese with his children.

Their Borgonzola is the first Canadian-made, Italian-inspired blue cheese. It's a semi-soft, bloomy, white rind cheese with slight blue veining in the paste.

The current management team of Quality Cheese, the family's fourth generation of cheese-makers, continues to follow Almerigo Sr.'s guidelines: know your ingredients well (that is, milk and bacterial cultures) and use your senses to create the best cheese.

111 Jevlan Dr.
Vaughan, ON
905-265-9991

FOUNDER AND PRESIDENT
Almerigo Borgo Sr.

CHEESEMAKERS
William Borgo and others

MILK TYPE
Pasteurized cow's milk

PRODUCTION LEVEL
Industrial

Federally registered

LOCAL ATTRACTIONS AND ACTIVITIES
- Canada's Paramount Wonderland—amusement park (Maple)
- Kortright Centre for Conservation (Kleinburg)
- McMichael Canadian Art Collection—featuring painitings of the Group of Seven (Kleinburg)

FOR MORE IDEAS, VISIT
www.ontariotravel.net

CHEESE PRODUCED

BOCCONCINI

BORGONZOLA
a semi-soft, bloomy rind, blue-veined cheese

BRIE

BURRINI

FRIULANO

MOZZARELLA
• Plain
• Smoked

PROVOLONE
• Plain
• Smoked

RICOTTA

SCAMORZA,
a semi-soft, rindless, gourd-shaped, pasta filata–style cheese

SMOKED CHEDDAR

AVAILABILITY

STORES
• Onsite store
  Monday to Saturday
  9 a.m. to 5 p.m.
• National grocery store
  chains

For distributor inquiries, please contact their sales team.

Est. 1983
Canada's Leading Goat Cheese Producer

425 Richardson Rd.
Orangeville, ON
1-877-438-3499 OR
519-941-9206

FOUNDERS
Adozinda, Tony and Olga Dutra

MILK TYPE
Pasteurized goat's milk

PRODUCTION LEVEL
Industrial

Federally registered

LOCAL ATTRACTIONS AND ACTIVITIES
- Hiking the trails of Mono Cliffs Provincial Park (Orangeville)
- Hockley Valley Resort (Orangeville)
- Old Downtown Gallery (Orangeville)
- Orangeville Fall Fair

FOR MORE IDEAS, VISIT
www.headwaterstourism.com
AND www.ontariotravel.net

THE LOVE FOR GOATS AND MAKING cheese followed Adozinda Dutra to Canada from her native Portugal. In 1983 she began producing cheese again with the milk from the family's goat herd. In 1987 her son, Tony, and his wife, Olga, joined Adozinda to process more cheese and find new markets to supply under the company name of Nova Cheese. In 1989 the owners of Woolwich Dairy approached the Dutras with an offer to sell their business to them. The Dutra family purchased Woolwich Dairy, giving them the opportunity to expand and take over production of the Chèvrai brand of goat cheese.

Woolwich Dairy is esteemed for its uniquely flavoured cheese and for introducing goat cheese to many Ontario shoppers.

CHEESE PRODUCED

BRIE

CHEDDAR
- Medium (White)

CHÈVRAI
a soft, unripened cheese
- Plain
- Fine Herbs
- Peppercorn
- Roasted Garlic

CROTTIN
- Plain
- Herbes de Provence
- Roasted Garlic

FETA

GOURMET GOAT AND MADAME CHÈVRE
a soft, unripened cheese
- Plain
- 4 Peppercorn Blend
- Bruschetta
- Cranberry Cinnamon
- Fine Herbs
- Herbes de Provence
- Roasted Garlic

MADAME CHÈVRE ELITE
a soft, unripened goat cheese layered with gourmet toppings
- Cranberry with Port
- Lemon Poppy Seed
- Mediterranean
- Roaster Red Peppers

MOZZARELLA

1- Brie; 2- Madame Chèvre Elite—Cranberry with Port; 3- Madame Chèvre Elite—Roasted Red Peppers; 4- Plain Chèvrai; 5- Fine Herbes Chèvrai; 6- Peppercorn Chèvrai

AVAILABILITY

STORES
- Regional health food stores
- National grocery store chains
- Whole Foods Market (Oakville and Toronto)

USED AT THE FOLLOWING RESTAURANTS
- One99 Broadway (Orangeville)
- Fairmont Royal York Hotel (Toronto)
- Verona's (Toronto)

For distributor inquiries, please contact the customer service department.

R.R. # 3
Shelburne, ON
519-925-9420

OWNERS
Philip Collman and Stephanie Diamant

CHEESEMAKER
Stephanie Diamant

MILK TYPE
Raw and pasteurized sheep's milk

PRODUCTION LEVEL
Artisanal farmstead

Provincially licensed

MILKY WAY IS LOCATED ON A CENTURY-old farmstead and has been in the Diamant family for 35 years. Stephanie left the farm to study and travel. While working on a farm in France, she ate cheese at every meal and fell in love with the taste and aroma of the classic Roquefort blue cheese. Back in Canada, she learned about sheep while working at another Ontario farm and became inspired to make sheep's milk cheese. Stephanie visited England to obtain hands-on experience from British cheesemakers, and in 1999 Milky Way began commercial production of cheese.

Stephanie and Philip monitor the health of their flock of East Friesian crossbreeds and have full control over their milk supply. Milky Way Farm is an example of an artisan company that is developing unique flavoured cheese reflecting the terroir of Dufferin County.

LOCAL ATTRACTIONS AND ACTIVITIES
- Chesslawn Vineyard and Winery (Caledon)
- Credit Valley Explorer Tour Train (Orangeville)
- Everdale Organic Farm and Environmental Learning Centre (Hillsburgh)
- Williams Mill artist studios (Glen Williams)

FOR MORE IDEAS, VISIT
www.thehillsofheadwaters.com
AND www.ontariotravel.net

CHEESE PRODUCED

USING RAW MILK

HONEYWOOD
a hard, natural rind, Pyrenees-style cheese

LAVENDER BLUE
a semi-soft to firm, blue cheese

USING PASTEURIZED MILK

BREBIS
a fresh, unripened cheese

CREEMORE
a semi-soft, bloomy rind cheese

FETA
based on a recipe from Stephanie's Greek aunt

VIOLET HILL
a soft to semi-soft, bloomy rind, ash-coated, pyramid-shaped cheese

1- Honeywood; 2- Violet Hill; 3- Creemore

AVAILABILITY

STORES

- Onsite store
  Call ahead for availability
- Creemore Farmers' Market (Creemore)
- Dags and Willow (Collingwood)

USED AT THE FOLLOWING RESTAURANTS

- Biele House (Collingwood)
- Eigensinn Inn (Singhampton)
- Splendido (Toronto)

For distributor inquiries, please contact Stephanie or Philip.

The Original / L'original
MARQUE
SINCE / DEPUIS
1874
76

BRIGHT CHEESE AND BUTTER HAS BEEN IN existence in the Oxford County community of Bright since 1876. The company is still owned by local dairy producers and shareholders. In its early years, cheese production was important as a method of preserving milk. In 1913, 179 tons of cheese was produced at the plant. In 1985 cheese production accounted for 95% of their output.

R.R. # 1
Bright, ON
519-454-8600

MANAGER
Larry Ropp

CHEESEMAKER
Randy Berg

MILK TYPE
Thermalized and pasteurized cow's milk

PRODUCTION LEVEL
Semi-industrial

Federally registered

LOCAL ATTRACTIONS AND ACTIVITIES
- Birtch Farms Estate Winery—fruit winery (Innerkip)
- Blossoms Apple Orchard and Herb Farm (Thamesford)
- Embro Highland Games
- Canterbury Folk Festival

FOR MORE IDEAS, VISIT
www.tourismoxford.ca AND
www.ontariotravel.net

CHEESE PRODUCED

USING THERMALIZED MILK

CHEDDAR (WHITE AND ORANGE)
- Mild
- Medium,
- Extra-Old
- 4-Year-Old
- 5-Year-Old

USING PASTEURIZED MILK

BRICK
- Plain
- Garlic
- Hot Pepper
- Onion and Parsley

COLBY

CURDS

GOUDA

HAVARTI

MARBLE

MONTEREY JACK

MOZZARELLA

Oxford County statue of Snow Countess

THE DEFINITIVE GUIDE TO CANADIAN ARTISANAL AND FINE CHEESE

AVAILABILITY

STORES
- Onsite store
  Monday to Friday
  9 a.m. to 5 p.m.
  Saturday 9 a.m. to 4 p.m.
- Local Foodland grocery
  stores
- Waterloo Farmers' Market

For distributor inquiries, please contact the sales team.

R.A. RULE

THE LANGENEGGER FAMILY HAVE BEEN making cheese in the same factory building since 1925. Tristano, with two other generations of the family, continues to produce cheese almost exactly the same way as when the company started 80 years ago.

Oak Grove is well known for its brick cheese (plain and flavoured), Limburger and Cook cheese. The latter is an old German-Mennonite recipe where the curd is fermented and boiled down to produce a soft and crumbly cheese. It's produced only with milk from the fall and winter seasons. Cows may eat dandelions in spring and summer, which alter the flavour of the milk. Oak Grove is one of the few companies producing Cook cheese.

29 Bleams Rd.
New Hamburg, ON
519-662-1212

OWNER
Tristano Langenegger

CHEESEMAKER
Orvil Blast

MILK TYPE
Pasteurized cow's milk

PRODUCTION LEVEL
Semi-industrial

Federally registered

LOCAL ATTRACTIONS AND ACTIVITIES
- Castle Kilbride National Historic Site—Victorian Italianate mansion (Baden)
- Ingersoll Cheese Factory Museum (Ingersoll)
- Ontario Mennonite Relief Sale and Quilt Auction (New Hamburg)
- New Hamburg Fall Fair
- Stratford Festival

For more ideas, visit
www.ontariotravel.net

CHEESE PRODUCED

BRICK
- Plain
- Caraway
- Hot Pepper
- Onion and Garlic

COOK
a soft, unripened cheese

LIMBURGER
a semi-soft, washed rind cheese

MONTEREY JACK

MOZZARELLA

NEW BRA
a semi-soft to firm, natural rind cheese

PARMESAN

ROMANO

AVAILABILITY

STORES
- Onsite store
  Monday to Friday
  9 a.m. to 5 p.m.
  Saturday 9 a.m. to 1 p.m.
- Milverton Foodland
  (Milverton)
- Mildmay Cheese House
  (Mildmay)

USED AT THE FOLLOWING
RESTAURANTS
- Mimi's Café (New Hamburg)
- Old Country (New Hamburg)
- The Waterlot (New Hamburg)

For distributor inquiries, please contact their sales team.

238

SHEPHERD GOURMET DAIRY WAS ESTAB-
lished by local sheep milk producers in order to
increase stability in their industry. Their solution was to build a cheese plant for using the
milk from their flocks. There is a close relation-
ship between the milk producers and cheese processor: every step from flock to cheese plant is
monitored. No antibiotics are used in the milk.

R.R. # 2
Tavistock, ON
519-462-1067

FOUNDER
Stewart Cardiff

MILK TYPE
Pasteurized goat's and
sheep's milk

PRODUCTION LEVEL
Semi-industrial

Federally registered

LOCAL ATTRACTIONS AND ACTIVITIES
- Dolls in Toyland—doll
  museum (Tilsonburg)
- Pumpkin Festival (Woodstock)
- Southwestern Ontario Fiddle
  and Stepdance Contest
  (Tavistock)
- World Crokinole
  Championship—a late
  19th-century table board game
  (Tavistock)

FOR MORE IDEAS, VISIT
www.tourismoxford.com
AND www.ontariotravel.net

CHEESE PRODUCED

USING GOAT'S MILK

CHEDDAR

FETA

MOZZARELLA

USING SHEEP'S MILK

FETA

KEFALOTYRI

MYTZITHRA
a fresh, unripened, salty, ricotta-style cheese

RICOTTA

AVAILABILITY

STORES
- Onsite store
    By appointment
- Choices (Vancouver)
- Co-op stores (Calgary)
- Costco (Canada-wide)
- Thrifty's Foods (Vancouver Island)

For distributor inquiries, please contact the company.

USED AT THE FOLLOWING RESTAURANT
- The Church (Stratford)

THE DEFINITIVE GUIDE TO CANADIAN ARTISANAL AND FINE CHEESE

C'ESTBON CHEESE LIMITED
Believe in Goodness
R.R.#3 ST. MARYS, ON N4X 1C6

4675 Line 3, R.R. # 3
St. Marys, ON
519-284-2599

OWNER/CHEESEMAKER
George Taylor

MILK TYPE
Pasteurized goat's milk

PRODUCTION LEVEL
Artisanal farmstead

Federally registered

GEORGE'S INTRODUCTION TO THE DAIRY industry was through his dad, who was employed as a manager at Ault Dairies. After 20 years in the television industry, George decided to return to the family farm in St. Marys. He switched the flock of sheep for a herd of Toggenburg and LaMancha goats. To learn more about cheese-making, George attended the Cheese Techno-logical Course offered by Guelph University.

The company is located at the family-operated Transvaal Farm. George has 100% control of the milk as he uses only the milk from his own herd. His cheese are made in small batches by hand.

LOCAL ATTRACTIONS AND ACTIVITIES
- Canadian Baseball Hall of Fame (St. Marys)
- "Once upon a Thames" storytelling festival (St. Marys)
- The Piper at the Falls—outdoor bagpipe presentation (St. Marys)
- The Quarry—Canada's largest outdoor, spring-fed swimming hole (St. Marys)

FOR MORE IDEAS, VISIT
www.townofstmarys.com
AND www.ontariotravel.net

CHEESE PRODUCED

BILLY JACK
a semi-soft, rindless, Monterey Jack–style cheese

CAERPHILLY
a Welsh, semi-soft, feta-style cheese

CHÈVRE
a fresh, unripened cheese

PIERRE TREMBLE
a firm, farmstead cheese

PYRAMID
a soft, surface ripened cheese

St. Marys

THE DEFINITIVE GUIDE TO CANADIAN ARTISANAL AND FINE CHEESE

AVAILABILITY

STORES

- Onsite store
  By appointment
- Joe's Table (London)
- Vincenzo's (Kitchener)
- Whole Foods Market
  (Oakville and Toronto)

USED AT THE FOLLOWING RESTAURANTS

- Rundles (Stratford)
- Smith and Latham
  (St. Marys)
- Woolfy's at Wildwood
  (St. Marys)

For distributor inquiries, please contact La Ferme/Black River Game Inc., 1-800-263-1263 or Festival City Dairy, 519-271-4426.

G. STRATHDEE

THE DEFINITIVE GUIDE TO CANADIAN ARTISANAL AND FINE CHEESE

Ewenity
Dairy Co-operative

EWENITY DAIRY CO-OPERATIVE WAS ESTAB-
lished in 2001 to assist in selling the local sheep
milk. Members of the co-op use environmentally friendly guidelines when raising, feeding
and milking their animals. They are fed natural ingredients and graze in the pastures during
spring and summer. As with many milk producers, the co-op sought ways to use the milk.
Cheesemaking was suggested as Stephanie, one
of the members, had been making cheese from
the milk of her own flock at Milky Way Farm.

❧

*I met Peter, Elizabeth's son, at St. Lawrence Farmers' Market in June
2003. This was my first introduction to Ewenity's products. I love the
playful names the co-op named their cheese: Eweda for Gouda (the
ewe being the female sheep), Ramembert for Camembert (the ram is
the male sheep) and Baa Baa Bleu for their seasonal blue cheese.*

R.R. # 1
Conn, ON
519-848-5694

FOUNDERS
Stephanie Diamant, Axel Meister
and Larry Kupecz

CHEESEMAKERS
Stephanie Diamant and
Elizabeth Bzikot

MILK TYPE
Raw and pasteurized sheep's
milk

PRODUCTION LEVEL
Artisanal

Provincially licensed

CHEESE PRODUCED

USING RAW MILK

EWEDA CRU
a firm, rindless, Gouda-style cheese

USING PASTEURIZED MILK

BAA BAA BLEU
a seasonal, soft, blue cheese

BREBIS FRAIS
a fresh, unripened cheese
- Plain
- Chives and Pepper
- Garlic

EWEDA
a firm, rindless, Gouda-style cheese

FETA

RAMEMBERT
a soft, bloomy rind, Camembert-style cheese

1- Feta; 2- Eweda; 3- Brebis Frais; 4- Ramembert; 5- Eweda Cru

AVAILABILITY

STORES
- Ewenity Dairy Co-op booth at St. Lawrence Farmers' Market (North building, Saturdays only) (Toronto)
- Dufferin Grove Organic Farmers' Market on Thursdays (Toronto)
- Regional health food store (Greater Toronto Area)
- Riverdale Farm Organic Market on Tuesdays (Toronto)

USED AT THE FOLLOWING RESTAURANTS
- Niagara Street Café (Toronto)
- Osgoode Hall (Toronto)

For distributor inquiries, please contact Elizabeth Bzikot, 519-848-5694.

THE DEFINITIVE GUIDE TO CANADIAN ARTISANAL AND FINE CHEESE

CARMINE MARZARO FOUNDED SALERNO Dairy in 1962. To this day, the cheeses are hand-made with the Old World touch, though adapted to modern technology. They offer nearly 50 different kinds of cheese. All are hallal and many are also certified kosher.

Their new retail outlet is also a delicatessen, offering freshly grilled panini sandwiches for the hungry lunch-time crowd. Their largest cheese is a 35-kilogram log of 6-month-old provolone, just big enough to feed a hungry company of infantry soldiers.

Who knew that Steeltown had its own cheese plant? An extra tasty reason to visit Hamilton.

20 Morley St.
Hamilton, ON
800-263-6536 OR
905-544-6281

FOUNDER
Carmine Marzaro

MILK TYPE
Pasteurized cow's, goat's and sheep's milk

PRODUCTION LEVEL
Industrial

Federally registered

LOCAL ATTRACTIONS AND ACTIVITIES
- Art Gallery of Hamilton
- Canadian Football League Hall of Fame (Hamilton)
- Dundurn Castle (Hamilton)
- Royal Botanical Gardens (Burlington)

FOR MORE IDEAS, VISIT
www.tourismhamilton.com
AND www.ontariotravel.net

CHEESE PRODUCED

USING COW'S MILK

BOCCOCETTE
a firm, natural rind cheese

BOCCONCINI
- Regular
- Cherry-size

BRICK

BURRINI

CACCIOCAVALLO

CACIOTTE
a semi-soft, rindless cheese

CASATA FRIULANO
a firm, natural rind cheese

CASTELLA
a firm, natural rind cheese

CROTONESE
a hard, natural rind cheese

FRESH CHEESE

MASCARPONE

MINI FRIULANO

MONTASIO
a firm, natural rind cheese

MOZZARELLA
- Low fat
- Partly skim
- Deluxe

OLD BRA
a hard, natural rind cheese

PEPATO
a Romano-style, hard, natural rind cheese with black peppercorns

PEPERONATO
a Romano-style, hard, natural rind cheese with chili flakes

(CONTINUED ON PAGE 247)

1- Cacciocavalo; 2- Provolone; 3- Pecorino; 4- Sette Fette; 5- Crotonese; 6- Scamorza;
7- Burrini; 8- Brick; 9- Bocette; 10- Friulano Cassata; 11- Peponato; 12- Sheep cheese;
13- Mini Friulano Cassata; 14- Goat cheese; 15- Romanello; 16- Montasio; 17- Mozzarella;
18- Provolette; 19- Tuma; 20- Trecce; 21- Bocconcini; 22- Mascarpone; 23- Ricotta;
24- Provoloncini; 25- Castella; 26- Caciotta; 27- Pepato

AVAILABILITY

STORES
- Onsite store
  Monday to Friday
  8 a.m. to 5 p.m.
  Saturday
  8 a.m. to 4:30 p.m.
- National grocery store
  chains

USED AT THE FOLLOWING
RESTAURANTS
- Maxwell (Hamilton)
- Shakespeare (Hamilton)

For distributor inquiries, please contact the company's sales team.

Salerno staff Angela & Robin

LOCAL ATTRACTIONS AND ACTIVITIES
- Art Gallery of Hamilton
- Canadian Football League Hall of Fame (Hamilton)
- Dundurn Castle (Hamilton)
- Royal Botanical Gardens (Burlington)

FOR MORE IDEAS, VISIT
www.tourismhamilton.com
AND www.ontariotravel.net

CHEESE PRODUCED
(cont'd)

PROVOLONE
- Regular, a large, long log of cheese
- Provolette, a rectangular block of provolone cheese
- Provoloncini, a smaller version of provolone
- Sette Fette, the traditional bell shape

RICOTTA
- Authentic
- Regular
- 15% milk fat
- Dry,10% milk fat
- Lean, 7% milk fat

ROMANELLO
a hard, natural rind, smaller version of Romano cheese

ROMANO SALEMO
a hard, natural rind cheese

SCAMORZA
a semi-soft, rindless, gourd-shaped, pasta filata–style cheese

TRECCE
- Regular size
- Mini

TUMA

USING GOAT'S MILK

GOAT'S MILK CHEESE
a hard, natural rind, Crotonese-style cheese

USING SHEEP'S MILK

SHEEP'S MILK CHEESE
a hard, natural rind, Crotonese-style cheese

Shopping at Salerno

THE DEFINITIVE GUIDE TO CANADIAN ARTISANAL AND FINE CHEESE

fromage
MONTASIO
cheese

WATER 40% EAU   M.F. 28% M.
MADE FROM: MILK, BACTERIAL CULTURE, RENNET, SALT.
FAIT DE LAIT, CULTURE BACTERIENNE, PRESURE, SEL.
KEEP COOL / CONSERVER AU FRAIS
PARON CHEESE CO. LTD.
HANNON, ONTARIO CANADA

400 Highway 20
Hannon, ON
905-692-4560

FOUNDERS
Natale and Louis Paron

MILK TYPE
Pasteurized cow's and goat's milk

PRODUCTION LEVEL
Semi-industrial

Provincially licensed

LOCAL ATTRACTIONS AND ACTIVITIES
- Battlefield House—a War of 1812 battlefield site (Stoney Creek)
- Hiking the Bruce Trail (Queenston to Tobermory)
- Laura Secord Homestead (Queenston)
- Niagara wine route

FOR MORE IDEAS, VISIT
www.tourismniagara.com
AND www.ontariotravel.net

PARON CHEESE IS ONE OF THE OLDEST Italian-style cheese companies in Ontario. Natale Paron established the company in the 1930s, above the Niagara Escarpment from the community of Stoney Creek. Italian-Canadians were settling in the Hamilton area and Paron knew they would be seeking ingredients reminiscent of their homeland. Being a cheesemaker himself, he set up shop, making traditional firm and hard cheese. Later on, he trained his son Louis to assist and eventually take over the company. Paron has won numerous awards, ribbons and trophies at industry competitions.

Visiting Paron Cheese, you will experience a traditional, family-owned enterprise. Tasting their cheese, you will discover Old World flavours, recreated in Canada.

My friend Joseph and I visited the Parons. Joseph, a native Hamiltonian, had driven by the plant and store many times on the way to visit the wineries of Niagara, but he'd never stopped in. We were in for a very pleasant and delicious discovery! The store is part of the ripening room. Wheels of Montasio, Friulano, Hard Goat, Casata and Parmesan cheeses sit on the racks, slowly ageing, waiting to be purchased. Smaller cuts are also available for sale. We were told many clients buy entire wheels and let them age even longer in their homes.

CHEESE PRODUCED

USING COW'S MILK

CACCIOCAVALO

CASATA
a semi-soft, natural rind cheese

FRIULANO

MONTASIO
a firm, natural rind cheese

PARMESAN

USING GOAT'S MILK

HARD GOAT
a firm, natural rind cheese

Paron cheese racks

1- Special Parmesan; 2- Cacciocavalo; 3- Hard Goat; 4- Grated Montasio; 5- Casata;
6- Parmesan; 7- Montasio; 8- Grated Parmesan

AVAILABILITY

STORES
- Onsite store
   Monday to Friday
   9 a.m. to 4:30 p.m.
   Saturday
   9 a.m. to 1 p.m.
   Sunday 9 a.m. to noon

For distributor inquiries, please contact the company.

THE DEFINITIVE GUIDE TO CANADIAN ARTISANAL AND FINE CHEESE

72 Church St.
Millbank, ON
1-877-437-5553

OWNER/HEAD CHEESEMAKER
Ruth Klahsen

MILK TYPE
Pasteurized goat's and sheep's milk

PRODUCTION LEVEL
Artisanal

Provincially licensed

LOCAL ATTRACTIONS AND ACTIVITIES
- Blyth Festival—Canadian drama festival (Blyth)
- Huron-Perth Counties—Farm to Table food tour
- Mennonite Information Centre (Millbank)
- Ontario Maze (Newton)

FOR MORE IDEAS, VISIT
www.visitperth.ca AND
www.ontariotravel.net

RUTH WORKED FOR SEVERAL YEARS AS A professionally trained chef, and she wanted to use both art and science to create food without the pressure of the traditional restaurant kitchen. She began her training by learning of the tremendous variety of cheese at Say Cheese, Hillary Alderson's cheese shop in London, Ontario.

After obtaining knowledge from other cheesemakers, Ruth began making her own cheese. She purchases milk from local Mennonite shepherds at a fair price and modifies traditional cow's milk cheese recipes to be used with sheep's milk.

I regularly go down to Toronto's St. Lawrence Market on Saturdays, to see Ruth and discover what her newest cheese creation is. I buy and serve them to my friends. Their reaction? 'This is not European? This is from Ontario?' I gleefully tell them the story of the new generation of Ontario cheesemakers like Ruth.

CHEESE PRODUCED

USING GOAT'S MILK

BANON
a French-style soft cheese cured in grape leaves

BIANCO NERO
A French Valençay-style, soft cheese, pyramid-shaped and covered with black vegetable ash

GOAT TOMME
a tomme-style soft cheese

USING SHEEP'S MILK

BAUMAN'S SMOKED
a firm, maple-smoked cheese, inspired by the traditional oszczpek, a Polish shepherds' cheese

BELLE
Ruth's tribute to a fresh chèvre, but made with sheep's milk

FRESCO
a fresh cheese

HALLOUMI
a fresh, Arabic-style cheese

NIKA
a version of Belle, with herbs and fermented organic garlic flowers

PARADISO
a semi-soft, Taleggio-style, washed rind cheese

PECORINO FRESCO/PEPATO FRESCO
a fresh, Pecorino-style cheese, very similar to a Mexican quesa fresca cheese

PIACERE
a French Fleur du Maquis–style, semi-soft cheese, covered with rosemary, savory, chili pepper and juniper berries

RICOTTA

SHEEPDIP
a fresh cheese spread with sun-dried tomatoes, capers and hot peppers

SMOKED RICOTTA

TOSCANO
an Italian Pecorino Toscano–style firm, natural rind cheese

USING A MIXTURE OF GOAT'S AND SHEEP'S MILK

BLISS
a soft, bloomy rind, Camembert-style cheese

1- Bauman's Smoked; 2- Pepato; 3- Piacere; 4- Paradiso; 5- Toscano; 6- Bianco Nero; 7- Banon; 8- Bliss

AVAILABILITY

STORES
- Onsite store at the Millbank Cheese and Cold Storage Monday to Saturday 9 a.m. to 5 p.m.
- All the Best Fine Foods (Toronto)
- de Luca's Cheese Market and Deli (Virgil)
- Sam and Son, Hamilton Farmers' Market (Hamilton)
- Smith's Cheeses at Covent Garden Market (London)
- St. Lawrence Farmers' Market, North Building, Saturdays (Toronto)

USED AT THE FOLLOWING RESTAURANTS
- Bijou (Stratford)
- J.K. Wine Bar (Toronto)
- Old Prune (Stratford)
- Rundles (Stratford)
- Scaramouche (Toronto)

For distributor inquiries, please contact Ruth.

MORNINGTON HERITAGE CHEESE AND DAIRY Co-operative is co-owned by the local goat milk producers and community members. The milk producers follow holistic practices and use no additives—keeping the milk as natural as possible.

Mornington Heritage Cheese and Dairy Co-operative is the largest goat milk producers' and processors' co-operative in Ontario.

72 Church St.
Millbank, ON
1-866-995-9903

FOUNDER
Bob Reid

MILK TYPE
Pasteurized goat's milk

PRODUCTION LEVEL
Semi-industrial

Federally registered

LOCAL ATTRACTIONS AND ACTIVITIES
- Guided historical walking tours (Stratford)
- Shakespeare to the Shoreline—themed driving tours (Perth and Huron counties)
- The Best Little Pork Shoppe (Shakespeare)
- Wine, Blues and All That Jazz Festival (Woodstock)

FOR MORE IDEAS, VISIT
www.visitperth.ca AND
www.ontariotravel.net

CHEESE PRODUCED

GOAT CHEDDAR
- Mild
- Medium
- Old
- Marble

CHÈVRE
a soft, unripened cheese
- Plain
- Garlic

GOAT CURDS

FETA
- Plain
- Sun-dried Tomato and Basil

GOAT GOUDA

MOZZARELLA

Oxford County Barn

AVAILABILITY

STORES
- Onsite store at the Millbank Cheese and Cold Storage
     Monday to Saturday
     9 a.m. to 5 p.m.
- Health section of regional grocery stores

For distributor inquiries, please contact the company directly.

CHEESEMAKING IS PART OF THE SCHEP family history. Margaret and Jacob's relatives in Holland make cheese and Margaret's mother was a world champion cheesemaker in 1975. In 1981 the Scheps immigrated to Canada with their children and began Holstein dairy farming near Thunder Bay. It's traditional in Holland to make cheese for home consumption with milk from your own herd. When they served their Gouda at parties, guests liked what they tasted and requested cheese for themselves.

When their two sons returned from college, Margaret began commercial production of Gouda in 1995. Her son Walter has joined her in the production of the family cheese. Thunder Oak Cheese Farm is the only producer of artisanal farmstead Gouda and Gouda curds in Ontario.

Boundary Dr.
Thunder Bay, ON
1-866-273-3329 OR
807-628-0175

OWNERS
Jacob and Margaret Schep

CHEESEMAKERS
Margaret and Walter Schep

MILK TYPE
Pasteurized cow's milk

PRODUCTION LEVEL
Artisanal farmstead

Provincially licensed

LOCAL ATTRACTIONS AND ACTIVITIES
- Amethyst Mine Panorama (Thunder Bay)
- Kakabeca Falls (Thunder Bay)
- Old Fort William Historical Park—reconstructed headquarters of the North West Company, during its fur empire heyday from 1803 to 1821 (Thunder Bay)
- Thunder Bay's Little Finland community

FOR MORE IDEAS, VISIT
www.thunderbay.ca AND
www.ontariotravel.com

CHEESE PRODUCED

GOUDA
- Mild (4 weeks old)
- Medium (3 months old)
- Old (6 months old)
- Extra-Old (20 months old)
- Black Pepper with Garlic and Onions
- Cumin
- Cumin and Cloves
- Dill and Garlic
- Dried Jalapeño
- Fenugreek
- Garden Herbs
- Garlic
- Nettle
- Red Pepper with Paprika, Garlic, Horseradish and Ginger
- Smoked
- Sun-dried Tomato

GOUDA CURDS
- Regular
- Cajun
- Garlic

QUARK

SWISS

Spirit of the North Parkway

1- Jalapeño Gouda; 2- Mild Gouda; 3- Garden Herbs Gouda; 4- Cumin and Cloves Gouda;
5- Red Pepper Gouda

AVAILABILITY

STORES
- Onsite store
  Monday to Saturday
  9 a.m. to 5 p.m
- George's Market
  (Thunder Bay)
- Quality Market
  (Thunder Bay)
- Whole Foods Market
  (Toronto)

USED AT THE FOLLOWING
RESTAURANTS
- Fairmont Royal York Hotel
  (Toronto)
- White Fox Inn
  (Thunder Bay)
- Airlane (Thunder Bay)

For distributor inquiries, please contact Margaret or Walter.

Manitoba

If you know of other Manitoba commercial cheesemakers,
send details to Gurth@CheeseofCanada.ca for the next edition.

258

61 Main St.
New Bothwell, MB
1-800-361-9542 OR
204-388-4666

CHEESEMAKERS
Ben Doerksen and Gil Dueck

MILK TYPE
Pasteurized and thermalized cow's and pasteurized goat's milk

PRODUCTION LEVEL
Industrial

Federally registered

LOCAL ATTRACTIONS AND ACTIVITIES
• Morris Stampede
• Niverville Fair
• New Bothwell Fair

FOR MORE IDEAS, VISIT
www.travelmanitoba.com

THE COMPANY BEGAN AS A CO-OPERATIVE of local dairy farmers in 1936. Over the years, it grew and became recognized for its commitment to producing high-quality cheese. Located in the centre of Manitoba's dairy belt, the freshest of milk is used from nearby dairy farms. Over 30 varieties of cheese are produced at their modern facility. In 2003 a natural smokehouse was built, providing the opportunity to offer new selections of smoked cheese to the public.

CHEESE PRODUCED

USING COW'S MILK

CHEDDAR
orange unless specified
- Mild
- Medium
- Old
- 1-Year-Old White, using thermalized milk
- 2-Year-Old White, using thermalized milk
- Light
- Marble
- Horseradish White
- Smoked
- 2-Year-Old Smoked White, using thermalized milk
- Unsalted

CURDS
- White
- Orange
- Marble

FARMERS

GOUDA
- Plain
- Smoked

HAVARTI
- Plain
- Dill
- Garlic-Chive

MONTEREY JACK
- Plain
- Jalapeño
- Smoked
- Smoked Jalapeño

MOZZARELLA
- Plain
- Part-skim
- Smoked

PANEER

USING GOAT'S MILK

FIRM GOAT CHEESE

GOAT CHEDDAR

Canola field with train and elevators

AVAILABILITY

STORES
- Onsite store
  Monday to Friday
  8:30 a.m. to 4:30 p.m.
- Regional grocery stores

USED AT THE FOLLOWING RESTAURANTS
- Blaze Bistro at the Delta Winnipeg
- Fairmont Hotel Winnipeg
- Tavern in the Park (Winnipeg)

For distributor inquiries, please contact the company's sales team.

THE DEFINITIVE GUIDE TO CANADIAN ARTISANAL AND FINE CHEESE

OAK ISLAND ACRES GOAT DAIRY IS THE only producer in Manitoba specializing in goat cheese. Richard and Beverley were involved in raising sheep and cattle in England, but the high price of land drove them to seek new ventures. They immigrated to Canada in 2003, seeking new agricultural opportunities. Seeing an increased demand for goat milk products, they purchased Oak Island Acres Goat Dairy. They raise Alpine, Nubian and La Mancha goats. Using the cheesemaking skills of Arni Hydamaka, Richard and Beverley offer a variety of cheeses. Professor Hydamaka, of the University of Manitoba's Department of Food Science, has written several research papers on the subject of cheese.

Îles des Chênes, MB
204-878-2498

OWNERS
Richard and Beverley Simcock

CHEESEMAKER
Arni Hydamaka

MILK TYPE
Pasteurized goat's milk

PRODUCTION LEVEL
Artisanal farmstead

Provincially licensed

LOCAL ATTRACTIONS AND ACTIVITIES
• Emu Village (Lac des Chênes)

FOR MORE IDEAS, VISIT
www.travelmanitoba.com

CHEESE PRODUCED

CHEDDAR
a 4-month-old cheese
- Plain
- Smoked

FETA

MOZZARELLA

SEMI-RIPENED GOAT CHEESE

SMOKED SEMI-SOFT GOAT CHEESE

SOFT CHÈVRE

Harvesting Canola

AVAILABILITY

STORES
- Onsite store
  Ring doorbell for service
- House of Nutrition (Winnipeg)
- Organza Foods (Winnipeg)
- Vita Health (Winnipeg)

USED AT THE FOLLOWING RESTAURANTS
- Fude Restaurant (Winnipeg)

For distributor inquiries, please contact Richard and Beverley.

Alberta

If you know of other Alberta commercial cheesemakers,
send details to Gurth@CheeseofCanada.ca for the next edition.

LEFT: DAVID THOMSPON HWY. NEAR NORDEGG (TRAVEL ALBERTA). ABOVE: TRAILRIDING IS MEDICINE HAT (TRAVEL ALBERTA).

264

7 Co-op Rd.
Didsbury, AB
1-800-661-4909
(Calgary office)

CHEESEMAKER
Ken Mumby

MILK TYPE
Pasteurized cow's milk

PRODUCTION LEVEL
Industrial

Provincially licensed

LOCAL ATTRACTIONS AND ACTIVITIES
• Didsbury Farmers' Market
• Didsbury Museum
• Gopher Hole Museum
  (Torrington)
• Olds Fair and Rodeo

FOR MORE IDEAS, VISIT
www.prairies2peaks.ca AND
www.travelalberta.com

THE ORIGINAL CHEESEMAKING FACILITY was established in the early 1900s. In 1960 the company was re-established, and in 1998 Foothills Creamery purchased Lone Pine Cheese, the latest incarnation. The brand was renamed as Rocky Mountain Cheese.

Ken Mumby entered the cheesemaking trade upon his discharge from the Royal Canadian Army in 1967. His brother told him of employment opportunities at the Warkworth Cheese Factory (Ontario). He was hired and has been making cheese ever since. Thirty-eight years later, he is creating delicious cheese in a province better known for its cattle than its dairy herds. With his staff, Ken produces cheese in the traditional way, by hand, using open cheese vats.

CHEESE PRODUCED

CHEDDAR
white and orange
- Mild
- Medium
- Aged
- 3-Year-Old
- 5-Year-Old
- Marble

COLBY/JACK

CURDS
white and orange

MOZZARELLA
- Plain
- Basil and Sun-dried Tomato
- Jalapeño
- Part-skim

QUARK
- 0.4% milk fat
- 4% milk fat
- 10% milk fat

Picnic at Reesor Lake

1- Quark; 2- Basil and Sun-dried Tomato Mozzarella; 3- Jalapeño Mozzarella; 4- Marble Cheddar; 5- Mild Cheddar; 6- Curds

AVAILABILITY

STORES
- AG Foods
  (Several locations in Alberta)
- Co-op (Olds)
- I.G.A. (Several locations
  in Alberta)

USED AT THE FOLLOWING
RESTAURANTS
- Macy's Family Restaurant
  (Didsbury)
- Jim's Pizza (Didsbury)

For distributor inquiries, please contact the Calgary office.

THE DEFINITIVE GUIDE TO CANADIAN ARTISANAL AND FINE CHEESE

R.R. # 1, Highway 11A
Sylvan Lake, AB
403-340-1560

OWNERS
Janny and John Schalkwyk

CHEESEMAKER
John Schalkwyk

MILK TYPE
Thermalized cow's milk

PRODUCTION LEVEL
Artisanal farmstead

Federally registered

THE SCHALKWYKS IMMIGRATED TO Canada from the Netherlands in 1995. They chose Alberta due to its wide open spaces. But John, who had been a cheesemaker for 25 years, was disappointed in the small selection of locally produced cheese and decided to rectify the situation. He and Janny established their own herd of Holstein cows and began producing cheese in 1998.

Their company has been successful and has been recognized by their peers. Their Goudas won the Canadian Cheese Grand Prix 2000 (Firm Cheese Category) and ranked tenth at Wisconsin's World Cheese Contest.

LOCAL ATTRACTIONS AND ACTIVITIES
- Beach volleyball tournaments (Sylvan Lake)
- Fort Normandeau Historic Site—a reconstructed North West Mounted Police fort, originally built during the Northwest Rebellion (Red Deer)
- Kerry Wood Nature Centre (Red Deer)
- Water activities and public beaches (Sylvan Lake)

FOR MORE IDEAS, VISIT
www.travelalberta.com

CHEESE PRODUCED

GOUDA

- Mild
- Medium
- Aged
- Basil
- Black Pepper
- Black Pepper and Garlic
- Cumin
- Dill
- Fenugreek
- Friesian Cloves
- Green Peppercorn
- Green Peppercorn with Cayenne
- Italian Herbs
- Onion, Garlic and Paprika
- Smoked

Alinda turning and wiping the cheeses; Cheese in moulds

1- Cumin; 2- Onion, Garlic and Paprika; 3- Smoked; 4- Dill; 5- Baby Gouda; 6- Green Peppercorn with Cayenne; 7- Green Peppercorn; 8- Friesian Cloves

AVAILABILITY

STORES

- Onsite store
  Monday to Saturday
  10 a.m. to 6 p.m.
- Currie Barracks Farmers' Market (Calgary)
- Janice Beaton Fine Cheeses (Calgary)
- Local grocery stores such as Co-op and AG Foods

USED AT THE FOLLOWING RESTAURANT

- Capri Centre (Red Deer)

For distributor inquiries, please contact World Wide Specialty Foods (Calgary), 403-255-6262.

G. PRETTI

THE DEFINITIVE GUIDE TO CANADIAN ARTISANAL AND FINE CHEESE

4304 52nd St.
Camrose, AB
780-672-1698

OWNER/CHEESEMAKER
Emanuela Leoni

MILK TYPE
Raw cow's milk

PRODUCTION LEVEL
Artisanal farmstead

Federally registered

LOCAL ATTRACTIONS AND ACTIVITIES
- Camrose Founders' Days
- Doors Open Camrose
- Wild bird watching
- World's Longest BBQ Festival

FOR MORE IDEAS, VISIT
www.tourismcamrose.com
AND www.travelalberta.com

A NATIVE OF THE PO VALLEY OF NORTHERN Italy, Emanuela moved to Alberta in 1987 with her husband, Franco, and their four sons. After several previous international moves, their sons were tired of relocating and had fallen in love with Alberta. They asked their parents to settle down in Canada's Wild Rose Country.

With the boys grown up, Emanuela decided to keep herself busy by learning how to make cheese. She convinced a family friend in Italy, a retired cheesemaker, to come and teach her. He was impressed with the quality and consistency of Alberta milk, and the fact that it was refrigerated. They made their first batch of cheese in 1996. Three years later, Emanuela had established her own cheesemaking facility on a local dairy farm.

Leoni-Grana is the first North American producer using the original Italian recipe. Cheese is produced only in April and May, when Emanuela believes the milk is the most flavourful. The cheese is made by hand. Two thousand litres of milk is processed daily, producing 120 kilograms, or 8 wheels, of cheese. After the forming and bathing in salt brine, the cheese is ripened for a minimum of 6 months to a maximum of 3 years. This unique Canadian product is stamped with the words Leoni-Grana and a maple leaf on its golden rind.

CHEESE PRODUCED

LEONI-GRANA
an Italian Grana Padano–style hard, natural rind cheese

Cheese wheels ripening

Leoni-Grana

AVAILABILITY

STORES

- You can order the cheese through the website: www.leonigrana.com

USED AT THE FOLLOWING RESTAURANTS

- Crowne Plaza Château Lacombe (Edmonton)
- Fairmont Château Whistler (Whistler, BC)
- Mission Hills Winery (Westbank, BC)
- Quarry (Canmore)
- River Café (Calgary)

For distributor inquiries, please contact Emanuela or Planet Foods (Calgary), 1-877-873-6348 or 403-281-7911.

G. PRETTY

British Columbia

If you know of other British Columbia commercial cheesemakers, send details to Gurth@CheeseofCanada.ca for the next edition.

2690 Almond Gardens Rd.
Grand Forks, BC
250-442-8112

OWNERS
Ric and Vickie Llewellyn

CHEESEMAKER
Vickie Llewellyn

MILK TYPE
Organic raw and pasteurized
cow's and goat's milk

PRODUCTION LEVEL
Artisanal farmstead

Federally registered

LOCAL ATTRACTIONS AND ACTIVITIES
- Big Rock Candy Mine—rock crystal collecting area (Grand Forks)
- Doukhobor Village Museum (Castlegar)
- Christina Lake, the warmest tree-lined lake in British Columbia

FOR MORE IDEAS, VISIT
www.city.grandforks.bc.ca
AND www.hellobc.com

IN 1983 RIC AND VICKIE FELL IN LOVE FOR the second time—this time with Jersey cows. Two years later, they settled in Grand Forks with their herd of animals. Jerseyland Organics was a hobby farm until 1994. They experimented in making different dairy products and discovered a potential market when they were asked to make cheese for the local Russian Doukhobor community. Many of them eat a vegetarian diet and cheese is an important source of protein. Commercial production began after the farm completed the transition to organic status, granted by the Certified Organic Association of British Columbia. In 1994 Jerseyland Organics became western Canada's first producer of organic cheese.

CHEESE PRODUCED

USING RAW COW'S MILK

ASIAGO

CHEDDAR
- Regular white
- Habañero and Jalapeño
- Leicester
- Onion and Garlic

FETA
- Plain
- Herbed

GOUDA
- Mild
- Medium
- Old
- Caraway
- Cumin
- Garlic and Dill
- Hemp
- Mixed Herbs
- Peppercorn

PARMESAN

USING PASTEURIZED COW'S MILK

CURDS
- Fresh
- Dry curd cottage cheese

USING RAW GOAT'S MILK

CHEDDAR

FETA

GOUDA
- Plain
- Garlic and Dill
- Mixed Herb

AVAILABILITY

STORES
- Onsite store
  June to Labour Day
  Monday to Friday
  8 a.m. to 4 p.m.
  Phone ahead on
  weekends
- Kootenay Co-op
- Les Amis du Fromage
  (Vancouver)
- Save-On-Foods (Nelson)

For distributor inquiries, please contact Ric.

USED AT THE FOLLOWING
RESTAURANTS
- Chef's Garden (Grand Forks)
- Bishop's (Vancouver)
- Fairmont Banff Springs
  Hotel (Banff)
- West (Vancouver)

THE DEFINITIVE GUIDE TO CANADIAN ARTISANAL AND FINE CHEESE

THE DEFINITIVE GUIDE TO CANADIAN ARTISANAL AND FINE CHEESE

FARMSTEAD
ARTISAN CHEESE
Handcrafted

HUBERT AND NORMAN ARE THE FATHER and son cheesemaker team of this young company. Since 1999 they have been producing artisanal farmstead cheese following traditional recipes. The company has received many awards from The British Empire Cheese Show (Belleville, Ontario) and the Canadian Cheese Grand Prix, but the awards most important to them are the comments of their customers.

A visit to their store is more than just sampling cheese. Be ready to experience the company's Good Time atmosphere! A rustic ambiance is created at the store with the "Village Cheese Model A" delivery truck, hand-painted cream cans, wooden butter churns and farmhouse cream separators. Ragtime music can even be heard from their authentic nickelodeon, an automated, mechanical band. Stop and enjoy lunch in the dining room or in the picnic area, ending the meal with a slice of apple pie topped off with their own ice cream or a slice of cheddar. Bus and school groups can call ahead for tours of the plant, where they can see the cheese being made the old-fashioned way.

The company offers a Cheese Club programme, whereby a different cheese is shipped to you or to another lucky recipient every month for 3, 6, 9 or 12 months. Fundraising projects through cheese sales are also offered. Contact them for more details.

3475 Smith Dr.
Armstrong, BC
1-888-633-8899 OR
250-546-8651

C.E.O.
Dwight Johnson

CHEESEMAKERS
Hubert and Norman Besner

MILK TYPE
Thermalized cow's and goat's milk

PRODUCTION LEVEL
Semi-industrial

Federally registered

LOCAL ATTRACTIONS AND ACTIVITIES
- Chickadee Ridge Miniature Horse Ranch (Armstrong)
- Historic O'Keefe Ranch (Vernon)
- Hunting Hawk Vineyards (Armstrong)
- Okanagan Opal Mine (Vernon)

FOR MORE IDEAS, VISIT
www.armstrongbc.com
AND www.hellobc.com

CHEESE PRODUCED

USING COW'S MILK

ALPINE MEADOW
a firm, rindless, Swiss-style cheese

TRADITIONAL CHEDDAR
- Village Mild
- Village Medium
- Village Aged
- Village Extra Aged
- Village Marble
- 2-, 3-, 4- and 5-year-old

FLAVOURED CHEDDAR
- Amber Ale Beer
- Apple and Cinnamon
- Bavarian Mustard
- Blueberry
- Cointreau
- Garden Dill
- Gewürztraminer Wine
- Original Canadian Maple
- Original Smokehouse
- Original Wild Salmon
- Merlot Wine
- Red Hot Pepper
- Savoury Garlic
- Tangerine Twist
- Westwold (Onion and Chive)

CREAM CHEESE
- Plain
- Dill
- Garlic
- Horseradish
- Onion and Chive

KONIG STRASSE
a German butter cheese

MONTEREY JACK
- Habañero 911 Monterey
- Jalapeño Monterey
- Mediterranean (with sun-dried tomato)
- Original Peppery Jack
- Suicidally Hot Horseradish
- Village Jack
- Wickedly Hot Horseradish

MOZZARELLA

VILLAGE HAVARTI

VILLAGE GRATED PARMESAN

USING GOAT'S MILK

DRUNKEN GOAT

CHEDDAR

EDAM

FETA

HAVARTI

PARMESAN

SMOKEN GOAT

SWISS

1- Original Peppery Jack; 2- Cotswold Cheddar; 3- Pacific Salmon Cheddar; 4- Merlot Wine; 5- Original Canadian Maple Cheddar; 6- Village Marble; 7- Aged Cheddar; 8- Original Smokehouse Cheddar; 9- Feta; 10- Curds; 11- Garlic Cheddar; 12- Pacific Salmon Cheddar; 13- Alpine Meadow; 14- Canadian Maple Cheddar; 15- Wickedly Hot Horseradish; 16- Suicidally Hot Horseradish Monterey Jack

AVAILABILITY

STORES
- Onsite store
  Daily
  8:30 a.m. to 5:30 p.m.
  Closed on major holidays
- Clancy's Gourmet Meats (Kelowna)
- Smith Cheese Inc. (London, Ontario)
- Thrifty Foods (Vancouver Island)

USED AT THE FOLLOWING RESTAURANTS
- Bukowski's Restaurant (Vancouver)
- Safeway's signature sandwiches (various locations throughout British Columbia)
- Sheraton Vancouver

For distributor inquiries, please contact Dwight Johnson.

THE DEFINITIVE GUIDE TO CANADIAN ARTISANAL AND FINE CHEESE

GORT'S
GOUDA CHEESE FARM

1470 50th St. S.W.
Salmon Arm, BC
250-832-4274

OWNER
Arie Gort

MILK TYPE
Raw and thermalized cow's milk

PRODUCTION LEVEL
Artisanal farmstead

Federally registered

THIS FAMILY-RUN BUSINESS HAS BEEN making cheese since 1981. They started by producing plain Gouda. Twenty-four years later, they offer 17 different flavoured Goudas, feta and Maasdammer: a light, nutty flavoured cheese. The Gorts brought with them a Dutch cheesemaking tradition of producing cheese on the farm. Their knowledge began with Arie's great-grandfather, the first cheesemaker in the family. Yolanda, Arie's daughter, is now learning the family's cheese secrets. Their cheeses have won awards at the Pacific National Exhibition and at the Canadian Cheese Grand Prix.

Arie will not sacrifice quality and believes in using only natural ingredients, with no preservatives added. His herd of cows consists of Brown Swiss and Canadian Milking Short horns. Tours of the facilities are offered three times a week at 10 a.m. in July and August. Other times are available by appointment.

LOCAL ATTRACTIONS AND ACTIVITIES
- Lake Shuswap
- Three Valley Gap—ghost town and hotel
- Roots and Blues Festival (Salmon Arm)
- Local wineries (Larch Hills Winery, Recline Ridge Winery and Granite Creek Estate Wines)

FOR MORE IDEAS, VISIT
www.shuswap.bc.ca
AND www.hellobc.com

CHEESE PRODUCED

USING THERMALIZED MILK

FETA
- Plain
- Basil and Tomato
- Garlic and Tomato
- Oregano

GOUDA
- Mild
- Medium
- Aged
- Light
- Cumin
- Cumin and Cloves
- Fenugreek
- Greek (onion, red pepper, parsley, peppercorns, thyme and oregano)
- Green Garlic
- Italian (tomato, garlic, basil, thyme and oregano)
- Jalapeño
- Jalapeño and Habañero
- Jalapeño, Cumin and Garlic
- Parsley (parsley, celery, onion, garlic, dill and chives)
- Peppercorn (peppercorn, onion and garlic)
- Red Pepper (red bell pepper, ginger, onion and garlic)
- Smoked

MAASDAMMER
a raw-milk cheese

Lake Okanagan

AVAILABILITY

STORES
- Onsite store
  Monday to Saturday
  8 a.m. to 5:30 p.m.
- Two EE Farm (Surrey)
- Whole Foods Market (Vancouver)

USED AT THE FOLLOWING RESTAURANTS
- Four Seasons Hotel (Vancouver)

For distributor inquiries, please contact the company.

SALMON ARM, B.C.

691 Salmon River Rd.
Salmon Arm, BC
250-832-0209

OWNER/CHEESEMAKER
Donat Keller

CHEESEMAKER
Stuart Bryant

MILK TYPE
Pasteurized goat's milk

PRODUCTION LEVEL
Artisanal farmstead

Federally registered

LOCAL ATTRACTIONS AND ACTIVITIES
- Canoe Creek Alpacas (Salmon Arm)
- Crannog Organic Ales (Sorrento)
- Shuswap Farm and Craft Market
- Shuswap Lake Provincial Park

FOR MORE IDEAS, VISIT
www.shuswap.bc.ca
AND www.hellobc.com

DONAT LEARNED THE CHEESEMAKING trade back home in Switzerland. He immigrated to Canada and established himself in British Columbia. Stuart started off in the dairy business and began making cheese in Chilliwack. They have developed many of their cheese recipes themselves. Donat and Stuart have established strict quality controls for the milk they use and have several milk producers under contract, paying them fair prices for the milk.

The store location in Chilliwack offers tours for organized groups. Please call ahead to make arrangements (604-823-7241). A window in the store permits viewing of the cheesemaking process. A dairy bar serves a variety of treats for all to enjoy.

CHEESE PRODUCED

CHÈVRE
soft, unripened cheese balls marinated in olive oil and herbs

GOAT FETA

GOAT MILK CHEDDAR

MILD GOAT CHEESE
a firm, ripened block of cheese

OKANAGAN GOAT
a soft, unripened cheese in the form of a log
- Plain
- Chanterelle or Porcini mushroom
- Garlic and Parsley
- Lemon and Pepper
- Olive Oil and Rosemary

WHITE MOULD RIPENED GOAT CHEESE
a soft, bloomy rind cheese

1- Chèvre; 2- Okanagan Goat—Lemon and Pepper; 3- Okanagan Goat—Plain; 4- Okanagan Goat—Garlic and Parsley; 5- Okanagan Goat—Olive Oil and Rosemary

AVAILABILITY

STORES
- Chiliwack store
  7350A Barrow Rd.
  Chilliwack, BC
      Open year-round
      Monday to Saturday
      10 a.m. to 5 p.m.
      Closed on major holidays
- Capers (West Vancouver)
- Nature's Fare (Kelowna, Kamloops, Penticton and Vernon)
- Save-On-Foods (locations throughout Alberta and British Columbia)
- Thrifty Foods (Vancouver Island)
- Urban Fare (Vancouver)

USED AT THE FOLLOWING RESTAURANTS
- Four Seasons Hotel (Vancouver)
- White Spot restaurants (multiple locations in Alberta and British Columbia)

For distributor inquiries, please contact Valoroso Foods, 250-860-3646.

170 Timberline Rd.
Kelowna, BC
250-764-3117

OWNERS
Ofri and Ofer Barmor

CHEESEMAKER
Ofer Barmor

MILK TYPE
Raw and pasteurized goat's milk

PRODUCTION LEVEL
Artisanal farmstead

Provincially licensed

AFTER LEAVING ISRAEL TO CREATE A better life for their family, the Barmors had a tough start in Canada. They established their cheesemaking operation and herd of goats on the slopes of Okanagan Mountain in 2003. Later that summer, a devastating forest fire destroyed their farm and damaged their house. Half a million acres of forest and 238 homes were burnt to a crisp. Fortunately, all of the Barmor's goats were safe, having previously been evacuated to another farm. By early October their facilities were being rebuilt, and their first batch of cheese was ready by mid-February 2004.

Ofer made similar cheese in Israel for 12 years. They chose goat milk because their daughter Carmel is lactose intolerant. The cheeses are produced using traditional French techniques, stressing making everything from scratch and by hand. Their production volume is small but of high quality.

Ofri ships holiday baskets and cheese platters across Canada. Tours of the dairy plant, the ageing cellar, the milking station and the goats are offered for groups of four people or more. A fee of $4 per person plus taxes is charged. Please call a week in advance to book a tour.

CHEESE PRODUCED

USING RAW MILK

CARMEL
an Italian-style hard cheese, aged for 3 months

CHEVRETAL
an Emmental-style hard cheese

HORIZON
a hard cheese with a horizontal black vein of vegetable ash; aged for 4 months

LIOR
an Italian-style hard cheese, wrapped with white-grayish mould

LIOR SPECIAL EDITION
a hard cheese with peppercorns and bay leaves; aged for at least 6 months

SMOKED CARMEL
an Asiago-style hard cheese; aged for at least 5 months

TUSCANY
a hard cheese in the style of an Italian Pecorino; aged for at least 6 to 8 months

VINTAGE
a hard cheese, aged for 4 to 5 months, then soaked in red wine for several days

USING PASTEURIZED MILK

BLUE VELVET
a Camembert-style cheese, wrapped in blue-grayish mould

CARMELIS FETA

CHABICHOU
a soft rind cheese with a delicate and slightly lemony taste

CHEVRY PROVENCE
a fresh cheese rolled in a mixture of herbes de Provence

(CONTINUED ON PAGE 283)

1- Lior; 2- Carmel; 3- Chevretal; 4- Blue Velvet; 5- Nutty Moon; 6- Goatgonzola

7- Horizon; 8- Grapeleaf Flute; 9- Vintage; 10- Turquoise Pyramid; 11- Moonlight

Ofri places cheese on shelf.

LOCAL ATTRACTIONS AND ACTIVITIES
- Kelowna Land & Orchard Co.
- Knox Mountain Park
- Lake Okanagan and Ogopogo—the legendary lake monster
- Okanagan Wine Route
- Wine and Thyme Cooking School (Westbank)

FOR MORE IDEAS, VISIT
www.tourismkelowna.com
AND www.hellobc.com

I enjoyed sampling their cheese with Sinclair Philip, innkeeper of Sooke Harbour House and Robert McCullough, Whitecap Book's publisher. This was a most delicious discovery at the Cuisine Canada 2004 Kelowna conference.

CHEESE PRODUCED

(cont'd)

CHEVRY TRUFFELS
a fresh cheese wrapped with dried dill and onion

GOATGONZOLA
a firm blue cheese

GRAPE LEAF FLUTE
a log-shaped rind cheese wrapped in a grape leaf

HEAVENLY
a St. Marcellin–style rind cheese

LOVELY
a heart-shaped rind cheese

MOONLIGHT
a soft, bloomy rind, brie-style cheese

NUTTY MOON
a soft, bloomy rind, brie-style cheese with nuts in the paste

RUBY
a soft cheese with dried cranberries and a white mould

YOGURT CHEESE
a fresh, unripened cheese

UNDER DEVELOPMENT

TURQUOISE PYRAMID

AVAILABILITY

STORES
- Onsite store
  March 1 to April 30
  Monday to Saturday
  11 a.m. to 5 p.m.
  May 1 to October 31
  Daily 10 a.m. to 6 p.m.
  November 1 to 30
  Monday to Saturday
  11 a.m. to 4 p.m.
  December to February
  closed
- Granville Island Market (Vancouver)
- Thrifty Foods (Vancouver Island)
- Whole Foods Market (Vancouver)

For distributor inquiries, please contact Ofri.

USED AT THE FOLLOWING RESTAURANTS
- Burrowing Owl (Oliver)
- Cedar Creek (Kelowna)
- Fresco (Kelowna)
- Mission Hill Family Estate (Westbank)

R.R. # 2, Chase Creek Rd.
Chase, BC
250-679-3841

OWNERS/CHEESEMAKERS
Theres and Hani Gasser

MILK TYPE
Organic pasteurized sheep's milk

PRODUCTION LEVEL
Artisanal farmstead

Federally registered

LOCAL ATTRACTIONS AND ACTIVITIES
- Adams River Rafting
- Chase Museum
- Sockeye salmon run on the Adams River
- Squilax Pow Wow

FOR MORE IDEAS, VISIT
www.chasechamber.com
AND www.hellobc.com

HANI AND THERES LEARNED ALL STAGES of the cheesemaking craft in Switzerland—from milking the sheep to making the cheese in the traditional open copper vats. In 1994 they moved to Canada to continue their trade.

Their herd of East Friesian dairy sheep and Lacaune sheep are kept outside year-round. Komondor guard dogs protect them from predators and border collies herd the sheep. The milk is certified organic by the Shuswap Thompson Organic Producers Association. Tours of the farm are available for organized groups. Please call ahead to arrange the visit.

CHEESE PRODUCED

AGED CHEESE

BRIE

FETA
- Droppings—small pieces
- Marinated in cold-pressed olive oil with garlic and rosemary

AVAILABILITY

STORES
- Onsite store
  Ring doorbell for service
- Capers (Vancouver)
- Coquitlam Farmers' Market
- Kamloops Farmers' Market
- Les Amis du Fromage (Vancouver)

For distributor inquiries, please contact Arla Foods, 905-669-9393 or 1-800-387-3699.

286

POPLAR GROVE
CHEESE

1060 Poplar Grove Rd.
Penticton, BC
250-492-4575

OWNER
Ian Sutherland

CHEESEMAKER
Shana Miller

MILK TYPE
Pasteurized cow's milk

PRODUCTION LEVEL
Artisanal

Federally registered

LOCAL ATTRACTIONS AND ACTIVITIES
- Joie Farm Cooking School (Naramata)
- Kettle Valley Steam Railway Tours (Summerland)
- Okanagan Wine Route
- Trans-Canada Hiking Trail

FOR MORE IDEAS, VISIT
www.penticton.ca AND
www.hellobc.com

POPLAR GROVE IS CANADA'S FIRST AND only wine and cheese company. Did this idea come about at a wine and cheese party? Ask Ian.

Shana always wanted to make cheese. She trained onsite, learning the techniques of hand-making the cheese. Each wheel is babied, taken care of with great attention. Her Harvest Moon is made only at the monthly full moon. Shana believes that the *affinage*, or ripening of the cheese, is very important. This is when its extra flavours develop as it ages in an environmentally controlled room.

CHEESE PRODUCED

DOUBLE CREAM CAMEMBERT

HARVEST MOON
a soft, washed rind cheese

NARAMATA BENCH BLUE
a soft, washed rind cheese with a slight blue taste

TIGER BLUE
a soft, washed rind, Stilton-style, blue cheese

1- Tiger Blue; 2- Harvest Moon; 3- Okanagan Double Cream Camembert; 4- Naramata Bench Blue

AVAILABILITY

STORES

- Onsite store
  May to October
  Daily 11 a.m. to 5 p.m.
  Closed remainder of
  the year
- Il Vecchio (Penticton)
- Les Amis du Fromage
  (Vancouver)
- Ottavio (Victoria)
- Oyama Sausage—Granville
  Island Public Market
  (Vancouver)
- Naramata General Store
  (Naramata)

For distributor inquiries, please contact the company.

USED AT THE FOLLOWING
RESTAURANT

- Mission Hill Family Estate
  (Westbank)

DUTCHMEN DAIRY LTD.

1321 Maier Rd.
Sicamous, BC
250-836-4304

OWNERS
Chris, Nelly and Jake Dewitt

CHEESEMAKER
Jay Houseman

MILK TYPE
Pasteurized cow's milk

PRODUCTION LEVEL
Semi-industrial

Federally registered

TO USE THE EXTRA MILK THEIR HERD OF Holstein cows produced, Chris and Nelly began cheese production in 1978. Their son, Jake, now works in the family business.

They use only the freshest milk and within 24 hours, it's transformed into cheese. The cheesemaking process is all done by hand. Through the viewing window located in their store, you can watch Jay creating their cheese.

LOCAL ATTRACTIONS AND ACTIVITIES
- Sicamous—Canada's Houseboat Capital, located on Lake Shuswap and Mara Lake
- Crazy Creek and Kay Falls (Sicamous)
- Silver Star Mountain Ski Resort (Vernon)

FOR MORE IDEAS, VISIT
www.shuswap.bc.ca
AND www.hellobc.com

CHEESE PRODUCED

CHEDDAR
- Mild (white and orange)
- Medium (white and orange)
- Sharp (white and orange)
- Bacon
- Cajun
- Chili Jack
- Dill Pickle
- Dill Seed
- Garlic
- Jalapeño

CURDS
- White
- Orange

MONTEREY JACK
- Plain
- Jalapeño

MOZZARELLA

AVAILABILITY

STORES
- Onsite store
  Spring and summer
  Daily 8 a.m. to 10 p.m.
  Autumn and winter
  Daily 8 a.m. to 6 p.m.
- I.G.A. grocery stores
  (within British Columbia)
- Shop Easy (Sicamous and
  Salmon Arm)

For distributor inquiries, please contact Jake.

USED AT THE FOLLOWING RESTAURANTS
- Moose Mulligan's Marine
  Pub (Sicamous)
- Loggers Restaurant at Hyde
  Mountain on Mara Lake
  Golf Course (Sicamous)

30854 Olund Rd.
Abbotsford, BC
1-888-668-4823 OR
604-854-6261

OWNERS
Peter and Jo-Ann Dykstra

CHEESEMAKER
Jason Dykstra

FOUNDERS
Jill Tyndale and Chris Watkins

MILK TYPE
Organic pasteurized goat's milk

PRODUCTION LEVEL
Artisanal farmstead

Provincially licensed

LOCAL ATTRACTIONS AND ACTIVITIES
- Abbotsford Farm and Country Market
- ChocolaTas—chocolate shop (Abbotsford)
- Clayburn Village Store and Tea Shop (Abbotsford)
- Circle Farm Tour (Fraser County)
- Lotusland Vineyards (Abbotsford)

FOR MORE IDEAS, VISIT
www.tourismabbotsford.ca
AND www.hellobc.com

GOAT'S PRIDE DAIRY AT MCLENNAN CREEK is an organic goat dairy producing bottled milk, cheese and yogurt. Jill and Chris bought their first goat as a source of milk for their son Luke, who was allergic to cow's milk. Beginning with that single goat, they ended up with a herd of over 170 Saanen, La Mancha, Alpine and Nubian goats. Their commercial operation began in 1997. They supplied milk to other dairies and processors, including Salt Spring Island Cheese Company and Happy Days Dairy. In 2001 they began processing their own milk into finished products. In 2004 Jason's Blue Capri won Best in Show at the American Dairy Goat Association annual cheese competition.

In January 2006 Jason's parents, Peter and Jo-Ann, purchased the business. The Dykstra family know the industry, having operated their own goat dairy farm for 15 years. They will continue to make the cheese established by Chris and Jill and you can look forward to Jason experimenting with creations of his own.

The farm is open for visits. Please do not bring your dogs.

CHEESE PRODUCED

BLUE CAPRI
a roquefort-style blue cheese

BLUE CAPRINA
a soft, German Cambozola-style blue cheese

CAPRABELLA
a low salt, feta-like cheese
- Plain
- Cranberry

CAPRAMONTE
a firm, cheddar-style cheese
- Plain
- Smoked

CHÈVRE
- Plain
- Black Pepper
- Garlic and Herbs
- Sun-dried Tomato and Basil

CHÈVROTINA
a soft, bloomy rind, Camembert-style cheese
- Plain buttons
- Plain log
- Ash Chèvrotina—identified by its distinctive ash goat image
- Blue Chèvrotina—a firm, blue, surface-ripened, pyramid-shaped cheese

FETA
- Plain
- Black Pepper
- Sun-dried Tomato and Basil

TOMME DE CHÈVRE
- Plain
- Black Pepper
- Caraway
- Red Pepper

Sunset paddling

AVAILABILITY

STORES
- Onsite store
  Monday to Saturday
  9 a.m. to 5 p.m.
  Closed on major holidays
- Capers (West Vancouver)
- Les Amis du Fromage (Vancouver)
- La Grotta del Fromaggio (Vancouver)
- Planet Organic Market (Coquitlam and Victoria)
- White Rock Farmers' Market

USED AT THE FOLLOWING RESTAURANTS
- C Restaurant (Vancouver)
- Rain City Grill (Vancouver)
- Ramada Inn (Abbotsford)

For distributor inquiries, please contact Peter or Jo-Ann.

NOW INTO THE THIRD GENERATION OF family cheesemaking in Canada, Scardillo Cheese has been a vibrant part of the Greater Vancouver Italian community since 1960. Rocky learned the cheesemaking craft from his father, Paulo, and is training his son, also named Paulo. The family tradition passes from generation to generation and follows the skills originally learned in Italy.

Scardillo Cheese is the last family-owned major cheese producer in British Columbia.

7865 Venture St.
Burnaby, BC
604-420-9892

OWNERS
Kathy and Rocky Scardillo

CHEESEMAKER
Rocky Scardillo

MILK TYPE
Pasteurized cow's milk

PRODUCTION LEVEL
Industrial

Federally registered

LOCAL ATTRACTIONS AND ACTIVITIES
- Burnaby Mountain Park, with its Kamui Mintara carved poles
- Burnaby Village Museum—self-guided tours of a 1920 village and restored 1912 carousel

FOR MORE IDEAS, VISIT
www.tourismvancouver.com/
visitors/about_vancouver/
municipalities/burnaby AND
www.hellobc.com

CHEESE PRODUCED

BOCCONCINI

CACCIOCAVALLO

MILD CHEDDAR
- White
- Orange

EDAM

FARM FRESH CURDS
- White
- Orange

FETA

MONTEREY JACK

MOZZARELLA

PRESSED MOZZARELLA

AMERICAN MOZZARELLA
full fat

RICOTTA

SCAMORZA
a semi-soft, natural rind, gourd- or oval-shaped cheese

TRECCE
- Plain
- Marinated in oil and spices

1- Mozzarella; 2- Feta; 3- Bocconcini; 4- Edam; 5- Ricotta; 6- Cacciocavallo; 7- Scamorza; 8- Pressed Mozzarella; 9- Trecce

AVAILABILITY

STORES
- Onsite store
  Monday to Friday
  9 a.m. to 2 p.m.
- Scardillo Cheese (Vancouver)
- Capers (West Vancouver)

USED AT THE FOLLOWING RESTAURANTS
- L'Artista (Burnaby)
- La Spaghetteria
  (New Westminster)

For distributor inquiries, please contact Kathy.

HILARY'S FINE CHEESES IS THE ONLY cheesemaking operation on south Vancouver Island. Hilary picks up the cow's milk from a local farming couple who manage a herd of grass-fed Holsteins. Goat milk is delivered to his plant once a week from a goat dairy located in the Lower Mainland.

Hilary's cheeses are inspired by the French Trappist monks and hand-ladled Camembert styles. Very little machinery is used (no pumps and no mechanical processes). The milk is treated very gently. Local wine and cider are used to wash different cheeses, giving them an even stronger regional identity.

ℝ

Hilary and I hit it off in our very first telephone conversation, when we discovered we had both graduated from Bishop's University. I knew his cousin when I studied there. Small world! "Raise a toast to Bishop's University, on the mighty Massawippi shore ..." Perhaps Hilary can remind me of the second verse of our university song.

1282 Cherry Point Rd.
Cobble Hill, BC
1-888-480-7600 OR
250-715-0563

OWNERS
Pat and Hilary Abbott

CHEESEMAKER
Hilary Abbott

MILK TYPE
Pasteurized cow's and goat's milk

PRODUCTION LEVEL
Artisanal

Provincially licensed

LOCAL ATTRACTIONS AND ACTIVITIES
- Local wineries (Blue Grouse Estate Winery, Cherry Point Vineyard, Vignetti Zanatta)
- Trans-Canada Hiking Trail
- Whitewater sea kayaking

FOR MORE IDEAS, VISIT
www.islands.bc.ca
AND www.hellobc.com

CHEESE PRODUCED

USING COW'S MILK

FROMAGE À LA CRÈME
a fresh, high-moisture cream cheese

RED DAWN
a semi-soft, tomme-style rind cheese, washed with local Merridale cider

SAINT-CLAIR
a soft, white mould, surface ripened cheese, named after Sinclair Philip, innkeeper of Sooke Harbour House

TRADITIONAL EASTERN CANADIAN CHEESE CURDS
made weekly according to a recipe and technique of a cheesemaker from Winchester, Ontario

YOUBOU
a full-fat, semi-soft blue cheese

USING GOAT'S MILK

BELLE ANN
a semi-soft, tomme-style cheese washed with Cherry Point Vineyard's blackberry port

CHÈVRE
a soft, high-moisture cream cheese

FETA

SAINT-MICHEL
a soft, white mould, surface ripened cheese, named after their son

Hilary Abbott and his cheese

FRESH FROM THE ISLAND
VANCOUVER ISLAND & THE GULF ISLANDS

1- Red Dawn; 2- Belle Ann; 3- Saint-Clair; 4- Saint-Michel; 5- Les Boutons de Vache

AVAILABILITY

STORES

- Onsite store
  Wednesday to Sunday
  11 a.m. to 4 p.m.
- Hilary's Cheese outlet,
  1725 Cowichan Bay Rd.,
  Cowichan Bay, Vancouver
  Island
- Duncan Farmers' Market
- Les Amis du Fromage
  (Vancouver)
- Oyama Sausage—Granville
  Island Public Market
  (Vancouver)
- Spinnakers (Victoria)

USED AT THE FOLLOWING RESTAURANT

- Glow (Nanaimo)

For distributor inquiries, please contact Pat or Hilary.

403 Lowry Rd.
Parksville, BC
250-954-3931

OWNERS
Clarke and Nancy Gourlay

CHEESEMAKER
Nancy Gourlay

MILK TYPE
Raw and pasteurized cow's milk

PRODUCTION LEVEL
Artisanal farmstead

Provincially licensed

LOCAL ATTRACTIONS AND ACTIVITIES
• Local seaside beaches
• Golf courses
• Wilderness hiking
• Salmon fishing

FOR MORE IDEAS, VISIT
www.islands.bc.ca
AND www.hellobc.com

THIS IS A FAMILY-RUN BUSINESS. CLARKE manages and milks their small herd of Holstein, Ayrshire, Brown Swiss and Canadienne cows. Nancy makes the cheese and their three boys help around the farm. Nancy's parents, Ray and Judy Haynes, coordinate the wholesaling of the cheese and the administration of the company.

It all began in 1999, when Nancy and Clarke returned from working in Switzerland for several years as international humanitarian aid workers. Nancy had been inspired by the delicious Swiss cheese, learned their techniques from Swiss cheesemakers and attended courses in Chilliwack, British Columbia. The milk, still warm from the cows, is processed into cheese and ripened on the farm.

The farm is open for visits. See the calves, watch Clarke milk the heifers and observe the cheese being made. Beware! Any visitors around the farm after 4 p.m. will be drafted and put to work.

CHEESE PRODUCED

USING RAW MILK

CAERPHILLY
a Welsh-style cheese (they have cousins living in Wales)

QUALICUM SPICE
a semi-soft cheese, flavoured with onions, garlic, paprika and sweet red pepper flakes

RACLETTE

RATHTREVOR
a firm, Swiss-style, rind ripened cheese, named after the local provincial park

USING PASTEURIZED MILK

BLUE CLAIR
a firm, roquefort-style blue cheese

FETA
- Plain
- Marinated in oil, garlic, sun-dried tomatoes and rosemary

FRESH CURDS

FROMAGE FRAIS
a fresh, unripened cheese

ISLAND BRIES
a soft cheese with a velvety white rind

MONTEREY JILL
a Monterey Jack–style semi-soft cheese, but softer in taste (more feminine according to the lady cheesemaker)

SAN PAREIL
a seasonal soft cheese with a mixed rind, as Nancy calls it, named after a local neighbourhood

UNDER DEVELOPMENT

MT. ARROWSMITH

Nancy and Clarke Gourlay

1- Mt. Arrowsmith; 2- Rathtrevor; 3- Marinated Feta; 4- Qualicum Spice; 5- Curds; 6- Fromage Frais; 7- Feta "Complet"; 8- Raclette; 9- Fromage Frais; 10- Caerphilly; 11- Island Bries

AVAILABILITY

STORES

- Onsite store
  Monday to Saturday
  10 a.m. to 4 p.m.
- Nanaimo Farmers' Market
- Ottavio's (Victoria)
- Parksville Farmers' Market
- Qualicum Farmers' Market
- West End Farmers' Market
  (Vancouver)

USED AT THE FOLLOWING RESTAURANTS

- Aerie Resort (Malahat)
- Bayside Oceanfront Inn
  (Parksville)
- Kingfisher Oceanside Resort
  (Courtenay)
- Tigh-Na-Mara Seaside Spa
  Resort (Parksville)
- Wickaninnish Inn (Tofino)

For distributor inquiries, please contact Ray, 1-877-248-4353 or 250-248-4353.

THE DEFINITIVE GUIDE TO CANADIAN ARTISANAL AND FINE CHEESE

635 McPhee Avenue
Courtenay, BC
1-866-244-4422 OR
250-344-4422

PRESIDENT
Edgar Smith

CHEESEMAKER
Paul Sutter

MILK TYPE
Pasteurized cow's milk

PRODUCTION LEVEL
Artisanal farmstead

Federally registered

LOCAL ATTRACTIONS AND ACTIVITIES
- Comox Air Force Museum and Heritage Park (Comox)
- Crown Isle Golf Course (Courtenay)
- Filberg Festival (Comox)
- Mt. Washington Alpine Resort (Mt. Washington)
- Mountain biking
- Salmon fishing

FOR MORE IDEAS, VISIT
www.tourism-comox-valley.bc.ca,
www.islands.bc.ca AND
www.hellobc.com

PAUL, A SWISS MASTER CHEESEMAKER, stresses that good cheese comes from good milk. He uses fresh milk from Beaver Meadow Farms, the Smith's third-generation farm. Their holistic natural system of farming means that no chemical pesticides, herbicides, antibiotics or growth hormones are used. The herds are rotated from pasture to pasture according to a system that monitors plant growth and recovery. Using this approach, their cows are clean and disease-free.

The Smith family are active stewards of the land, ensuring the health of their forests, streams and grasslands. The farm received the Certified Heritage Farm designation, the TLC Conservation Partner designation and a Countryside Canada award.

With the influx of eastern Canadians to the region, Paul started making fresh curds to satisfy all the requests. The company's superb cheeses have won awards at the British Empire Cheese Show, the Canadian Cheese Grand Prix and The Royal Agricultural Winter Fair.

CHEESE PRODUCED

AMSTERDAMMER
a ripened, firm cheese with a buttery aroma

BOERENKAAS
a ripened, firm cheese with a slight tangy finish

BUTTER CHEESE

CHEDDAR
• Mild
• Medium

COMOX BRIE

COMOX CAMEMBERT

FRESH CURDS

LA SCALA
New for 2006; a blend of Irish Derby and Italian-style Asiago cheese

TRIPLE CREAM CAMEMBERT

VERDELAIT
a ripened, firm cheese offered in several flavours
• Christmas Spice
• Cracked Pepper
• Cumin Seed
• Fall
• Garlic and Chive
• Pacific Pepper, new for 2006;
  a mix of habañero and black
  pepper
• Summer
• Wasabi (Japanese green
  horseradish)

Paul Sutter and Edgar Smith

1- Boerenkaas; 2- Cracked Pepper Verdelait; 3- Wasabi Verdelait; 4- Comox Brie;
5- Amsterdammer; 6- Cumin Seed Verdelait; 7- Curds; 8- Garlic and Chives Verdelait;
9- Triple Cream Camembert; 10- Comox Camembert; 11- Cheddar

AVAILABILITY

STORES
• Onsite store
    Monday to Friday
    1 to 4 p.m.
• Campbell River Farmers'
  Market (Vancouver Island)
• Les Amis du Fromage
  (Vancouver)
• Peninsula Farmers' Market
  (Central Saanich, Vancouver
  Island)
• Thrifty Foods (several
  locations throughout British
  Columbia)

USED AT THE FOLLOWING RESTAURANTS
• Atlas Café (Courtenay)
• Bee Hive Café
  (Campbell River)
• Canoe Club (Victoria)
• Hastings House (Ganges,
  Salt Spring Island)

For distributor inquiries, please contact their sales team at 1-866-244-4422.

THE DEFINITIVE GUIDE TO CANADIAN ARTISANAL AND FINE CHEESE

1306 Beddis Rd.
Salt Spring Island, BC
250-537-4987

OWNERS
Susan and Julia Grace

CHEESEMAKER
Julia Grace

MILK TYPE
Organic raw and pasteurized
cow's milk

PRODUCTION LEVEL
Artisanal farmstead

Provincially licensed

SUSAN AND JULIA MAKE CHEESE FROM their own herd of Jersey cows. When my wife, Joanne, saw her first Jersey calf, she fell in love with it. "It's so cute!" she said. "It looks like Bambi." Susan also fell under their spell when the Graces adopted their first Jersey heifer. They operated a community-shared agriculture (CSA) farm. Susan took care of the cow and Julia made butter, yogurt and cheese for their CSA members.

In 1998 they began production of certified organic cheese commercially. The herd has now grown to 12 milking heifers, providing milk high in fat and protein. Each cow produces approximately 18 litres of milk daily. From this rich milk, Moonstruck Organic produces cheese with depth of flavour and silky textures.

LOCAL ATTRACTIONS AND ACTIVITIES
- Ganges Farmers' Market (Salt Spring Island)
- Island Gourmet Safaris
- Salt Spring Island Vineyard
- Salt Spring Island's studios and art galleries

FOR MORE IDEAS, VISIT
www.gulfislands.net,
www.islands.bc.ca AND
www.hellobc.com

CHEESE PRODUCED

USING RAW MILK

BEDDIS BLUE
a semi-soft, blue cheese

BLOSSOM'S BLUE
a firm, Stilton-style, blue cheese

FARMSTEAD FETA

TOMME D'OR
a hard, aged cheese

WHITE GRACE
a hard, unpressed cheese

USING PASTEURIZED MILK

ASH-RIPENED CAMEMBERT
a soft, bloomy rind cheese

BABY BLUE
a soft, surface ripened, blue cheese

FROMAGE BLANC
a fresh, unripened cheese

FROMAGE BLEU
a fresh, blue cheese

SAVOURY MOON
a soft, bloomy rind cheese

WHITE MOON
a soft, bloomy rind cheese

Moonstruck Organic's Jersey cows

Julia Grace's cheese: 1- Fromage Blanc; 2- Fromage Bleu; 3- Savoury Moon; 4- Ash-Ripened Camembert; 5- Beddis Blue; 6- White Moon; 7- Blossom's Blue; 8- Baby Blue; 9- Tomme d'Or; 10- White Grace

AVAILABILITY

STORES

- Ganges Farmers' Market (Salt Spring Island)
- Ottavio's (Victoria)
- Salt Spring Island Cheese Co.
- Salt Spring Island Vineyard
- Thrifty Foods (selected locations on Vancouver Island)

USED AT THE FOLLOWING RESTAURANTS

- The Aerie (Malahat)
- C Restaurant (Vancouver)
- Hastings House (Ganges, Salt Spring Island)
- Sooke Harbour House (Sooke)
- Spinnakers Brew Pub (Victoria)

For distributor inquiries, please contact Julia.

DAVID WANTED TO RAISE HIS CHILDREN IN the countryside, so he sold his Toronto fine food shops and catering services and moved to British Columbia. In 1996 he began producing cheese, making it by hand in small batches. He knows the importance of an attractive presentation; his soft cheeses are packaged in clear plastic and beautifully decorated with flowers, basil, roasted garlic and hot chilis. One sees them and the word "wow" emerges from one's mouth.

David started with sheep's milk. Over a six-year period, he learned how to make consistently good cheese. But sheep are seasonal milk producers, so he experimented with goat's milk. He pays above-market prices for his goat's milk to ensure a good supply and the survival of the producers. From 2001 to 2004 his facility was working at maximum capacity, but demand was exceeding supply. In 2004 he expanded his facilities to meet the requests for his cheese.

285 Reynolds Rd.
Salt Spring Island, BC
250-653-2300

OWNER/CHEESEMAKER
David Wood

MILK TYPE
Pasteurized goat's and sheep's milk

PRODUCTION LEVEL
Artisanal

Provincially licensed

LOCAL ATTRACTIONS AND ACTIVITIES
• ArtSpring festival
• Garry Oaks Winery
• Salt Spring Island Festival of the Arts
• Salt Spring Studios Tour
• Sea kayaking

FOR MORE IDEAS, VISIT
www.gulfislands.net,
www.islands.bc.ca AND
www.hellobc.com

CHEESE PRODUCED

USING GOAT'S MILK

CROTTIN-STYLE CHEESE
a soft, unripened cheese
- Plain
- Oregano

USING GOAT'S AND SHEEP'S MILK

FETA

SURFACE RIPENED CHEESE, SOFT CHEESE
- Blue Mould
- White Mould

USING SHEEP'S MILK

SEMI-HARD CHEESE

USING GOAT'S MILK WITH SOME SHEEP'S MILK

SOFT FRESH CHEESE
- Plain
- Basil
- Flower
- Hot Chili
- Peppercorn
- Roast Garlic
- Sun-dried Tomato
- White Truffle

Owner and cheesemaker David Wood

1- Semi-Hard Cheese; 2- Plain Crottin; 3- White Mould, Surface Ripened Cheese; 4- Blue Mould Surface Ripened Cheese; 5- Roast Garlic Soft Fresh Cheese; 6- Basil Soft Fresh Cheese; 7- Hot Chili Soft Fresh Cheese; 8- Flower Soft Fresh Cheese; 9- Under development; 10- Saint-Joan (Under development); 11- Peppercorn Soft Fresh Cheese

AVAILABILITY

STORES
- Onsite store
  Summer
  7 days a week
  Winter
  Weekends only
- Ganges Farmers' Market (Salt Spring Island)
- Fine food shops in Vancouver, Victoria and Whistler
- Thrifty Foods (selected locations on Vancouver Island)

USED AT THE FOLLOWING RESTAURANTS
- Glow (Nanaimo)
- Lumière (Vancouver)
- Sooke Harbour House (Sooke)
- The Aerie Resort (Malahat)

For distribution inquiries, please contact David.

G. PRETTY

Other Canadian Cheesemakers

QUEBEC

FERME CARON
Saint-Louis-de-France, QC
819-379-1772

FROMAGERIE DU COIN
Sherbrooke, QC
819-346-0416

FROMAGERIE LA P'TITE IRLANDE
Weedon, QC
418-338-0527

FROMAGERIE LES MÉCHINS
Les Méchins, QC
418-729-3855

FROMAGERIE MIRABEL 1985 INC.
Saint-Antoine, QC
450-438-5822

FROMAGERIE PROULX
Saint-Georges-de-Windsor, QC
819-828-2223

FROMAGERIE SAINT-JACQUES
INTERNATIONAL
Saint-Jacques-de-
    Montcalm, QC
450-839-2729

JAC LE CHÈVRIER
Saint-Flavien, QC
418-728-1807

LA TRAPPE À FROMAGE
Gatineau, QC
819-243-6411

ONTARIO

A.M. JENSEN LTD.
(WILTON CHEESE FACTORY)
Simcoe, ON
1-866-625-0165

ARLA FOODS INC.
Concord, ON
1-800-387-3699 OR
905-669-9393

BLACK RIVER CHEESE COMPANY
Milford, ON
613-476-2575

ELDORADO GOLDEN CHEESE CO.
Eldorado, ON
613-473-2973

GALATI CHEESE COMPANY LTD.
Windsor, ON
519-973-7510

MAPLE DALE CHEESE
(HENRY FOODS)
Plainfield, ON
613-477-2454

PINE RIVER CHEESE AND
BUTTER CO-OP
Ripley, ON
519-395-2638

MANITOBA

VOLGA ENTERPRISES LTD.
Winnipeg, MB
204-256-4559

Cheese Related Information

CANADIAN CHEESE FESTIVALS

Here is a list of festivals dedicated to cheese. If you know of any others in Canada, please forward the details to Gurth@CheeseofCanada.ca.

- Festival des fromages de Warwick (Warwick, QC) www.festivaldesfromages.qc.ca
- Foire Vin Fromage (Saint-Jérôme, QC) www.foirevinfromage.ca
- St. Albert Curd Festival (St. Albert, ON) www.curdfestival.com
- Toronto Wine and Cheese Show (Toronto, ON) www.towineandcheese.com

CHEESE APPRECIATION CLASSES

If you would like to learn more about cheese, here are companies I know of offering classes. Contact your local cooking schools or community colleges. They may also offer special classes such as these ones.

- Cheese of Canada—special Canadian cheese tasting seminars led by the author, matched to wine, whiskey or beer selected by a certified sommelier. A fun and tasty event for friends, co-workers or clients. www.CheeseofCanada.ca
- Artisan Cheese Marketing—Cheese Education Guild Certificate (Toronto, ON) www.artisancheesemarketing.com
- Cheese Culture (Toronto, ON) www.cheeseculture.ca
- George Brown College's Chef School (Toronto, ON) www.coned.georgebrown.ca
- Janice Beaton's Fine Cheeses (Calgary, AB) www.jbfinecheese.com
- Les Amis du fromage (Vancouver, BC) www.buycheese.com
- Manitoba Liquor Control Commission
- West Vancouver School District Community Learning

CHEESEMAKING COURSES

Want to learn how to make cheese for your own personal consumption or possibly to become a professional cheesemaker? Visit the following websites for more information.

- Cheesemaking workshops—Glengarry Cheesemaking and Dairy Supply (Alexandria, ON) www.glengarrycheesemaking.on.ca
- Cheesemaking Technology—Guelph Food Technology Centre (Guelph, ON) www.gftc.ca
- Institut de technologie agroalimentaire (Saint-Hyacinthe, QC) www.ita.qc.ca

CANADIAN CHEESE COMPETITIONS

Some cheesemakers enjoy entering their products into competitions, to be judged by professionals or by the public. Competitions are a great way for promoting cheese.

- British Empire Cheese Show (Belleville, ON) coordinated by the Central Ontario Cheesemakers Assoction (905-377-1029)
- Canadian Cheese Grand Prix (Dairy Farmers of Canada) www.dairygoodness.ca
- Canadian Western Agribition (Regina, SK) www.agribition.com
- Royal Agricultural Winter Fair (Toronto, ON) www.royalfair.org
- Sélection Caseus, open only to Quebec fine cheese (Warwick, QC) www.festivaldesfromages.qc.ca

CANADIAN CHEESE ORGANIZATIONS

CENTRAL ONTARIO CHEESEMAKERS ASSOCIATION
c/o Ms. Wendy Gibbons
21 Ravine Dr., R.R. # 2,
Baltimore, ON, K0K 1C0
905-377-1029

ONTARIO CHEESE SOCIETY
P.O. Box 225
Grimsby, ON, L3M 4G3
905-945-3633 or 1-888-387-2317
www.ontariocheese.org

LA SOCIÉTÉ DES FROMAGES DU QUÉBEC
8585, boulevard St-Laurent, office # 310
Montreal, QC, H2P 2M9
514-381-6350
www.societedesfromages.com

Recipes

Hors d'œuvres

THE DEFINITIVE GUIDE TO CANADIAN ARTISANAL AND FINE CHEESE

Joanne and I first experienced this classic Bavarian cheese dish at a brewpub in Nuremberg, Germany. It was part of a brotzeit *platter, a combination of sliced meats and cheeses, pickles, pretzels and rye bread, served with a pint of beer.*

1 lb. (450 g) Ramembert, rind removed
6 oz. (180 g) cream cheese, at room
    temperature
¼ cup (60 mL) unsalted butter, at room
    temperature
1 ½ tsp. (7.5 mL) whole caraway seeds
1 tsp. (5 mL) whole cumin seeds
4 green onions, finely chopped
½ onion, finely diced
¼ cup (60 mL) dark beer
2 tsp. (10 mL) sweet paprika
2 garlic cloves, minced
kosher salt and freshly ground black
    pepper, to taste
pretzels, slices of rye or pumpernickel
bread, carrot and celery sticks,
    sliced radishes

1. Let the Ramembert warm up to room temperature, approximately 1 hour.
2. In a medium bowl, combine the cheeses, butter, caraway and cumin seeds, onions, beer, paprika and garlic. Mash with either a fork or a potato masher until well mixed.
3. Season with salt and pepper.
4. Cover and refrigerate for 2 hours or overnight, to let the different flavours blend together.
5. Using an ice cream scoop, spoon onto a platter and serve with pretzels, sliced bread, raw vegetables and a pint of your favourite beer.

using Ewenity Dairy Co-operative Ramembert, produced in Conn, Ontario

Makes approximately 3 cups (750 mL)

PREP TIME
30 minutes + minimum of 2 hours of refrigeration

COOKING TIME
None

MAKE AHEAD
Recipe can be made 1 or 2 days ahead, covered and refrigerated.

GURTH'S NOTES
- Use a good strong dark beer. My favourite for this dish is Maudite, a beer brewed in Quebec.
- If you like a little smoky flavour, use smoked paprika powder.

using Leoni-Grana, produced in Camrose, Alberta

Makes about 25 pieces

PREP TIME
30 minutes

COOKING TIME
20 minutes

MAKE AHEAD
These can be made and cooked 2 days ahead. Store in an airtight container at room temperature. Reheat in the oven for 5 minutes at 300°F (150°C) prior to serving. Spray lightly with oil to give them more moisture.

GURTH'S NOTES
• Substitutions for Leoni-Grana cheese would be any good dry, hard cheeses such as Parmigiano Reggiano, Montasio and Pecorino Romano.
• Make it spicier by adding 2 pinches of cayenne.

Joanne and I cannot resist these little treats! They are one of our favourite finger foods. Be careful, they are addictive. You taste one, you devour six.

1 ¼ cups (310 mL) all-purpose flour, sifted
½ tsp. (2.5 mL) baking powder
¼ tsp. (1 mL) kosher salt
1 tsp. (5 mL) sweet paprika
½ tsp. (2.5 mL) ground cumin
pinch cayenne pepper
¼ cup (60 mL) grated Leoni-Grana cheese
¼ cup (60 mL) olive oil
1 egg, beaten
2 to 3 Tbsp. (30 to 45 mL) ice cold water
25 pimento stuffed olives

1. Preheat the oven to 350°F (180°C).
2. Line a large cookie sheet with parchment paper.
3. Combine the flour, baking powder, salt, paprika, cumin, cayenne and cheese in a bowl and stir until well mixed.
4. Add the oil, egg and ice water. Stir until the dough comes together.
5. Dry the olives with paper towels.
6. Flatten 2 tsp. (10 mL) of dough with your fingers into a disk 2 inches (5 cm) in diameter.
7. Place an olive in the middle and enclose in dough.
8. Roll between your palms to seal the seams and make a uniformly smooth ball.
9. Place on a cookie sheet and repeat with remaining olives and dough.
10. Bake until lightly browned, about 20 minutes.
11. Remove from the oven and permit to cool slightly. Pop them in your mouth and be ready to smile!

THE DEFINITIVE GUIDE TO CANADIAN ARTISANAL AND FINE CHEESE

This recipe comes from the files of Edgar Smith, president of Natural Pastures. It took me a while to decipher the origins of the name of this cheese. If you break it down into it syllables, ver-de-lait, *it means 'glass of milk' in French.*

4 large eggs, beaten
¾ cup (180 mL) 18% cream
6 oz. (180 g) cooked crabmeat
2 green onions, finely sliced
½ red bell pepper, diced
¼ tsp. (1 mL) hot chili pepper sauce
1 cup (250 mL) grated Cracked Pepper Verdelait
24 to 27 store-bought tartlet shells, thawed

1. Preheat the oven to 350°F (180°C). Place the rack at middle height.
2. In a large bowl, combine the eggs, cream, crabmeat, onions, red peppers, chili sauce and cheese.
3. Spoon the mixture into tartlet shells.
4. Place filled tartlets on a baking sheet and bake for 12 to 15 minutes or until the egg mixture is set.
5. Remove from the oven and let cool for 3 minutes on a wire rack.

using Natural Pastures Cracked Pepper Verdelait, produced in Courtenay, British Columbia

Makes 24 to 27 tartlets

PREP TIME
15 minutes

COOKING TIME
15 minutes

MAKE AHEAD
The filling can be made 1 day ahead, covered and refrigerated. Crab quiches can be cooked 1 day ahead, covered and refrigerated. Reheat in 300°F (150°C) oven for 5 to 10 minutes.

using Fromagerie Ferme des chutes cheddar, produced in Saint-Félicien, Quebec

Makes approximately 48 squares

PREP TIME
35 minutes + 24 hours of refrigeration

COOKING TIME
15 to 20 minutes

MAKE AHEAD
Fondue squares can be made 2 days ahead, covered and refrigerated. Dip them in the egg wash and bread them just before baking.

GURTH'S NOTE
• Have a selection of dipping sauces (such as BBQ, red, green or fruit salsa) ready for more tasty fun.

This recipe comes from the files of Pierre Bouchard, cheesemaker at Fromagerie Ferme des chutes.

4 cups (1 L) 2% milk
4 oz. (100 g) unsalted butter
pinch kosher salt and freshly ground
    black pepper
⅔ cup (160 mL) all-purpose flour
⅔ cup (160 mL) cornstarch
8 oz. (225 g) grated Parmesan cheese
8 oz. (225 g) grated Chute à Michel
    cheddar
2 eggs, lightly beaten
2 cups (500 mL) breadcrumbs

1. Butter a 9- × 13-inch (3.5-L) deep-sided heatproof pan.
2. In a large saucepan over medium-low heat, combine milk, butter, salt and pepper. Heat until lightly bubbling.
3. In a large bowl, mix the flour, cornstarch, grated parmesan and cheddar cheese.
4. Add the dry ingredients all at once to the hot milk mixture and cook, stirring frequently, until a cheese crust forms at the bottom of the pot, approximately 20 minutes.
5. Pour the hot cheese mixture into prepared pan; permit to cool at room temperature. Refrigerate, covered, for 24 hours.
6. Heat the oven to 350°F (180°C).
7. Line a baking sheet with parchment paper.
8. Cut the hardened cheese mixture into squares.
9. Dip each square into beaten eggs and coat with breadcrumbs.
10. Place on baking sheet and bake for 15 to 20 minutes or until the cheese has softened.

This is the cooperative's Bluenoser (Nova Scotian) twist on a classic European fondue.

1 large round loaf of bread
8 oz. (225 g) cream cheese, softened at
　　room temperature
1 cup (250 mL) sour cream
1 tsp. (5 mL) Worcestershire sauce
½ tsp. (2.5 mL) hot chili pepper sauce
¼ tsp. (1 mL) garlic salt
12 oz. (346 g) Old Cheddar cheese,
　　grated
5 oz. (140 g) cooked shrimp meat
5 oz. (140 g) cooked crabmeat

1. Preheat the oven to 350°F (180°C).
2. Slice the top off the loaf of bread and reserve. Scoop out the inside, leaving a 1-inch (2.5-cm) layer all around the edge. Use bread for dipping.
3. In a large mixing bowl, beat the softened cream cheese. Add the sour cream, Worcestershire sauce, hot chilli pepper sauce and garlic salt.
4. Mix in grated cheese, shrimp and crabmeat until just combined.
5. Fill the bread shell with the cheese-seafood mixture.
6. Place the top on the loaf and wrap the bread in foil.
7. Place on a cookie sheet and bake for 70 minutes or until the mixture is thoroughly heated.
8. Serve with reserved bread cubes and crackers.

using Farmers Cooperative Dairy Old Cheddar, produced in Truro, Nova Scotia

Serves 8 to 10 people as an hors d'oeuvre

PREP TIME
20 minutes

COOKING TIME
70 minutes

MAKE AHEAD
Bread pot fondue filling can be prepared 1 day ahead, covered and refrigerated. Bring to room temperature, pour into bread and heat as above.

using Fromagerie l'Ancêtre Organic 3-Year-Old Cheddar, produced in Bécancour, Quebec

Makes 16 to 20 pieces

PREP TIME
15 minutes + time to freeze

COOKING TIME
10 to 15 minutes

MAKE AHEAD
The cheese logs can be made 1 week ahead, covered and frozen.

GURTH'S NOTE
• Try other cheese, such as mozzarella, raclette, Edam, Gouda or provolone.

Tasty food can be simply made and these simple snacks are so tasty! After years of asking my mother-in-law for the recipe for this Deall holiday tradition, Kathleen agreed to share it with all of us. Once a year these treats are served, and I look forward to eating them every time.

2 cups (500 mL) grated cheddar
1 tsp. (5 mL) Worcestershire sauce
3 Tbsp. (45 mL) 35% cream
pinch and a bit cayenne (Not too much!)
1 Tbsp. (15 mL) prepared mustard
1 loaf sliced white or whole wheat bread, crusts removed

1. Combine the cheese, Worcestershire sauce, cream, cayenne and mustard in a bowl. Stir to form a smooth paste.
2. Using a rolling pin, flatten and roll each slice of bread until very thin.
3. Spread the cheese mixture onto each long rectangle of bread.
4. Roll the slices up tightly.
5. Place in a container seam-side down and freeze.
6. Preheat oven to 350°F (180°C).
7. Place frozen cheese logs seam-side down on a baking sheet and bake in the oven for 10 to 15 minutes or until cheese has melted and bread is slightly toasted.

This modified recipe is based on one from Donat Keller, owner/cheesemaker of Happy Days Goat Dairy. The recipe is quite innovative using goat cheese in a steamed pork dumpling.

14 oz. (400 g) ground pork
7 oz. (200 g) shrimp, peeled, deveined
    and mashed
2 tsp. (10 mL) kosher salt
2 Tbsp. (30 mL) granulated sugar
2 Tbsp. (30 mL) corn flour
1 tsp. (5 mL) toasted sesame seed oil
1 Tbsp. (15 mL) light soya sauce
5 oz. (140 g) Goat cheese
2 green onions, finely sliced
1 package Chinese dumplings or
    wonton wraps

1. In a large bowl, combine the ground pork and mashed shrimp.
2. Using a mixer, blend the meats, salt, sugar, flour, oil and soya sauce until sticky.
3. Add the cheese and sliced onions; mix well.
4. Place 1 tsp. (5 mL) of the filling in the centre of a dumpling skin.
5. Lightly dampen the edges with water and bring them together to form a small bundle. Press the edges to seal.
6. Place several dumplings in an oiled steaming basket and steam for 10 minutes.
7. Serve hot with your favourite dipping sauce.

using Happy Days Goat Dairy Okanagan Goat cheese, produced in Salmon Arm, British Columbia

Makes 45 to 50 dumplings

PREP TIME
30 minutes

COOKING TIME
10 minutes per batch of dumplings

MAKE AHEAD
The dumplings can be prepared 4 hours ahead, covered with a damp towel and refrigerated. The dumplings can also be made ahead, placed in rows on a waxed paper–lined baking sheet and frozen. Once frozen, transfer to a freezer bag.

GURTH'S NOTE
• These are great to make ahead and freeze. Invite friends over for a dumpling-making party.

QUARK & FUNDY SMOKED SALMON GÂTEAU

using Armadale Farm Quark cheese, produced in Roachville, New Brunswick

Makes 8 to 10 portions

PREP TIME
40 minutes + 1 hour of refrigeration

COOKING TIME
20 minutes

MAKE AHEAD
The crêpes can be made 1 week ahead, stacked with waxed paper between each crêpe, wrapped in plastic wrap and frozen. The gâteau can be made 1 day ahead, covered and refrigerated.

I modified this recipe from one I learned from Stephen Langley, one of my chef professors at George Brown College's Chef School. I thought it most appropriate to match a New Brunswick cheese with Bay of Fundy smoked salmon.

CRÊPES:
2 eggs, lightly beaten
1 cup (250 mL) milk
½ cup (125 mL) water
3 Tbsp. (45 mL) melted unsalted butter, cooled
½ tsp. (2.5 mL) kosher salt
1 cup (250 mL) all-purpose flour

FILLING:
1 cup (250 mL) quark cheese
1 medium red onion, finely diced
3 Tbsp. (45 mL) finely chopped fresh dill
27 oz. (750 g) Atlantic smoked salmon, sliced
sprigs of fresh dill

CRÊPES:
1. In a small bowl, combine the eggs, milk, water and butter.
2. In a second bowl, mix the salt and the flour. Pour in the egg mixture and stir until well blended; cover and refrigerate for an hour.
3. Strain into a clean bowl to remove any lumps.
4. In a medium skillet, over medium-high heat, brush the skillet with a little extra butter. Pour in 3 Tbsp. (45 mL) of batter and swirl so the entire surface of the pan is covered with crêpe batter.
5. Cook until lightly golden along the edges; flip and cook for 30 seconds.
6. Remove from heat, permit to cool and cover with wax paper.
7. Repeat with the remaining batter.

FINAL ASSEMBLY:
1. On a large plate or platter, place 1 crêpe and spread a small amount of cheese onto it.
2. Sprinkle with the diced onion and chopped dill and cover with 3 to 4 slices of the smoked salmon.
3. Place a second crêpe on top.
4. Repeat the layers until all the ingredients are used, ending with a crêpe.
5. Slice into pie-shaped pieces and garnish each serving with a sprig of dill.

THE DEFINITIVE GUIDE TO CANADIAN ARTISANAL AND FINE CHEESE

This recipe was developed because Joanne and I love garlic and Oka cheese so much. Don't panic about 2 whole bulbs! Roasted garlic has a sweet and nutty taste. It is a delicious soup to serve during the fall and winter. Enjoy!

2 whole garlic bulbs, cloves separated
  and peeled
2 Tbsp. (30 mL) olive oil
1 cup (250 mL) dry white wine
4 cups (1 L) chicken or vegetable
  stock
1 cup (250 mL) 35% cream
kosher salt and freshly ground black
  pepper to taste
3 garlic cloves, peeled and sliced in
  half
4 slices rye bread, toasted
½ lb. (225 g) Oka cheese, grated
4 Tbsp. (60 mL) cream sherry

1. Preheat the oven to 350°F (180°C).
2. Wrap the peeled cloves in lightly oiled foil and roast for 50 to 60 minutes, or until soft.
3. Mash the roasted garlic in a small bowl. Set aside.
4. In a large soup pot, heat the oil over medium-low temperature and add the mashed garlic; cook for 1 minute. Pour in the wine and bring to a boil. Cook until the volume is reduced by half.
5. Add the stock and let simmer for 15 minutes. Remove from the heat and cool for 5 minutes.
6. Purée in a blender or food processor until smooth. Return the soup to the pot. Pour in the cream, heat over medium-low temperature and stir. Season with salt and pepper.
7. Rub the toasted bread and the inside surface of the soup bowls with garlic halves.
8. Place ⅛ of the grated cheese in each of the 4 heatproof bowls. Ladle 1 cup (250 mL) of soup into each bowl.
9. Preheat the oven to broil.
10. Pour 1 Tbsp. (15 mL) of the sherry into each bowl. Cover with a bread slice. Sprinkle the remaining cheese over the bread and broil until the cheese is bubbling and slightly brown.

using Agropur's Oka cheese, produced in Oka, Quebec

Serves 4

PREP TIME
30 minutes

COOKING TIME
90 minutes

MAKE AHEAD
The soup can be made 2 days ahead, covered and refrigerated. Garnish with the cheese and crouton just prior to serving.

GURTH'S NOTE
• If Oka is not available, use a good stringy cheese such as Saint-Paulin, Gouda, mozzarella or Swiss.

using Salerno Dairy provolone cheese, produced in Hamilton, Ontario

Makes 8 to 10 double portions

PREP TIME
40 minutes + 3 hours for the dough to rise

COOKING TIME
40 minutes

MAKE AHEAD
The sandwich can be made 1 day ahead, covered and refrigerated.

GURTH'S NOTES
• Havarti, Esrom, Gouda and Monterey Jack are other tasty cheese substitutes.
• Use your favourite cold cut meats (i.e. roast turkey, roast beef, roast chicken …).
• For the pesto, substitute olive tapenade, mustard or roasted red pepper sauce.

I made this sandwich for a party Joanne and I hosted. Everyone loved biting into the bread, stuffed with cold cuts and cheese. Our friend Jay stayed close to the table for extra helpings of what he called 'the sandwich." Serve these on a platter and watch them being devoured by your hungry friends during the CFL Grey Cup match.

SPONGE:
1 cup (250 mL) all-purpose flour
¼ cup (60 mL) durum semolina flour
pinch kosher salt
2 Tbsp. (30 mL) active dry yeast
1 cup (250 mL) lukewarm water

DOUGH:
4 cups (1 L) all-purpose flour
¼ cup (60 mL) durum semolina flour
1 ¼ cups (310 mL) lukewarm water
3 Tbsp. (45 mL) extra virgin olive oil
pinch kosher salt

SANDWICH:
6 Tbsp. (90 mL) pesto
8 oz. (225 g) peppercorn salami
11 oz. (300 g) provolone cheese slices
11 oz. (300 g) Black Forest ham, sliced
4 Tbsp. (60 mL) extra virgin olive oil

SPONGE:
1. In a medium bowl, combine the all-purpose flour, semolina and salt. Make a well in the centre.
2. In a small bowl, dissolve the yeast in the water; pour into the centre of the well.
3. Stir the flour mixture into the yeast to form a sponge. Cover with a tea towel and place in a draft-free, warm location for an hour or until doubled in size.

DOUGH:
1. In a large bowl, combine both flours. Make a well in the centre. Spoon the sponge into the centre and add the water, oil and salt.
2. Stir the flour mixture into the sponge mixture until it's well incorporated and the dough forms into a ball.
3. Using a little extra flour, dust the dough and knead with the palm of your hand for 10 minutes or until the dough becomes smooth and elastic. Dust with more flour if the dough becomes too sticky.
4. In a large, lightly oiled bowl, place the kneaded dough and let rise in a warm, draft-free location for 90 minutes or until doubled in size.
5. Punch the dough down and place on a floured surface.

SANDWICH:
1. Knead the dough with a little more flour and stretch it by using a rolling pin until it is 6 inches (15 cm) wide by 3 feet (90 cm) long. Cut in half; you'll have 2 pieces, each being 6 inches (15 cm) wide by 1.5 feet (45 cm) long.
2. Cover the surface of each piece of dough with pesto up to 1 inch (2.5 cm) from each end. Place slices of salami down the centre, then add a layer of provolone and finally the ham.
3. Roll each piece of dough up tightly, sealing the ends by crimping and tucking them underneath the stuffed dough.
4. Preheat the oven to 400°F (200°C) and set the rack at middle height.
5. Place the stuffed dough on an oiled baking sheet and brush with the remaining oil. Cover with plastic wrap and a tea towel and let rise in a draft-free, warm location for 30 minutes or until doubled in size.
6. Remove the plastic wrap and towel and bake for 35 to 40 minutes or until the bread is golden.
7. Remove from the oven, let cool for 5 minutes and slice crosswise.

THE DEFINITIVE GUIDE TO CANADIAN ARTISANAL AND FINE CHEESE

Serve this piping hot with a big slice of Baked Grey Cup Stuffed Provolone Sandwich (previous page).

2 Tbsp. (30 mL) unsalted butter
2 onions, diced
2 cups (500 mL) sliced celery
4 garlic cloves, minced
4 boiled potatoes, peeled and diced
8 cups (2 L) 2% milk
1 bottle dark beer (such as Alberta's Big Rock)
3 cups (750 mL) grated Cheddar cheese
1 tsp. (5 mL) Worcestershire sauce
kosher salt and freshly ground black pepper, to taste

1. In a large soup pot, melt the butter over medium heat. Add the onions and celery, cover, and cook for 5 to 7 minutes or until softened.
2. Stir in the minced garlic and cook for 1 minute.
3. Add the diced potato and cook for 3 minutes.
4. Pour in the milk and beer. Stir and simmer until the liquid is hot.
5. Add the grated cheese and stir some more.
6. Adjust the flavour with Worcestershire sauce, salt and pepper.

using Rocky Mountain Cheddar, produced in Didsbury, Alberta

Serves 6 generously

PREP TIME
40 minutes

COOKING TIME
30 minutes

MAKE AHEAD
The chowder can be made 1 day ahead, covered and refrigerated.

GURTH'S NOTE
• If you don't live in Wild Rose Country, meaning Alberta, use your favourite local old cheddar and dark beer.

using Fromagerie La Petite Heidi chive-flavoured Sainte-Rose chèvre, produced in Sainte-Rose-du-Nord, Quebec

Makes 4 portions

PREP TIME
15 minutes

COOKING TIME
none

MAKE AHEAD
The roll filling can be made 1 day ahead, covered and refrigerated.

GURTH'S NOTES
• For hors d'oeuvre, use the filling to stuff mini-pitas or brioche.
• Other flavoured soft chèvre, quark or cream cheese can be used.

Line Turcotte, co-owner and cheesemaker at Fromagerie La Petite Heidi, sent me a collection of recipes she created using her cheese. She highlighted this one as being one of her favourites.

½ cup (125 mL) peeled and sliced celery
⅔ cup (160 mL) cooked lobster, broken in pieces
5 oz. (140 g) chive-flavoured chèvre at room temperature
4 black olives, pitted and sliced
4 hot dog buns

1. In a bowl, combine the celery, lobster meat, cheese and sliced olives.
2. Spoon the mixture into the hot dog buns.
3. Serve—and be prepared to be asked to make more.

THE DEFINITIVE GUIDE TO CANADIAN ARTISANAL AND FINE CHEESE

George DeMelo, co-owner and cheesemaker at Portuguese Cheese, faxed this recipe to me. Years ago when I worked at a downtown Toronto restaurant, I baked a cheeseless version of this bread, known in Portugal as broa.

2 Tbsp. (30 mL) vegetable oil
1 small onion, finely diced
1 small red bell pepper, diced
1 jalapeño chili pepper, finely diced
1 garlic clove, minced
1 cup (250 mL) all-purpose flour
1 cup (250 mL) white cornmeal
1 Tbsp. (15 mL) baking powder
1 tsp. (5 mL) kosher salt
3 large eggs, lightly beaten
1 ½ cups (375 mL) buttermilk
8 oz. (225 g) Corvo cheese, grated

1. Preheat the oven to 375°F (190°C).
2. Grease a 9- × 5- × 3-inch (23- × 13- × 6-cm) loaf pan.
3. In a small frying pan, heat the oil at medium temperature and add the onion, red bell pepper and jalapeño chili. Cover and cook for 5 to 7 minutes or until the onions have softened.
4. Add the garlic and cook for 1 minute. Remove from the heat and let cool.
5. In a large bowl, mix the flour, cornmeal, baking powder and salt.
6. In a medium bowl, combine the beaten eggs with the buttermilk. Stir the onion-pepper mixture into the egg-buttermilk mixture.
7. Pour the liquid mixture into the dry ingredients and stir only enough to combine.
8. Add the grated cheese and mix only enough to disperse the cheese throughout the batter.
9. Pour the batter into the prepared pan.
10. Bake for 50 minutes or until a toothpick inserted in the centre comes out clean.
11. Remove from the oven and let stand for 5 minutes.
12. Remove the bread from the pan and place on a rack to cool.

using Portuguese Cheese Company Corvo cheese, produced in Toronto, Ontario

Serves 6 to 8

PREP TIME
15 minutes

COOKING TIME
65 minutes

MAKE AHEAD
The bread can be made 1 day ahead, covered and kept at room temperature.

GURTH'S NOTE
• If you do not have buttermilk, mix 1 ½ cups (375 mL) milk with 4 tsp. (20 mL) white vinegar.

using Les Fromages de l'Érablière's Cru des érables, produced in Mont-Laurier, Quebec

Makes 32 pieces

PREP TIME
20 minutes

COOKING TIME
15 minutes per baking sheet

MAKE AHEAD
The Croque-Monsieur can be prepared a day ahead, covered and refrigerated. Bake just before serving.

GURTH'S NOTE
• Substitute Oka, raclette or Münster for Cru des érables.

This dish consists of three of my favourite ingredients: cheese, maple flavouring and turkey, all inside a freshly baked croissant. This is a very tasty and simple brunch item to prepare.

4 packages frozen crescent roll dough, thawed
8 oz. (225 g) Cru des érables
16 deli slices of roasted turkey, cut in half

1. Preheat the oven according to the directions on crescent roll packaging.
2. Remove the rind from the cheese and cut into 32 pieces.
3. Wrap each piece of the cheese tightly with a piece of turkey.
4. Unroll 1 package of the dough, as per manufacturer's instructions.
5. Place a turkey-cheese roll at the wide end of each triangular piece of dough.
6. Roll towards the narrow end, sealing the edges. Place on a parchment lined baking sheet, seam-side down.
7. Repeat with the remaining dough.
8. Bake for 10 to 15 minutes or until the crescents are golden.
9. Remove from the oven and let cool for 3 minutes before serving.

THE DEFINITIVE GUIDE TO CANADIAN ARTISANAL AND FINE CHEESE

Main Courses

THE DEFINITIVE GUIDE TO CANADIAN ARTISANAL AND FINE CHEESE

Fish and cheese? Even Joseph, my good friend and a fellow foodie, had never heard of this combination. Fish and cheese, who would have thought of it. Don't knock it until you have tried it!

1 Tbsp. (15 mL) unsalted butter
½ shallot, finely diced
1 Tbsp. (15 mL) all-purpose flour
1 cup (250 mL) milk
7 oz. (200 g) brie cheese, rind removed
    and cut into small wedges
1 Tbsp. (15 mL) canola oil
pinch kosher salt and freshly ground
    black pepper
2 fresh halibut fillets (6 oz./180 g
    each), skinned
4 sprigs fresh dill
1 egg, lightly beaten
¼ cup (60 mL) breadcrumbs
extra sprigs of fresh dill

1. In a small saucepan, melt the butter over medium-low heat. Add the diced shallots and cook covered for 3 minutes, or until softened.
2. Stir in the flour and cook for 2 minutes.
3. Gradually whisk in the milk in small amounts. Stir well to prevent lumps from forming.
4. Add in the cheese, cover and let cook for 15 minutes, stirring occasionally. The sauce has thickened enough when it coats the back of a spoon. Season with salt and pepper. Reduce the heat to minimum.
5. In an ovenproof skillet, heat the oil over medium-high heat. Sprinkle salt and pepper on both sides of the fillets.
6. Cook the fish in a hot skillet for 2 to 3 minutes on each side. Remove the skillet from the heat. Place dill sprig over the halibut.
7. In a small bowl, combine the beaten egg and breadcrumbs. Spread on top of the dill.
8. Preheat the oven to 400°F (200°C).
9. Place the rack on the second-highest level. Place the skillet in the oven and cook for 4 minutes.
10. Increase the heat to broil; cook until the breadcrumbs are golden in colour, 1 to 2 minutes.
11. Remove from the oven and place the fish on plates. Spoon the sauce over half of the fillet and garnish with a sprig of fresh dill.

using Damafro Brie Le Connaisseur cheese, produced in Saint-Damase, Quebec

Serves 2

PREP TIME
20 minutes

COOKING TIME
20 minutes

MAKE AHEAD
The sauce can be made 1 day ahead. Cover and refrigerate.

GURTH'S NOTE
• I serve this dish on a bed of bulghur and wild rice with a jicama, carrot and red cabbage salad. Very tasty!

using Forfar Dairy 4-Year-Old Cheddar, produced in Portland, Ontario

Makes 6 to 8 portions

PREP TIME
20 minutes

COOKING TIME
50 minutes

MAKE AHEAD
Mac'n'Garlic'n'Beans can be made 1 day ahead, covered and refrigerated.

GURTH'S NOTE
• Try using a cheddar flavoured with jalapeño, cajun spices or bacon.

Joanne loves making casserole dishes like this one. She prepares it after brunch on Sunday for that evening's dinner. All the pans are washed before the meal is placed in the oven. It makes great leftovers for the next day's lunch.

3 Tbsp. (45 mL) extra virgin olive oil
3 Tbsp. (45 mL) all-purpose flour
3 cups (750 mL) milk
10 oz. (280 g) Four-Year-Old Cheddar, grated
¼ cup + ½ cup (60 mL + 125 mL) Parmesan cheese, grated
1 lb. (450 g) cooked elbow macaroni
3 garlic bulbs, cloves separated, peeled and roasted
1 ½ cups (375 mL) cooked romano beans

1. In a large saucepan, heat the oil over medium-low temperature and add the flour. Stir and cook for 3 minutes or until the flour bubbles along the edges of pan.
2. Drizzle the milk in gradually, whisking to reduce the chance of lumps form forming.
3. Stir in the cheese and the ¼ cup (60 mL) of the Parmesan.
4. Let the sauce cook for 10 minutes or until it has thickened.
5. Preheat the oven to 350°F (180°C).
6. In a large bowl, combine the cooked macaroni, roasted garlic and beans. Stir in the cheese sauce.
7. In a 9- × 13-inch (3.5-L) buttered rectangular dish, spoon the mixture; sprinkle the remaining ½ cup (125 mL) of Parmesan on top.
8. Place the dish on a baking sheet, cover with foil and bake for 30 minutes.
9. Remove the foil and cook for an additional 5 minutes or until the top becomes slightly crispy.
10. Remove from the oven and let cool for 10 minutes prior to serving.

THE DEFINITIVE GUIDE TO CANADIAN ARTISANAL AND FINE CHEESE

Here is a Canadian twist to the classic Chicken Cordon Bleu. I love the crunchiness that the cracked wheat, rye and flax of the Red River Cereal give to the dish.

4 chicken breasts, deboned and
   skinned
¼ tsp. (1 mL) kosher salt
¼ tsp. (1 mL) freshly ground pepper
4 oz. (100 g) Chèvre Doux cheese cut
   into 4 pieces
1 cup (250 mL) breadcrumbs
1 cup (250 mL) Red River Cereal
1 ½ cups (375 mL) all-purpose flour
2 eggs, lightly beaten with 1 Tbsp.
   (15 mL) of water
3 Tbsp. (45 mL) canola oil

1. Preheat the oven to 425°F (220°C).
2. With the tip of a sharp paring knife, make a small incision into the side of each chicken breast. Insert the blade deeper into the meat and swivel it carefully, enlarging the opening to create an interior pocket in the breast.
3. Season the breasts and pockets with salt and pepper.
4. Stuff each pocket with a piece of cheese.
5. In 3 separate wide containers, place the all-purpose flour in one, the beaten eggs in a second and the combined breadcrumbs and Red River Cereal in the third.
6. Coat each breast with flour, dip it into the egg mixture and coat with the breadcrumbs-cereal mixture.
7. In a large skillet, heat the oil over medium-high temperature.
8. Fry the breasts until golden on one side, flip them over and place the skillet in the oven.
9. Roast for 12 to 15 minutes, or until the internal temperature tests 165° (74°C) on a meat thermometer or until the meat is no longer pink in the middle.
10. Remove from the heat, cover and let rest for 10 minutes before serving.

using Fromagerie Tournevent Chèvre Doux cheese, produced in Chesterville, Quebec

Serves 4

PREP TIME
20 minutes

COOKING TIME
20 minutes

MAKE AHEAD
The chicken breasts can be prepared 1 day ahead, covered and refrigerated.

using Bothwell Cheese Gouda, produced in New Bothwell, Manitoba

Serves 6

PREP TIME
30 minutes + 1 hour of refrigeration

COOKING TIME
75 minutes

MAKE AHEAD
The crêpes can be made 1 week ahead, individually separated with waxed paper, stacked, wrapped in plastic wrap and frozen.

GURTH'S NOTE
- The wild rice is cooked in large quantities of boiling water for approximately 45 minutes or until the rice grain splits and is slightly chewy.

This recipes comes from the files of Chef Jason Wortzman, Director of Sales and Marketing at Bothwell Cheese. I like this recipe, for it shows another way to use wild rice.

1 egg, lightly beaten
1 Tbsp. (15 mL) extra virgin olive oil
¾ cup (180 mL) milk
1 ½ cups (375 mL) all-purpose flour
½ tsp. (2.5 mL) salt
1 ¼ cups (310 mL) cooked wild rice
14 oz. (400 g) old-fashioned cooked ham, thinly sliced
14 oz. (400 g) button, cremini or oyster mushrooms, sliced and sautéed
16 oz. (450 g) Gouda, grated

1. Preheat the oven to 350°F (180°C)
2. In a large bowl, combine the egg, oil and milk.
3. In a medium bowl, mix the flour and salt. Add the dry mixture to the liquids and stir well until smooth. Cover and refrigerate for 1 hour.
4. Strain the crêpe mixture into a clean bowl, removing all the lumps. Stir in the cooked wild rice.
5. Heat an oiled 8- inch (20-cm) crêpe pan on medium-high temperature. Ladle ¼ cup (60 mL) of batter to just cover the bottom of the pan.
6. Cook until the crêpe is no longer wet and the edges begin to brown. Flip and cook the other side for 2 minutes. Place on a large plate.
7. Continue making crêpes with the remaining batter.
8. On each crêpe, place a thin layer of ham; spoon the cooked mushrooms over top and cover with the grated Gouda.
9. Loosely roll the crêpes and place on an oiled baking sheet.
10. Cover with foil and bake in the oven for 15 to 20 minutes or until the cheese has melted. Serve hot!

THE DEFINITIVE GUIDE TO CANADIAN ARTISANAL AND FINE CHEESE

The tanginess and saltiness of the Beddis Blue makes this dish a delicious fall and winter meal. I decided to forgo the traditional wine in the recipe for I had none. I did have good beer in the house though!

1 Tbsp. (15 mL) extra virgin olive oil
1 Tbsp. (15 mL) unsalted butter
1 medium onion, diced
1 tsp. (5 mL) minced garlic
1 cup (250 mL) arborio rice
1 cup (250 mL) strong Bock-style beer
3 ½ to 4 cups (875 mL to 1 L) chicken
    or vegetable stock, hot
1 cup (250 mL) cooked chicken pieces
3 cups (750 mL) baby spinach, packed
1 cup (250 mL) Blue cheese, rind
    removed and crumbled

1. In a large pot, heat the oil and butter over medium-low temperature until the butter has melted.
2. Add the onions and cook, covered, for 5 to 7 minutes, until softened.
3. Stir in the garlic and cook for a minute.
4. Add in the rice and stir until each grain is coated with the oil and butter.
5. Stir in the beer and increase the heat to medium. Cook until nearly all the beer has been absorbed by the rice.
6. Start adding the stock, one ladle at a time. Stir until all the liquid has been absorbed before adding another ladle. Repeat until the rice is just a little crunchy (al dente).
7. Add the cooked chicken and stir until warmed through.
8. Mix in the spinach and stir until cooked.
9. Just prior to serving, stir in the cheese into the risotto mixture.

using Moonstruck Organic's Beddis Blue cheese, produced on Salt Spring Island, British Columbia

Serves 4 generously

PREP TIME
10 minutes

COOKING TIME
45 minutes

MAKE AHEAD
This recipe is best made just before serving.

GURTH'S NOTES
- Substitutions for Beddis Blue would be firm blue cheese, such as Ermite, Geai Bleu or Highland Blue.
- Use a good, strong, dark beer. Try Ontario's urBock, Quebec's Maudite, or your favourite local beer.

*using Fromagerie La Vache à Mail-
lotte Allégretto and Fredondaine
cheese, produced in La Sarre, Quebec*

Serves 4 to 6

PREP TIME
15 minutes

COOKING TIME
35 minutes

MAKE AHEAD
The tart can be prepared and
baked 1 day ahead, covered and
refrigerated.

*This is a delicious tart to make when local field-ripened
tomatoes are available. Serve it with a green salad
and a glass of wine for a great summer lunch. This
recipe comes from the files of the Fromagerie.*

1 store-bought pie shell
3 Tbsp. (45 mL) Dijon mustard
½ cup + ½ cup (125 mL + 125 mL)
    grated Allégretto cheese
4 to 6 large beefsteak tomatoes,
    seeded and thinly sliced
⅓ to ½ cup (80 to 125 mL) finely
    sliced fresh basil
¾ cup + ¼ cup (180 mL + 60 mL)
    grated Fredondaine cheese
kosher salt and freshly ground black
    pepper, to taste

1. Preheat the oven to 375°F (190°C).
2. In a pie pan, fit the pie shell. Spread with the mustard and
   cover with the ½ cup (125 mL) of Allégretto cheese.
3. Arrange ½ the sliced tomatoes over top and cover with ½ the
   sliced basil.
4. Top with ¾ cup (180 mL) of the Fredondaine cheese. Season
   with salt and pepper.
5. Repeat the layering of the tomatoes and basil, reserving several
   tomato slices for the top layer.
6. Cover with the remaining ½ cup (125 mL) of Allégretto.
7. Place the remaining tomato slices on top and sprinkle with the
   ¼ cup (60 mL) of Fredondaine.
8. Bake for 35 minutes. Serve warm or at room temperature.

THE DEFINITIVE GUIDE TO CANADIAN ARTISANAL AND FINE CHEESE

This recipe is a signature dish of Patrick Fregni, chef of their dining room.

4 potatoes, thinly sliced, peel on
6 oz. (180 g) aiguillette of smoked
   duck
4 oz. (100 g) Migneron de Charlevoix,
   cut into 4 pieces
2 oz. (60 g) red wine jelly
4 sprigs fresh rosemary
2 pinches herbes de Provence

1. Place oven rack at the second highest position.
2. In a large saucepan of boiling water, cook the potato slices until firm. Remove and let cool.
3. Heat the oven to broil.
4. On 4 oven-safe plates, arrange the potato slices in a fan shape. Top with the smoked duck and a piece of Migneron de Charlevoix.
5. Broil until the cheese has melted.
6. Let cool for a minute and paint the plate with the red wine jelly.
7. Stick a sprig of rosemary in the centre of the dish and sprinkle the plate with herbes de Provence.
8. Serve immediately.

using Maison d'Affinage Maurice Dufour Migneron de Charlevoix cheese, produced in Baie-Saint-Paul, Quebec

Serves 4

PREP TIME
20 minutes

COOKING TIME
10 minutes

MAKE AHEAD
Potatoes can be cooked, cooled in ice-cold water, patted dry, covered and refrigerated 2 hours before serving.

GURTH'S NOTE
• The aiguilettes are long strips of duck meat, cut close to the breast bone.

using Fromagerie Fritz Kaiser Miranda cheese, produced in Noyan, Quebec

Serves 6

PREP TIME
20 minutes

COOKING TIME
75 minutes

MAKE AHEAD
The dish can be prepared 1 day ahead, covered and refrigerated. Add the croutons just prior to baking.

This recipe is modified from one of my mom's classic Sunday night dinners. Its aroma always enticed me to be first at the dinner table. As this recipe uses Swiss cheese, I thought it would be appropriate to use a cheese made by Fritz Kaiser, a cheesemaker originally from Switzerland.

1 Tbsp. (15 mL) extra virgin olive oil
1 tsp. (5 mL) kosher salt
½ tsp. (2.5 mL) freshly ground black pepper
1 Tbsp. (15 mL) herbes de Provence
12 chicken thighs, skinned and boneless
2 medium onions, thinly sliced
1 ½ cups (375 mL) sliced button mushrooms
½ cup (125 mL) sliced shiitake mushrooms
2 cups (500 mL) grated Miranda cheese
15 oz. (425 g) cream of chicken soup
1 ½ cups (375 mL) seasoned croutons

1. Preheat the oven to 350°F (180°C).
2. In a small bowl, combine the oil, salt, pepper and herbes de Provence.
3. In a 9- × 13-inch (3.5-L) casserole dish, place the chicken thighs and drizzle with the oil-herb mixture.
4. Cover with the onions, mushrooms and grated cheese.
5. Pour the soup over the chicken mixture.
6. Sprinkle with the croutons. Cover the casserole with foil.
7. Bake in the oven for 60 minutes. Remove the foil and continue cooking for 15 minutes to permit the croutons and cheese to become crispy.
8. Remove from the oven and let cool for 10 minutes prior to serving.

THE DEFINITIVE GUIDE TO CANADIAN ARTISANAL AND FINE CHEESE

This recipe is modified from one in the files of Wool-wich Dairy.

2 Tbsp. (30 mL) unsalted butter
2 garlic cloves, minced
⅓ cup (80 mL) chopped mushrooms
⅓ cup (80 mL) chopped zucchini
½ green bell pepper, diced
3 green onions, chopped
1 carrot, shredded
2 Tbsp. (30 mL) chopped parsley
kosher salt and freshly ground black
    pepper, to taste
8 pork cutlets
5 oz. (140 g) Chèvrai cheese
2 oz. (60 g) mozzarella, grated

using Woolwich Dairy's Chèvrai cheese, produced in Orangeville, Ontario

Serves 4 to 6

PREP TIME
20 minutes

COOKING TIME
40 minutes

MAKE AHEAD
The pork rolls can be prepared 1 day ahead, covered and refrigerated.

1. Preheat the oven to 350°F (180°C).
2. In a skillet, melt the butter over medium-high heat. Cook the garlic, mushrooms, zucchini and bell pepper for 3 minutes or until softened.
3. Add the green onion and shredded carrot and cook for 1 minute. Remove from the heat and add the parsley. Adjust the seasoning with salt and pepper.
4. With a mallet, pound each cutlet until approximately 6 × 3 inches (15 × 7 cm) in size.
5. Spread the Chèvrai over each cutlet.
6. Place 1 Tbsp. (15 mL) of the vegetable mixture at one end of the cutlet and roll it up.
7. Place seam-side down in an 8-inch square (2-L) baking dish.
8. Repeat with remaining the cutlets and vegetables.
9. Sprinkle the remaining vegetable mixture around the rolls.
10. Bake uncovered for 30 minutes, basting with the pan juices intermittently.
11. Sprinkle each roll with the mozzarella and continue baking until the mozzarella has melted. Serve hot.

using Ivanhoe Cheese Garlic Monterey Jack, produced in Ivanhoe, Ontario

Serves 4

PREP TIME
15 minutes

COOKING TIME
25 minutes

MAKE AHEAD
The quesadilla filling can be made 2 days ahead, covered and refrigerated.

GURTH'S NOTE
• If you are noted for falling asleep at the Christmas Family Dinner, you can blame the turkey. Turkey meat has tryptophan, a precursor to serotonin, needed in the brain to induce and maintain sleep. I now have a scapegoat, or should I say a scapeturkey!

Joanne and I love garlic and Mexican food. This is a perfect way to use leftover turkey from Thanksgiving or Christmas. Gobble gobble fiesta olé!

2 Tbsp. (30 mL) canola oil
½ onion, diced
2 cups (500 mL) cooked turkey, cubed
1 cup (250 mL) cooked black refried beans
½ cup (125 mL) grated Monterey Jack
1 green onion, chopped
dried chili flakes, to taste
kosher salt and freshly ground black pepper, to taste
4 tortilla wraps
sour cream (optional)
diced tomatoes (optional)
avocado, mashed with lemon juice (optional)

1. In a small skillet, heat 1 Tbsp. (15 mL) of the oil over medium-low temperature.
2. Add the diced onion and cook covered for 5 to 7 minutes, or until tender.
3. In a large bowl, combine the cooked onion, turkey, refried beans, Garlic Monterey Jack and green onion.
4. Season with the chili, salt and pepper.
5. In a medium skillet, heat the remaining 1 Tbsp. (15 mL) of oil over medium temperature.
6. Spoon ¼ of the turkey mixture on half of the wrap and fold the tortilla in half.
7. Place the tortilla wrap in the skillet. Cook for 7 to 10 minutes or until the cheese begins to melt.
8. Flip the quesadilla and cook for a further 5 minutes.
9. Serve with your favourite Tex-Mex garnishes.

Side Dishes

PUMPKIN & ROASTED GARLIC POLENTA WITH TOSCANO

This dish was inspired by Ontario's fall produce and Ruth Klahsen's delicious Toscano cheese. I created it for a cooking demonstration I presented at The Royal Agricultural Winter Fair (Toronto). Serve it as a delicious savoury meal for the fall and winter season. Enjoy!

1 garlic bulb, cloves separated and peeled
1 Tbsp. (15 mL) olive oil
4 to 5 cups (1 to 1.25 L) water or vegetable stock
1 tsp. (5 mL) kosher salt
1 cup (250 mL) coarse corn grits/meal
2 cups (500 mL) pie pumpkin, peeled, seeded and cut into ½-inch (1.25-cm) cubes
½ cup (125 mL) grated Toscano cheese
¼ cup (60 mL) plain yogurt
kosher salt and freshly ground black pepper, to taste

1. Preheat the oven to 325°F (160°C).
2. Wrap the garlic cloves in oiled foil and place in the oven. Roast for 50 minutes.
3. Mash the softened garlic in a small bowl. Set aside.
4. In a large pot, bring the salted water to a boil. Slowly pour in the corn grits in a steady stream, whisking constantly to make sure no lumps form.
5. Add the pumpkin cubes and roasted garlic. Stir and cover.
6. Cook for 30 to 40 minutes, stirring occasionally, until the mixture is very thick and the pumpkin is cooked.
7. Remove from the heat and stir in the cheese and yogurt. Season with salt and pepper. Serve hot.

using Monforte Dairy Toscano cheese, produced in Millbank, Ontario

Serves 4 as a side dish

PREP TIME
20 minutes + 50 minutes for roasting garlic

COOKING TIME
45 minutes

MAKE AHEAD
The garlic can be roasted and mashed 2 days ahead, covered and refrigerated.

GURTH'S NOTE
• Aged Montasio, Leoni-Grana and tomme de chèvre would be very tasty cheese substitutes.

using Cheeselady Cumin Gouda, produced in North Winsloe, Prince Edward Island

Serves 8

PREP TIME
30 minutes

COOKING TIME
95 minutes

MAKE AHEAD
The dish can be made 1 day ahead, covered and refrigerated. Reheat in a 300°F (150°C) oven for 60 minutes.

GURTH'S NOTE
• Try other flavours of Gouda, such as smoked, herbs or cumin and cloves.

2 Tbsp. (30 mL) extra virgin olive oil
1 onion, thinly sliced
3 large garlic cloves, minced
1 cup (250 mL) chicken or vegetable stock
1 cup (250 mL) dry white wine
2 tsp. (10 mL) herbes de Provence
1 ¼ cups (310 mL) 35% cream
1 tsp. (5 mL) kosher salt
½ tsp (2.5 mL) freshly ground black pepper
1 lb. (450 g) baking potatoes, peeled and grated
1 fennel root, finely sliced
6 oz. (180 g) Gouda, grated

1. Preheat the oven to 350°F (180°C). Place the rack at middle height.
2. Butter a 9- × 13-inch (3.5-L) rectangular baking dish.
3. In a large saucepan, heat the oil over medium temperature. Cook the onion, covered, for 3 to 5 minutes or until soft.
4. Add the garlic and cook for an additional 1 minute.
5. Add the stock, wine and herbs; reduce the heat to a low simmer.
6. Pour in the cream and season with salt and pepper; remove from the heat.
7. Add the potatoes and fennel to the cream mixture. Return to the stove and simmer for 10 minutes.
8. Spoon ½ of the mixture into the buttered dish. Cover with ½ of the Gouda. Layer with the remaining mixture and sprinkle with the remaining cheese.
9. Bake for 75 minutes or until the top browns, the liquid bubbles and the potatoes are tender.
10. Let rest for 15 minutes before serving.

THE DEFINITIVE GUIDE TO CANADIAN ARTISANAL AND FINE CHEESE

This dish is a favourite after Joanne and I run races with Jared and Aislinn, our nephew and niece. Our bodies crave the carbs.

8 large potatoes, cut into long
   triangular wedges
6 Tbsp. (90 mL) canola oil
3 Tbsp. (45 mL) unsalted butter
3 Tbsp. (45 mL) all-purpose flour
3 cups (750 mL) cold vegetable or
   chicken stock
1 Tbsp. (15 mL) soya sauce
1 tsp. (5 mL) Worcestershire sauce
kosher salt and freshly ground black
   pepper, to taste
2 cups (500 mL) cheese curds

1. Preheat the oven to 425°F (220°C).
2. In a large bowl, toss the potato wedges with 2 Tbsp. (30 mL) of oil.
3. Pour the remaining oil in a large roasting pan. Place in the oven.
4. Once the oil is hot, carefully toss the oiled potato wedges into the pan.
5. Cook for 30 to 40 minutes, flipping the wedges occasionally to cook them evenly on both sides, until gold and crispy.
6. In a saucepan, melt the butter over medium heat. Stir in the flour and cook for 2 minutes.
7. Slowly drizzle in the cold stock, stirring constantly to prevent lumps.
8. Cook for 15 to 20 minutes, stirring occasionally, or until thickened.
9. Season with the soya and Worcestershire sauces, salt and pepper.
10. Divide the cooked potato wedges amongst 4 large plates.
11. Cover with cheese curds and ladle on the brown gravy.

using Les Blancs d'Arcadies cheese curds, produced in Caraquet, New Brunswick

Serves 4

PREP TIME
15 minutes

COOKING TIME
40 minutes

MAKE AHEAD
The gravy can be made 1 day ahead, cooled, covered and refrigerated.

GURTH'S NOTE
• Now that flavoured cheese curds (such as garlic, bacon, chili, etc.) are available, the flavour possibilities abound.

using Chèvrerie Dion Le Délice Chèvre, produced in Montbeillard, Quebec

Serves 8

PREP TIME
20 minutes + 8 hours of refrigeration

COOKING TIME
30 to 35 minutes

MAKE AHEAD
The cheesecake can be made 2 days ahead, covered and refrigerated.

GURTH'S NOTE
• Have extra jam or jelly in the pantry? Use it to cover the cheesecake instead of the sliced fruit.

This recipe comes from the files of the Dion Family. Imagine adding pureed blueberries or strained raspberries to the mixture.

1 cup (250 mL) Chèvrerie Dion's plain-flavoured Le Délice cheese, softened at room temperature
1 tsp. (5 mL) pure vanilla extract
2 Tbsp. (30 mL) fresh lemon juice
¾ cup (180 mL) granulated sugar
pinch salt
3 eggs
1 store-bought graham cracker crumb crust (precooked)
slices of your favourite fresh fruit (such as strawberries, kiwi, etc.)

1. Preheat the oven to 350°F (180°C).
2. In a large bowl, blend the cheese, vanilla, lemon juice, sugar and salt until well combined.
3. Blend in the eggs, one at a time, until well incorporated.
4. Pour the mixture into the precooked pie crust.
5. Bake for 30 to 35 minutes or until the centre still jiggles slightly.
6. Remove from the oven and let cool. Refrigerate for 8 hours.
7. Cover with the fruit slices and serve.

Gay Cook, an Ottawa food writer and Cuisine Canada colleague, gave me permission to modify her Leeds Grenville Apple Torte recipe. It was originally published in Fifty-Five Plus *(September 2004). For more information about Gay, visit her website: www.gaycook.com.*

TORTE CRUST:

½ cup (125 mL) unsalted butter, softened at room temperature
⅓ cup (80 mL) granulated sugar
¼ tsp. (1 mL) pure vanilla extract
1 cup (250 mL) all-purpose flour
¼ cup (60 mL) strawberry or raspberry jam

FILLING:

8 oz. (225 g) Holmestead Cheese Sales feta, rinsed
¼ cup (60 mL) granulated sugar
2 eggs
½ tsp. (2.5 mL) pure vanilla extract
⅓ cup (80 mL) granulated sugar
½ tsp. (2.5 mL) ground cinnamon
4 cups (1 L) peeled, cored and sliced McIntosh apples
⅓ cup (80 mL) sliced almonds, or chopped walnuts or pecans
½ cup (125 mL) 35% cream (optional)

using Holmestead Cheese Sales feta, produced in Aysleford, Nova Scotia

Serves 8

PREP TIME
30 minutes

COOKING TIME
35 minutes

MAKE AHEAD
The torte can be made 1 day ahead, covered and refrigerated. Bring to room temperature prior to serving.

TORTE CRUST:

1. Preheat the oven to 425°F (220°C).
2. In a bowl, beat the butter, sugar and vanilla until well combined. Blend in the flour, mixing well.
3. Press the mixture on the bottom of a 9-inch (2.5-L) springform pan and 1 inch (2.5 cm) up the sides. Spread a thin layer of jam over the bottom.

FILLING:

1. In a food processor, beat the feta until creamy. Blend in the ¼ cup (60 mL) of sugar, eggs and vanilla.
2. When well mixed, spread over the jam in the pan.
3. In a small bowl, combine the ⅓ cup (80 mL) of sugar and cinnamon.
4. In a large bowl, toss the apple slices with the sugar-cinnamon mixture.
5. Place the apples over the feta mixture, pressing the apples gently to even the surface. Sprinkle the nuts over the top.
6. Bake for 10 minutes. Reduce the heat to 400°F (200°C) and continue to bake for 25 minutes or until the apples are tender when pierced with the tip of a sharp knife.
7. Remove from the oven and let cool.
8. Remove the springform pan and serve with whipped cream if desired.

using La Moutonnière's La Neige de brebis cheese, produced in Sainte-Hélène-de-Chester, Quebec

Serves 6 to 8

PREP TIME
15 minutes

COOKING TIME
80 minutes

COOLING TIME
90 minutes

MAKE AHEAD
The flans can be made 2 days ahead, covered and refrigerated.

GURTH'S NOTE
- Substitute a small amount of vanilla, maple syrup, lavender petals or crème de cassis for the lemon zest.

This recipe is modified from one in La Moutonnière's files.

FLAN:
8 large eggs
¾ cup (180 mL) granulated sugar
16 oz. (450 g) La Moutonnière's La Neige de brebis cheese
1 lemon, zest only
1 ¼ cups (310 mL) 35% cream

ORANGE COULIS:
10 oranges, juice only
¾ cup (180 mL) granulated sugar

TO SERVE:
clementine slices

FLAN:
1. Preheat the oven to 300°F (150°C). Line a deep roasting pan with a tea towel.
2. In a large bowl, beat the eggs and sugar with a mixer until the mixture becomes pale yellow, approximately 5 to 7 minutes.
3. Drain the cheese and blend with the egg mixture, lemon zest and cream.
4. Fill the small ramekins ¾ full with the mixture and place in the prepared roasting pan.
5. In a kettle, boil 4 cups (1 L) of water. Pour the hot water into the roasting pan until the water level reaches halfway up the sides of the ramekins.
6. Carefully place the pan in the oven and cook for 60 minutes.
7. Remove the pan from the oven; remove the ramekins from the hot water bath and let cool on a wire rack at room temperature. Cover and refrigerate.

ORANGE COULIS:
1. In a small saucepan, combine the orange juice and sugar; cook over medium-high heat for 15 to 20 minutes or until reduced in volume by half.
2. Let cool, cover and refrigerate.

TO SERVE:
1. To unmould the flan, insert a butter knife between the edge of the ramekin and the flan. Place a plate upside down over the ramekin. Flip the plate and ramekin over so the plate is right-side up. Tap the ramekin and the flan should gently fall out. Repeat the procedure if necessary.
2. Drizzle with the orange coulis and garnish with the clementine slices.

Glossary of Terms

AFFINAGE The French term for ageing and ripening cheese.

ASIAGO A hard, natural rind, cow's milk cheese originally from northern Italy. Used for grating and cooking.

BLOOMY RIND A white downy rind that develops on surface ripened cheese when spores of *Penicilium candidum* bacteria are sprayed on the cheese's surface.

BOCCONCINI A semi-soft, unripened, pasta filata–style, cow's milk cheese originally from Italy.

BRICK A firm, rindless, cow's milk cheese originally from the United States; traditionally pressed with masonry bricks.

BRIE A soft, bloomy rind, cow's milk cheese; originally from the Brie region of France.

BROCCIO A fresh, Corsican whey cheese made with sheep's or goat's milk.

BURRINI A semi-soft, rindless, gourd-shaped, pasta filata–style, cow's milk cheese with a ball of butter in the centre. Orignally from Italy.

CACCIOCAVALLO A firm, rindless, gourd-shaped, pasta filata–style, cow's milk cheese. Originally from Italy.

CAMBOZOLA A soft, bloomy rind, cow's milk German cheese with a few streaks of blue veins in its paste. A cross between a French Camembert and an Italian Gorgonzola.

CAMEMBERT A soft, bloomy rind, cow's milk cheese from France.

CHÈVRE A soft, goat's milk, unripened cheese.

COLBY A mild, cow's milk, firm, rindless cheddar; softer than a regular cheddar.

COTTAGE CHEESE Traditionally a cow's milk, fresh, unripened cheese.

CREAM CHEESE Traditionally a cow's milk, fresh, unripened cheese.

CROTTIN A French goat cheese made in the shape of a small flattened ball.

CROTONESE A semi-firm, natural rind, Italian Pecorino cheese, traditionally made with goat's and sheep's milk; flavoured with pepper.

CURDS The semi-solid portion of coagulated milk used in the production of cheese.

EDAM A firm, rindless, cow's milk cheese originally from Holland.

EMMENTAL Originally a firm, natural rind, cow's milk cheese from Switzerland, displaying large eyes in its paste.

ESROM A Danish version of a semi-soft, washed rind, cow's milk Port-Salut cheese.

EYES Holes formed by gases released during the ageing of cheese. Most evident in Swiss, Emmental, Appenzeller and Gruyère cheese.

FARMERS A firm, cow's milk, rindless cheese, produced by pressing cottage cheese.

FEDERALLY REGISTERED Conforming to cheese production and sanitation standards set by the Canadian federal government. The cheese can be sold in any province.

FETA A soft cheese, traditionally made in Greece with goat's or sheep's milk; stored in a saltwater brine.

FLEUR DU MAQUIS A soft, natural rind, cow's milk Corsican cheese covered with herbs and spices.

FRIULANO A firm, brushed rind, cow's milk cheese, originally from Italy.

GOUDA A firm, rindless, cow's milk cheese following the traditional Dutch recipe.

GRANA PADANO A hard, natural rind, cow's milk cheese made north of Italy's Po River.

HALLAL Food prepared according to the dietary laws of Islam.

HAVARTI A semi-soft, cow's milk, rindless cheese created in Denmark.

JARLSBERG A firm, natural rind, cow's milk cheese; the Norwegian version of Emmental.

KEFALOTYRI A Greek, hard cheese; usually used for grating.

KOSHER Food prepared under a rabbi's supervision that fulfills the requirements of Jewish biblical law.

MAROILLES A semi-soft, washed rind, cow's milk cheese from the region of Flanders, Belgium.

MIXED RIND A surface ripened cheese that has been both washed with a liquid and sprayed with a bacterial culture.

MONTEREY JACK A semi-soft, rindless, cow's milk cheese, originating in Monterey, California.

MORBIER A semi-soft, washed rind, cow's milk, French cheese with a distinctive layer of edible vegetable ash in the centre.

MOZZARELLA Originally an Italian cow's milk, semi-soft, rindless cheese. The traditional Italian Buffala di mozzarella is made with water buffalo milk and stretched using the pasta filata technique. Most North American mozzarella is made with skim milk and used on pizza.

MUENSTER A semi-soft, washed rind, cow's milk cheese, originally from the Alsace region of France.

NATURAL RIND A thick, hard rind that forms naturally on cheese aged for a long time (such as Leoni-Grana).

PANEER An East Indian, fresh, unripened cheese made of cow's milk.

PARMESAN A hard, natural rind, cow's milk cheese, similar to a Parmigiano Reggiano, but not made in the Parma region of Italy.

PASTA FILATA An Italian term for stretched curd cheese such as provolone. The curds are heated, then stretched to the desired consistency.

PASTE The interior portion of a cheese.

PECORINO A hard, natural rind, Italian cheese made with sheep's milk.

PECORINO TOSCANO A hard, natural rind, sheep's milk cheese made in the Tuscany region of Italy.

PORT-SALUT A semi-soft, washed rind, cow's milk cheese, originally made by the monks of Port du Salut, France.

PROVINCIALLY LICENSED Conforming to cheese production and sanitation standards set by individual Canadian provinces. The cheese can only be sold retail within the boundaries of that province.

PROVOLONE A firm, rindless, cow's milk, pasta filata–style cheese.

QUARK A fresh, unripened cow's milk cheese, developed in Germany.

QUESA FRESCA A Mexican soft, rindless cheese, eaten within a few days of making.

RACLETTE A semi-soft, washed rind, cow's milk cheese; originally from Switzerland.

REBLOCHON A French soft, cow's milk cheese.

RICOTTA Traditionally a fresh, unripened, cow's milk Italian cheese made from the whey.

RIND The exterior portion of a cheese. Edible if not coated with wax. Produced naturally or by the addition of moulds.

RINDLESS No rind develops on the outside of the cheese (mozzarella for example).

ROMANO A hard, natural rind cheese made in Italy with cow's, sheep's or goat's milk.

SAINT-MARCELLIN A soft cheese made in the Rhône-Alpes region of France; made originally with goat's milk, now mostly with cow's milk.

SELLES-SUR-CHER A semi-soft, ash-coated, goat's milk, French cheese from the Loire region.

SWISS A cow's milk, firm, rindless cheese with large eyes in the paste—caused by gas during the ageing of the cheese.

TALEGGIO A semi-soft, surface ripened, cow's milk cheese from the Lombardy region of Italy.

TERROIR The environmental growing conditions (type of soil, amount of precipitation and sunshine received, length of growing season, proximity to salt water) of a specific geographic region.

TOMME A semi-soft to firm cheese originally produced in the mountainous Savoy and Pyrenees regions of France. Made with cow's, goat's or sheep's milk.

TORTILLONS A semi-soft, unripened, pasta filata–style, cow's milk cheese from Quebec.

TRECCE A soft, pasta filata–style, cow's milk cheese whose long threads are braided by hand.

TUMA A fresh, unripened, cow's milk cheese, similar to ricotta; originally from Italy.

VALENCAY A semi-soft to firm, goat's milk, French cheese, made in the shape of a pyramid.

WASHED RIND A surface ripened cheese washed with a liquid (saltwater brine or alcohol) to promote the growth of mould during ageing.

WHEY The liquid portion of coagulated milk, used in the production of ricotta.

Bibliography

Bizier, R. and R. Nadeu. *Répertoire des fromages du Québec.* Éditions du Trécarré: Outremont, 2004.

Daigle, R., R. Hendrickson, et al. *Fundamentals of Canadian Cheeses and Their Uses in Fine Cuisine.* Les Éditions de la Chenelière Inc: Montreal, 1992.

Dairy Bureau of Canada. *Canadian Cheeses—Fact and Fancy.*

Harbutt, J. *Cheese—A Feast of International Dishes.* Hermes House: London, 2001.

Herbst, S.T. *The New Food Lover's Companion.* 2nd ed. Barron's Educational Services, Inc.: 1995.

Ingram, G. and Steven and Sarah Labensky. *Webster's New World Dictionary of Culinary Terms.* Prentice Hall: New Jersey, 1997.

Menzies, H. *By the Labour of Their Hands: The Story of Ontario Cheddar Cheese.* Quarry Press: Kingston, 1994.

Index

THE DEFINITIVE GUIDE TO CANADIAN ARTISANAL AND FINE CHEESE

THE DEFINITIVE GUIDE TO CANADIAN ARTISANAL AND FINE CHEESE